Excel Tips, Tricks, and Traps

Ron Person

Que ® Corporation
Carmel, Indiana

Excel Tips, Tricks, and Traps

Library of Congress Catalog No.: 89-60366
ISBN 0-88022-421-5

92 91 90 5 4 3 2

Interpretation of the printing code: the rightmost double-digit number is the year of the book's printing; the rightmost single-digit number, the number of the book's printing. For example, a printing code of 89-4 shows that the fourth printing of the book occurred in 1989.

Excel Tips, Tricks, and Traps is based on Excel 2.1.

About the Author

Ron Person

Ron Person has written more than 10 books for Que Corporation, including *Using Excel: IBM Version*, *Using 1-2-3 Release 3*, and *Using Microsoft Windows*. His firm, Ron Person & Co., based in San Francisco, trains and supports corporations nationally and internationally in Excel and other strategic Windows and OS/2 Presentation Manager applications. Ron Person & Co. is noted for their training and materials for end-users, trainers, developers, and support personnel. Ron has an M.B.A from Hardin-Simmons University and an M.S. in physics from Ohio State University. He is a frequent speaker at financial and computer conferences.

Publishing Director
David P. Ewing

Acquisitions Editor
Terrie Lynn Solomon

Editors
Shelley O'Hara
Eric Schoch

Editorial Assistant
Stacey Beheler

Technical Editors
Robert M. Cole
Jeffrey B. Nylund

Book Design and Production
David Kline
Lori Lyons
Jennifer Matthews
Shelley O'Hara
Mitzi Parsons
Dennis Sheehan

Indexer
Sherry Massey

Composed in Times Roman and Helvetica
by Que Corporation

Table of Contents

Acknowledgments

Excel Tips, Tricks, and Traps had many contributors, all among the pioneers who used Excel and saw a better way of working. I'd like to thank the following individuals and many clients for their contributions to the development of this book:

Microsoft's development, sales, and support people who have developed a strategic suite of products that clearly shows there is a better way to get work done.

Don Baarns for his contributions to the macro and advanced macro chapters. His tips on debugging and dialog box performance were enlightening.

Ralph Soucie for his additions to the macro and advanced macro chapters. Ralph added depth to these chapters with information on the dialog box editor and using alert boxes.

Will South for his vision of how Excel and a new generation of software can improve business performance. Our long-distance discussions have stretched my knowledge.

Robert M. Cole and Jeffrey B. Nylund for their expertise and consistency in the PC and Macintosh technical reviews.

Gary Vickers and Boris Erlank for their vigor in using Excel in process monitoring.

Edith Lewis for her tips on Excel charting.

Shelley O'Hara for her excellent job of editing, layout, and desktop publishing. It's only fitting that this book be produced on a personal computer.

Terrie Lynn Solomon and Dave Ewing for their encouragement, trust, and assistance in writing a continuing family of books for Que Corporation, the highest quality personal computer book publisher.

Trademark Acknowledgments

Que Corporation has made every effort to supply trademark information about company names, products, and services mentioned in this book. Trademarks indicated below were derived from various sources. Que Corporation cannot attest to the accuracy of this information.

1-2-3 is a registered trademark of Lotus Development Corporation.

dBASE II and dBASE III are registered trademarks of Ashton-Tate Company.

HP LaserJet is a trademark of Hewlett-Packard Co.

IBM ProPrinter is a trademark and PC is a registered trademark of International Business Machines.

Macintosh and LaserWriter are registered trademarks of Apple Computer, Inc.

Microsoft Excel, Microsoft Windows, Microsoft Windows Write, and Multiplan are registered trademarks of Microsoft Corporation.

SideKick is a registered trademark of Borland International, Inc.

Conventions Used in This Book

A number of conventions are used in *Excel Tips, Tricks, and Traps* to help you learn the program.

Direct quotations of words that appear on-screen are printed in a special typeface. Information you are asked to type is printed in **boldface**. The letter you use to select a command or option also appears in **boldface**: **E**dit **C**opy.

This book covers both Presentation Manager, Windows, and Macintosh versions of Excel. If a particular tip pertains to just one environment, this is noted in the tip. If the keystrokes to perform an operation differ for each version, both Windows and Presentation Manager (PC) and Macintosh keys are provided.

Introduction

Excel leads a new generation of software applications. Some Fortune 500 companies and international clients have demonstrated that the future belongs to this new generation. These companies' MIS departments are planning and developing now for the transition to the graphics environment of Windows, Presentation Manager, and Macintosh.

Many businesses are already experiencing large productivity gains by using Excel and other Windows applications. For example, one client in particular reduced the time to generate monthly management accounting reports from three days to half a day. This client previously used Lotus 1-2-3, Chartmaster, and Allways; now the business has automated the process with Excel.

The difference between Excel and character-based applications such as Lotus 1-2-3 is just short of astounding. After training well over 1500 people in hands-on spreadsheet skills and consulting on spreadsheets for 6 years, I recognize the differences between character-based and graphics-based applications and the advantages of graphics-based applications. People immediately accept Excel's graphical user interface. Beginning users return to work and immediately begin doing productive work with Excel. Such acceptance and immediate usability is rare with character-based spreadsheets.

The difference is accessible power. New users not only accept Excel quickly, but they also move up the productivity curve faster. Beginning Excel users do work that takes 1-2-3 users years of experience to reach. In Windows, Presentation Manager, and Macintosh applications, a new user can see all the available options after a single menu choice. By contrast a character-based application, such as Lotus 1-2-3 Release 3, may require the user to make as many as seven menu choices. At no time can the user see all the options. Many people use Lotus for years and never know the commands that they missed.

The growth of Windows and Presentation Manager reached its winning momentum in the first quarter of 1989. In the first quarter of 1989, more 80286 and 80386 computer systems capable of running the new generation of software were sold than were sold of the previous generation of 8088 and 8086 computers. At the same time more new Windows applications were released than new DOS applications.

Who Should Read This Book

Excel Tips, Tricks, and Traps is a dictionary of techniques to help you solve business problems. This book helps you push the high-end of Excel's already impressive capabilities and is a perfect companion to *Using Excel: IBM Version*, which contains tutorials as well as hundreds of tips and tricks.

The beginning or occasional Excel user can best use *Excel Tips, Tricks, and Traps* as a handbook of business aids. If you are a beginning user and reach a functional limit with Excel, such as moving a legend to the upper left corner, pull out this book to find a tricky solution. When you change paper orientation from portrait to landscape and the fonts change, pull out this book to learn why. Chapters such as those on creating and designing worksheets (Chapter 2), formatting (Chapter 3), and enhancing charts (Chapter 10) contain tips useful to all Excel users. These tips and tricks give you the extra edge that makes your finished results more impressive.

The intermediate Excel user will gain the most from this book. If you are an intermediate user, you are already moving up Excel's rapid learning curve and are looking for ways to push the limits of Excel's standard menus and recorded macros. You will find that by combining techniques or by using commands in innovative ways you can push Excel beyond its already impressive capabilities.

The advanced Excel user will gain from the sharing of techniques that increase performance or that improve the efficiency of macros. At the advanced level, it's often the insight gained from a single technique that allows a developer to simplify a project, break through a barrier, or improve efficiency. Excel's capability to create menus and custom dialog boxes and its capability to link applications using Dynamic Data Exchange or macro control of another application raise the limits of what advanced Excel users can do.

How To Use This Book

Use this book like a dictionary. Refer to it when you have a problem. The book is built by grouping tips, tricks, and traps into function-related chapters. These chapters do not necessarily correlate to the menus. If you need tutorial assistance or an in-depth explanation about a command, refer to *Using Excel: IBM Version*, the most comprehensive book on Excel for Windows and the Presentation Manager.

All readers of this book should take the time to look through the table of contents to learn what solutions the book contains. When you have a problem, you will know where to look.

Excel Tips, Tricks, and Traps is written for Excel users in the Windows, Presentation Manager, and Macintosh environments. Because of the graphics interface, users can move between hardware systems and continue to use Excel without retraining.

Shortcut keys are referred to throughout the book—first with Windows and Presentation Manager shortcut keys (noted by PC in parentheses), followed by the Macintosh shortcut keys (noted by Macintosh in parentheses).

Screen figures have been taken from operating Excel under Windows 2.1 on a Compaq computer with an EGA display.

Where To Find Other Information

Other related books, all published by Que Corporation, will increase your power and productivity with Excel:

Using Excel: IBM Version by Ron Person and Mary Campbell contains over 800 pages of Excel information starting from operating Windows and a mouse up to recording and modifying macros. Each section of the book begins with a Quick Start tutorial designed to teach you fundamental concepts step-by-step. The tutorials are built so that you can complete them with a minimum of reading and a maximum of hands-on learning in 40 minutes or less. After completing a tutorial, you can refer to the many in-depth chapters for more information. *Using Excel: IBM Version* contains hundreds of tips, tricks, and traps—each set apart from the text in an easy-to-find box.

Using Excel: Macintosh Version takes the same step-by-step approach as *Using Excel: IBM Version*. This book teaches you how to design worksheets, set up a database, create graphs, and develop macros with the Macintosh version of Excel.

Excel QuickStart, written for the beginning user, takes a graphics approach to teaching Excel. From over 100 two-page illustrations, you learn the basic Excel operations.

Excel Business Applications: IBM Version, a book and disk set, introduces the concepts and techniques for building Excel business models. You can run or customize the ready-to-run financial models provided with this book.

1

Operating Excel

Excel operates within the Windows environment on personal computers and within the desktop of Macintosh computers. Both of these environments are much easier to use than text-oriented computer environments. An additional advantage is that what you learn in one application will transfer to another Windows or Macintosh application.

Within both of these environments, you can display multiple documents, resize and move document windows, and use shortcut keys on frequently used procedures. This chapter describes these operations and shortcuts.

Starting Excel

In both PC and Macintosh Excel, you can use shortcuts to save you time in anything you do. For additional information on loading files, see Chapter 7.

1.1 Tip: **To load a worksheet file when you begin Excel, start the program with the file name.**

From Windows MS-DOS Executive in PC Excel, you can start the program and a selected worksheet together by selecting the worksheet's file name and pressing Enter or double-clicking your mouse on the file name. To do this, the directory that contains Excel must be in the PATH command in the AUTOEXEC.BAT file. If you install Excel correctly, the PATH is changed automatically.

From DOS, you can start Excel with a worksheet by changing to the Excel directory, typing the following, and pressing Enter:

EXCEL filename.ext

filename.ext is the file name of the Excel worksheet you want opened. If the worksheet is in a different directory, include the file's path name, as in the following command:

EXCEL C:\WINDOWS\89TAX\QTR1.XLS

From the desktop in Macintosh Excel, you can start the program with a specific worksheet by double-clicking on the worksheet's icon or name.

1.2 Tip: **If you want to work on several files, start Macintosh Excel and load several files.**

You can start Excel and load multiple Excel files on the Macintosh with these steps:

1. Open the folder that contains the files you want to open.
2. Select specific files by pressing Shift and clicking your mouse.

   Or

   Select all files by pressing Command+A. Then press Shift and click on the files you want to deselect.
3. Press Command+O to open all selected files and start Excel.

Getting Help

Excel provides extensive help information, almost like having a helpful guide at your beck and call. You can get general help information, specific help about a particular topic, and help about Excel equivalents to Lotus 1-2-3 commands. You can even use a shortcut key to change the mouse pointer so that you can point to commands about which you need help.

1.3 Tip: **If you need help with a command, press F1 to display an index of help.**

Press F1 while in the worksheet to display an index of help topics. (Macintosh users can press F1 or Command+/.) The **H**elp option is available on the PC Excel menu or as **W**indows **H**elp on the Macintosh Excel menu.

In PC Excel, select underlined topics with the Tab key and press Enter, or click on the desired topic. As each new list of topics and subtopics appear, select the topic in which you are interested. The mouse pointer displays as a hand when placed on a help topic you can choose (see fig. 1.1). Remove the Help window by choosing the **C**lose command or by pressing Alt+F4.

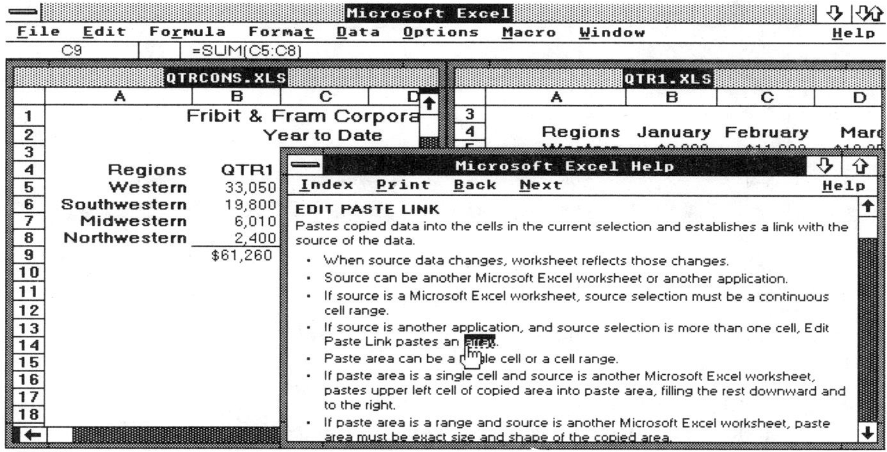

Fig. 1.1. *Selecting a help topic.*

In Macintosh Excel, choose the help topics you want from the scrolling list box. Remove the Help window by choosing the Close box or the Cancel button.

1.4 Tip: **To find related help or read definitions in the Help window, select words with a solid or dashed underscore.**

Words in a Help window with a solid underscore can lead you to additional Help windows. Choose these words by selecting them with the Tab key and pressing Enter or by clicking on them. Back up to the previous Help window with the **B**ack command.

Words or phrases underscored with a dashed line contain a definition. Select the underscored word by tabbing to it or clicking on it. To display the pop-up definition, hold down the Enter key or mouse button while pointing at the item. Figure 1.2 shows the definition of linked documents.

To see a listing of shortcut keys, choose Help for the keyboard and then select the type of shortcuts you want to see.

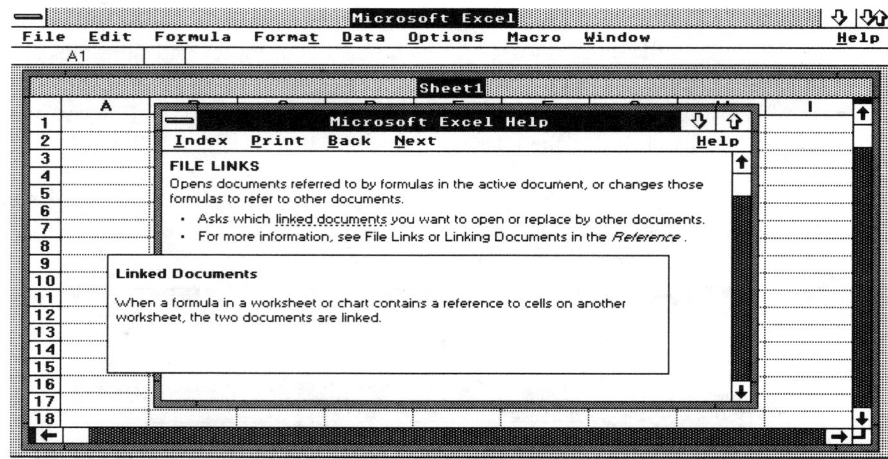

Fig. 1.2. A definition displayed from a Help window.

1.5 Tip:

For a hard copy, print the information in the Help window.

Print information in the Help window by choosing the **P**rint command in the Help window. For instance, you may want to print a copy of the shortcut keys.

1.6 Tip:

Instead of searching the Help index, use Shift+F1 to get context-sensitive help.

To get help for a specific command or area of the screen, press Shift+F1. On the Macintosh, you can press Shift+F1 or Command+?. A large question mark that indicates Help mode appears over the mouse pointer, as shown in figure 1.3. Click the question-mark pointer on the command or screen area for which you want help. The appropriate Help window appears.

PC users can get help about an open dialog box by pressing F1 for Help. Close the Help window by choosing the **C**lose command or by pressing Alt+F4.

Macintosh users can get help about an open dialog box by pressing F1 or Command+/. To close the window, choose the Cancel button or the Close box.

1.7 Tip:

When you receive an error message, use F1 to display additional information about the problem.

When error boxes appear on-screen, press F1 (PC) or Command+/ (Macintosh) to get additional information that describes the problem.

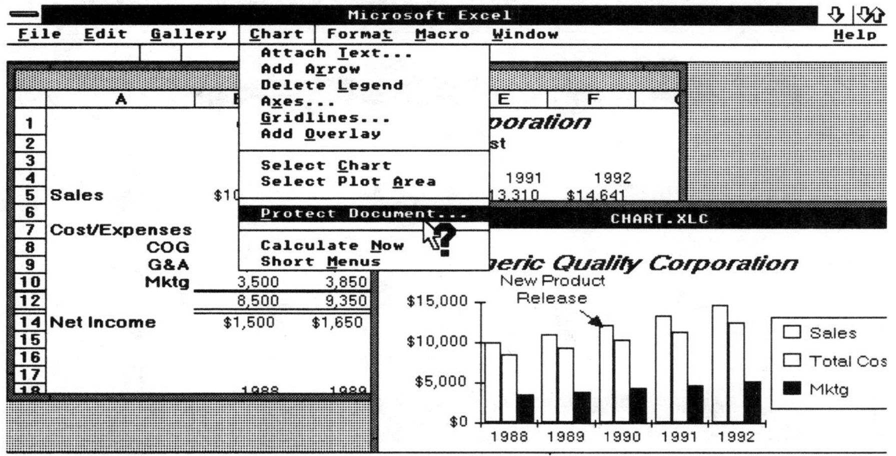

Fig. 1.3. Context sensitive help.

Arranging and Sizing Windows

One of the advantages to the Windows and Macintosh desktop environments is your ability to open multiple documents in Excel. You can be working with more than one worksheet, chart, and macro sheet at the same time. Using multiple windows is almost as easy as moving and arranging sheets of paper on your desktop. This section describes both basic window operations and shortcuts to make your work more productive.

1.8 Tip: **To move and size windows quickly, use the mouse.**

Figure 1.4 shows a PC Excel document window with boxes and title bar. You can control document windows in PC Excel with the actions listed in table 1.1. Table 1.2 shows the keys you can use to control windows in PC Excel.

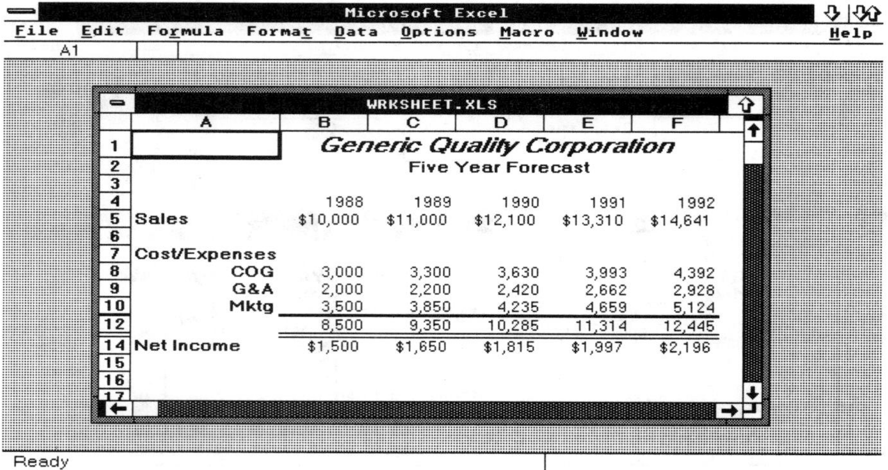

Fig. 1.4. PC Excel document window with boxes and title bar.

Table 1.1
Controlling PC Excel Windows

Movement	*Action*
Maximize a window	Double-click on title bar (top bar in window)
Maximize a window	Double-click on Size box (lower right corner)
Restore the size	Double-click on Size box
Close a window	Double-click on Document Control menu (left of title bar for worksheet)
Move the window	Drag the title bar
Move an edge	Drag the gray edge border
Change the size	Drag the Size box
Restore Excel from maximized to window	Click on Restore icon (double arrows at top right)
Minimize Excel to icon	Click on Minimize arrow (single down arrow at top right)

Movement	*Action*
Maximize an Excel window	Click on Maximize arrow (single up arrow at top right—not shown in fig. 1.4)
Restore a document window from maximized	Click on Document Control menu (to left of **F**ile in maximized window), choose **R**estore
Maximize Excel icon	Double-click on Excel icon (not shown in fig. 1.4)

Table 1.2
Controlling Windows in PC Excel

Action	*Key Excel window*	*Key Document window*
Restore	Alt+F5	Ctrl+F5
Move	Alt+F7	Ctrl+F7
Size	Alt+F8	Ctrl+F8
Minimize	Alt+F9	NA
Maximize	Alt+F10	Ctrl+F10
Close	Alt+F4	Ctrl+F4

Figure 1.5 shows a Macintosh window with boxes and the title bar. You can control windows in Macintosh Excel with the mouse actions in table 1.3.

Fig. 1.5. Macintosh windows showing boxes and title bar.

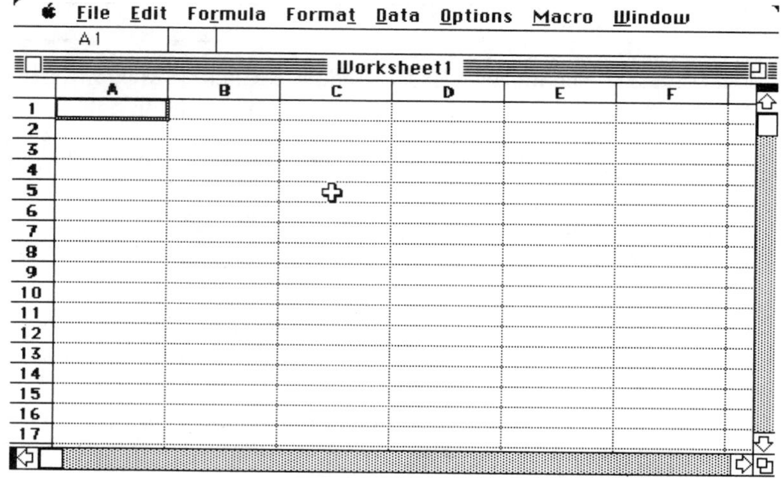

Table 1.3
Controlling Windows in Macintosh Excel

Movement	*Mouse Action*
Maximize a window	Click on Zoom box (on right in title bar)
Restore the size	Click on Zoom box (on right in title bar)
Close a window	Click on Close box (on left in title bar)
Move the window	Drag the title bar
Resize a window	Drag the Size box (lower right corner)

1.9 Tip: **Use automatic tiling to have Excel arrange the windows for you.**

You can arrange windows on-screen by dragging them by the title bar, or you can use automatic tiling. Excel automatically arranges worksheets on-screen when you choose the **W**indow **A**rrange All command. As figure 1.6 shows, each window is resized and arranged so that all windows show. If you have an even number of windows, the active window is placed at the top left. With an odd number of windows, the active window appears vertically at the left.

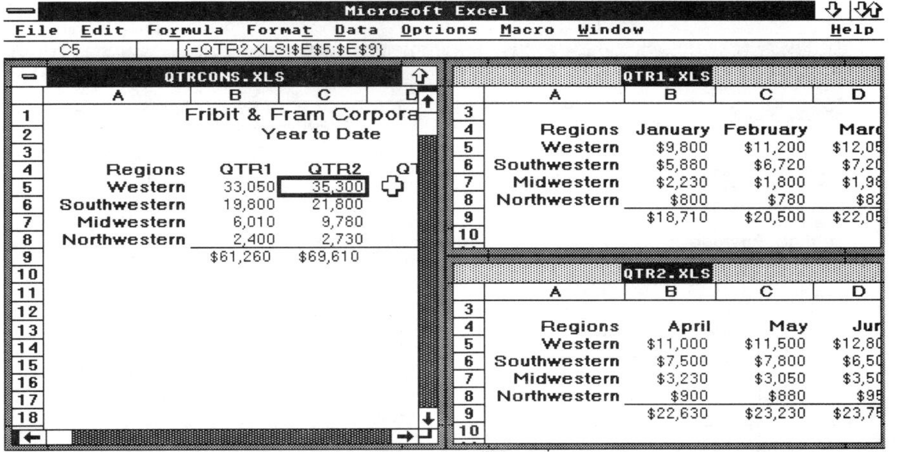

*Fig. 1.6. Windows arranged with the **W**indow **A**rrange All command.*

1.10 Tip: To see more than one part of a worksheet, split the screen into two window panes.

You can see more than one part of a window by splitting it into panes. The pane divider appears as a solid black bar at the top of the vertical scroll bar and at the left end of the horizontal scroll bar. You might want to split the worksheet, for example, to view both the criteria and extract ranges of a database file or to see both the data-entry area and the results area simultaneously.

To reposition the pane divider, drag the solid black bar to the place where you want to split the window. Release the mouse button when you have positioned the split. Figure 1.7 shows the mouse pointer at the right edge of the window after pulling down a pane divider.

If you want to use the PC keyboard to split windows, press Alt+- (Alt+hyphen) to select the Document Control menu. Then choose the Spli**t** command. Press arrow keys to move the grayed split bar. Press Enter to fix the split in place.

Panes scroll in pairs, either vertically or horizontally. Activate the pane in which you want to work by pressing F6 for the next pane or Shift+F6 for the previous pane.

Choose the **O**ptions **F**reeze Panes to lock panes in position. The **O**ptions Unfreeze Panes command unlocks panes. Remove panes by dragging the black bar past the arrow on the extreme end of the pane's scroll bar. Or using the keyboard, press Alt+- and then press the arrow key until the split moves off the screen.

Fig. 1.7.
Splitting a worksheet into panes.

Microsoft Excel
File Edit Formula Format Data Options Macro Window Help
D24 =G23
AMORTIZ3.XLS

	B	C	D
5	Principal		$30,000
6	Annual interest rate		9.75%
7	Term (years)		7
8	Periods (per year)		12
9	Start date		9/30/87
10	Monthly Payment		$494.17
11	No. of Payments		84
12			

	B	C	D	E	F	G	H
13–14	Payment no.	Payment dates	Beginning balance	Interest	Principal	Ending balance	Cumulative interest
22	8	Apr-88	28,203.76	229.16	265.01	27,938.74	1,892.09
23	9	May-88	27,938.74	227.00	267.17	27,671.58	2,119.10
24	10	Jun-88	27,671.58	224.83	269.34	27,402.24	2,343.93
25	11	Jul-88	27,402.24	222.64	271.53	27,130.71	2,566.57
26	12	Aug-88	27,130.71	220.44	273.73	26,856.98	2,787.01
27	13	Sep-88	26,856.98	218.21	275.96	26,581.03	3,005.22
28	14	Oct-88	26,581.03	215.97	278.20	26,302.83	3,221.19

Ready

1.11 Tip: **If the headings disappear in a split pane, make them reappear by moving the pane divider.**

If a split between window panes passes through row or column headings, the headings may be hidden, as though they were turned off by the **O**ptions **D**isplay Row & Column **H**eadings command. To make the hidden headings reappear, move the pane divider either closer to the window's center or as far as the divider will go toward an edge.

Operating Menus and Dialog Boxes

When you learn how to operate Excel menus and dialog boxes, you've learned how to operate 30 to 40 percent of any Windows or Macintosh application. The menus and dialog boxes work the same in all these applications. This synergy in learning gives you a head start in becoming productive on multiple applications.

Excel menus and dialog boxes give you something that no other electronic worksheet has—ACCESSIBLE POWER. In Excel you have to choose only a single command to get a dialog box that displays all the options available for that command. This means that Excel users from beginning to advanced can immediately see all the available features. No longer do you have to wind your way through long pathways of commands to find a single option. This section discusses tips, tricks, and traps to use when selecting options.

1.12 Tip: **Increase your speed by touch-typing through the menus.**

PC users can press the Alt key to activate the menu bar. Macintosh users press the period (.) key on the numeric keypad. (If you have a NumLock key, make sure that it is off when you press the period key.) Then you can select commands by typing the command or menu's underlined letter or by pressing arrow keys to select the command and then pressing Enter.

Excel also activates the menu bar if you press the slash (/) key. You can customize which key activates the menu by choosing the **O**ptions **W**orkspace command. Select the **A**lternate Menu Key command and change the slash (/) to a different key.

At any time, you can press the Esc key to cancel the menu bar.

1.13 Tip: **Avoid confusion with 1-2-3 by using the Alt key to activate the menu bar.**

If you are an experienced Lotus 1-2-3 user, pressing the slash (/) key to activate Excel's menu can inhibit your learning and confuse you in both Excel and 1-2-3. By pressing the slash key your mind begins to replay familiar 1-2-3 keystroke sequences. You will find learning Excel easier if you activate the menu with the Alt key. This key is used by all Windows and Presentation Manager applications.

1.14 Tip: **If you are a new user, choose partial menus.**

Excel comes with both full and short sets of menus. Choose the **O**ptions Full **M**enus command to see the full set, or choose the **O**ptions Short **M**enus command to see a partial set. The short set of menus does not contain more advanced commands and may be less intimidating for new users.

The Full **M**enus and Short **M**enus commands occupy the same location on the **O**ptions menu. Each appears when appropriate.

1.15 Tip: **Use quick key combinations to speed operations**

Quick key combinations perform operations or choose commands when you hold down one key and press a second. Quick key combinations are listed throughout this book in the appropriate topic area.

The first key held down for a quick key usually indicates a general type of action, as indicated in table 1.4.

Table 1.4
Quick Key Combinations

PC key	*Macintosh key*	*Type of Action*
Alt	Command	Choose commands and dialog box options
Shift	Shift	Extend a selection, perform the opposite action, or move in the opposite direction
Ctrl	Option	Execute quick formatting, execute a macro (PC) or execute a macro when in combination with Command (Macintosh)

1.16 Tip: **Use function keys as PC Excel command shortcuts.**

Use the function keys in table 1.5 as shortcuts for frequently used commands in PC Excel. Remember to hold down the Shift, Ctrl, or Alt keys as you press the function key. Additional shortcut keys are listed throughout the book in the appropriate topics. (If you are a former 1-2-3 user, notice that many of the single function keys are the same as they are in 1-2-3.)

Table 1.5
PC Excel Function Keys

Key	*Function*
F1	**H**elp
Shift+F1	Context-sensitive help
Alt+F1	**F**ile **N**ew (Chart)
Alt+Shift+F1	**F**ile **N**ew (Worksheet)
Alt+Ctrl+F1	**F**ile **N**ew (Macro sheet)
F2	Edit formula
Shift+F2	Fo**r**mula **N**ote
Ctrl+F2	**W**indow **S**how Info
Alt+F2	**F**ile Save **A**s
Alt+Shift+F2	**F**ile **S**ave
Alt+Ctrl+F2	**F**ile **O**pen
Alt+Ctrl+Shift+F2	**F**ile **P**rint
F3	Fo**r**mula **P**aste Name
Shift+F3	Fo**r**mula Pas**t**e Function
Ctrl+F3	Fo**r**mula **D**efine Name
Ctrl+Shift+F3	Fo**r**mula **C**reate Names
F4	Fo**r**mula **R**eference
Ctrl+F4	Control **C**lose (document window)
Alt+F4	Control **C**lose (application window)
F5	Fo**r**mula **G**oto
Shift+F5	Fo**r**mula **F**ind (cell contents)
Ctrl+F5	Control **R**estore (document window)
Alt+F5	Control **R**estore (application window)
F6	Next pane
Shift+F6	Previous pane
Ctrl+F6	Next document window
Ctrl+Shift+F6	Previous document window
F7	Fo**r**mula **F**ind (next cell)
Shift+F7	Fo**r**mula **F**ind (previous cell)
Ctrl+F7	Control **M**ove (document window)
Alt+F7	Control **M**ove (application window)
F8	Extend mode (toggles)
Shift+F8	Add mode
Ctrl+F8	Control **S**ize (document window)
Alt+F8	Control **S**ize (application window)

Table 1.5—*Continued*

Key	*Function*
F9	**O**ptions Calculate **N**ow
Shift+F9	**O**ptions Calculate **D**ocument
Alt+F9	Control Mi**n**imize (application window)
F10	Activate menu bar
Ctrl+F10	Control Ma**x**imize (document window)
Alt+F10	Control Ma**x**imize (application window)
F11	**F**ile **N**ew (Chart)
Shift+F11	**F**ile **N**ew (Worksheet)
Ctrl+F11	**F**ile **N**ew (Macro sheet)
F12	**F**ile Save **A**s
Shift+F12	**F**ile **S**ave
Ctrl+F12	**F**ile **O**pen
Ctrl+Shift+F12	**F**ile **P**rint
Alt+Esc	Activate next application window
Shift+Alt+Esc	Activate previous application window

1.17 Tip: **Use the function keys as Macintosh Excel command shortcuts.**

Use the function key combinations shown in table 1.6 as shortcuts for frequently used commands. Function keys are available on the Macintosh Extended keyboard. Remember to hold down the Command, Shift, or Command and Shift keys as you press the function key. Additional shortcut keys are listed throughout the book in the appropriate topics.

Table 1.6
Macintosh Function Keys

Key	*Function*
F1	**E**dit **U**ndo
Shift+F1	Context-sensitive help
F2	**E**dit Cu**t**
Shift+F2	Fo**r**mula **N**ote
Command+F2	**W**indow **S**how Info

Key	*Function*
F3	**E**dit **C**opy
Shift+F3	Fo**r**mula Pas**t**e Function
Command+F3	Fo**r**mula **D**efine Name
Command+Shift+F3	Fo**r**mula **C**reate Names
F4	**E**dit **P**aste
Command+F4	**F**ile **C**lose (active window)
F5	Fo**r**mula **G**oto
Shift+F5	Fo**r**mula **F**ind (cell contents)
Command+F5	Restore (decrease window size)
F6	Next pane
Shift+F6	Previous pane
Command+F6	Next document window
Command+Shift+F6	Previous document window
F7	Fo**r**mula **F**ind (next cell)
Shift+F7	Fo**r**mula **F**ind (previous cell)
Command+F7	Move active document window
F8	Extend mode (toggles)
Shift+F8	Add mode
Command+F8	Size active document window
F9	**O**ptions Calculate **N**ow
Shift+F9	**O**ptions Calculate **D**ocument
F10	Activate menu bar
Command+F10	Enlarge active document window
F11	**F**ile **N**ew (Chart)
Shift+F11	**F**ile **N**ew (Worksheet)
Command+F11	**F**ile **N**ew (Macro sheet)
F12	**F**ile Save **A**s
Shift+F12	**F**ile **S**ave
Command+F12	**F**ile **O**pen
Command+Shift+F12	**F**ile **P**rint
Command+M	Activate next document window
Command+Shift+M	Activate previous document window

1.18 Tip: **Use keyboard shortcuts in dialog boxes.**

As a touch typist, you may find it more convenient to keep your fingers on the keyboard as you make dialog box entries. Keyboard shortcuts you can use in a dialog box are shown in table 1.7. Shortcuts you can use in a text box are shown in table 1.8.

Table 1.7
Dialog Box Keyboard Shortcuts

Action	*PC Key*	*Macintosh Key*
Move to next item	Tab	NA
Move to previous item	Shift+Tab	NA
Move between option buttons	Arrow	NA
Toggle active check box	Space bar	NA
Move to name in list box	Letter that name begins with	Letter that name begins with
Select item with underlined letter	Alt+letter	Command+letter
Choose button with thick border (usually OK button)	Enter	Enter
Choose Cancel	Esc	Command+.

Table 1.8
Text Box Keyboard Shortcuts in PC Excel

Action	*Key*
Move	Left- or right-arrow key
Select letter	Shift+arrow
Move to beginning	Home
Move to end	End
Select to beginning/end	Shift+Home/End

Action	*Key*
Delete character to right	Del
Delete character to left	Backspace
Cut to clipboard	Shift+Del
Copy to clipboard	Ctrl+Ins
Paste clipboard at cursor	Shift+Insert

1.19 Tip: **Be quick—don't wait for the dialog box.**

Using the mouse to select from dialog boxes works well while learning or exploring, but it's much faster to type your command and option selections without waiting for the dialog box to appear. For example, in PC Excel pressing Alt, t, b, o, Enter (Forma**t** **B**order **O**utline) produces an outlined border much more quickly than if you waited for the dialog box.

1.20 Tip: **Make quick entries in dialog boxes.**

Many dialog boxes first display with the most frequently changed text box completely selected. Typing immediately replaces the text or number that is selected. For example, the Copies number in the **F**ile **P**rint dialog box always appears selected. This enables you to press Alt (PC) or the period on the numeric keypad (Macintosh), f, p, 6, Enter to print six copies.

1.21 Tip: **Make fast choices from scrolling list boxes.**

Scrolling list boxes, like the Fo**r**mula Pas**t**e Function box in figure 1.8, present lists of easily forgotten or misspelled choices. To choose quickly, use the keys in table 1.9.

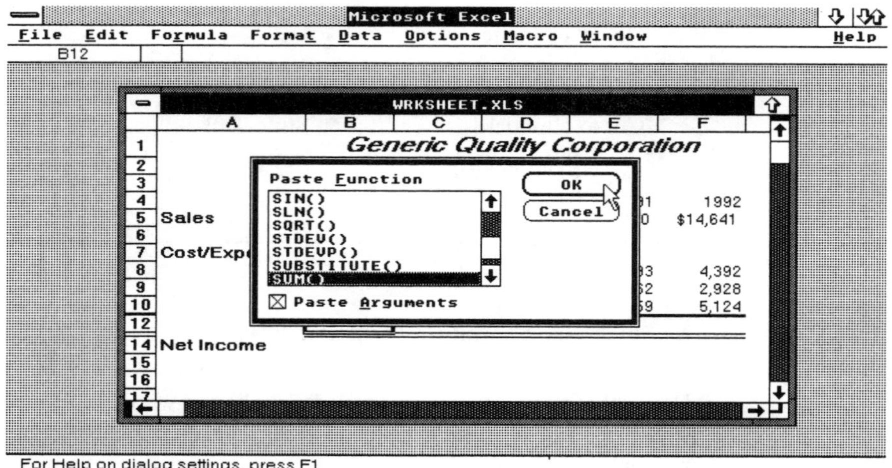

*Fig. 1.8. Formula Paste **F**unction box with SUM() selected.*

Table 1.9
Scrolling List Box Keyboard Shortcuts

Action	*Key*
First choice	Home (Macintosh: Any number key on keypad)
First choice starting with a specific letter	That letter
Last choice	End (Macintosh: No equivalent)

For example, to enter the SUM( ) function with its arguments, select any function in the list box so that it is highlighted. Then press s to move to the first function that starts with s. Press the down-arrow key until SUM( ) is selected. (In PC Excel, you can continue to press s until SUM is selected.)

With the mouse, you can scroll through the list box using the scroll bar. After SUM( ) is selected, select the Paste **A**rguments box and choose OK.

2

Creating and Editing a Worksheet

When building a simple worksheet or designing a complex integrated system composed of many worksheets, macros, and charts, it's important to plan ahead. The tips in the first part of this chapter help you plan your application. The shortcuts and tips throughout the rest of the chapter speed the actual production time.

Excel is easy to learn if you begin with the mouse and if someone explains the concepts of menus and dialog boxes. After working for a while, you may feel that there should be a faster way to work—there is. Sections of this chapter describe how to speed many processes such as editing and copying.

Designing Worksheets

A little worksheet planning can help prevent serious design problems later. As some of the steps here describe, building a worksheet using proper procedures can help you detect errors and bugs as you build the system. If you are building worksheets or systems that involve linking worksheets and using databases, be sure to read the chapters that discuss those topics.

2.1 Tip: **Follow a plan to build a worksheet without errors.**

Improve your chances of building a worksheet without errors by adhering to the ideas in the following plan.

1. Decide the needed output and input.

   Decide what you want for output, what is needed for input, and how you will find the solution. What are the assumptions that underlie your intended calculations? What variables will you want to change (interest rates, inflation rates, sales growth factors, and so on)?

2. Draw a thumbnail sketch or map.

   Make a simple sketch that shows the areas you'll need in your worksheet and their layout. Areas might include a data-entry area, a place for calculations, data tables, look-up areas, and a database. If your solution requires multiple worksheets with linked data, diagram which data is passed between specific worksheets, where the data comes from, and where it goes.

   The sketch helps you see areas of conflict when you later want to make a change. You can annotate the sketch or map later with range names or cell addresses to make it easy to move within the worksheet with the Goto key. The kite-tail layout described later in this chapter is a useful architecture for most worksheets.

3. Build a text skeleton.

   Type text headings and labels where you expect them to go. These labels needn't be in exactly the right location. You always can move them later. These labels act as a skeleton on which you can place data and formulas.

4. Enter sample data.

   Use sample data that's in the range of real data, but is easier to analyze. If the sample data is in the worksheet before you enter formulas, formulas return their results as soon as you enter them. If you have not entered sample data, a formula may return an error. Therefore, you don't know whether the formula is written correctly. Using round numbers such as 5000 and 2 when you enter sample data lets you immediately check the result of a formula such as =2*5000. More complex numbers, such as 2.354 and 5932.5, make it more difficult to tell whether a formula is correct.

5. Enter formulas, tables, and databases.

   To see the result of formulas as you enter them, first enter formulas that depend on data and then enter formulas that depend on other formulas.

6. Check for realistic results.

   Determine whether the formulas produce the correct results.

7. Format for appearance.

   To save time, select multiple nonadjacent areas (see the tips in the next section) and format them one at a time. Use the ROUND function or select **O**ptions **C**alculation **P**recision as Displayed to ensure that the numbers displayed and printed are the same numbers used in calculation. (Rounding errors can cause serious financial problems in all electronic worksheets. Excel's **O**ptions **C**alculation **P**recision as Displayed command handles the problem quickly.)

8. Cross-check, audit, and document your worksheet.

   Enter real data in the worksheet and cross-check the results against a hand-calculated answer. Use the techniques described in Chapter 6 to audit your worksheet for hidden errors. Document the worksheet for yourself and others by writing instructions or by marking cells that contain assumptions with the Fo**r**mula **N**otes command.

9. Save an archive copy of your worksheet.

   If your worksheet is important, took considerable time, or will be used by others, make a copy of the original, save it to a disk, and store it in a safe location for security and future reference.

2.2 Tip: Separate large worksheets into smaller linked worksheets.

Separating large worksheets into multiple smaller worksheets is the best way to work. If you use multiple linked worksheets, you gain the following:

- Faster delivery of worksheet programs. You can build large programs one component at a time and then begin working with the component worksheets. This way, you don't have to wait for the entire system to be built and debugged.
- More available memory. You have more memory because you load only necessary worksheets.

- Easier debugging. Your worksheet is easier to debug because you can test and debug each sheet individually rather than test the entire system.
- Components that are easier to upgrade. You can change one of the small worksheets without affecting all the others.
- Faster recalculation. You can recalculate more quickly because worksheets are smaller. Moreover, you may need to recalculate only the worksheet with which you are working instead of all worksheets.

Chapter 5 describes numerous ways of creating and editing multiple worksheets. Chapter 4 shows powerful techniques for linking and analyzing data between worksheets by using arrays. Chapter 9 explains how to extract data from worksheets.

2.3 Trick: Use a kite-tail layout to separate functional areas.

If you cannot separate a large worksheet into smaller linked worksheets, you may want to use a kite-tail architecture similar to that shown in figure 2.1. Figure 2.1 shows one large worksheet with areas that are functionally similar.

Each square in the kite-tail is an area of the worksheet that contains many cells. With the kite-tail structure, you can insert or delete rows or columns in any area without affecting any other area.

Reserve a square in the kite-tail for each functional part of the worksheet. For example, the top left square might contain data entry; the second can contain calculations; and the third can contain a database. The last square should be the data extract range for the database. Putting this area last prevents an unlimited data extract from accidentally deleting data below the area.

Excel's matrix memory management ensures that blank worksheet areas outside the squares do not use memory. If the rightmost cell is to the left of column 160 (column FD), normal memory management is used. If your worksheet exceeds 160 columns, refer to Chapter 13 for changes you can make to improve performance.

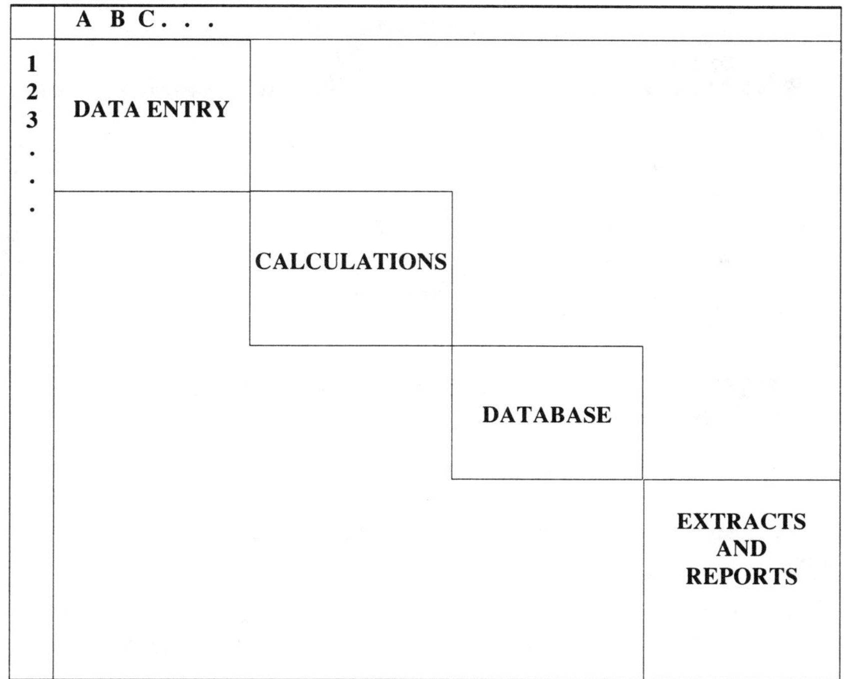

Fig. 2.1. *A worksheet with a kite-tail design.*

Selecting Cells and Ranges

With the tips and tricks in this section, you find out how to speed the process of selecting cells, how to view the corners of a selected range, and how to select areas in rapid succession.

2.4 Tip: **Select cells quickly with Goto.**

Use the Goto key—F5 for PC users, Command+G for Macintosh users—to move quickly to a new location. After pressing the Goto key, the dialog box in figure 2.2 appears. Choose a name from the list box or type the address in the **R**eference box and choose OK.

Fig. 2.2.
*The **Goto** dialog box.*

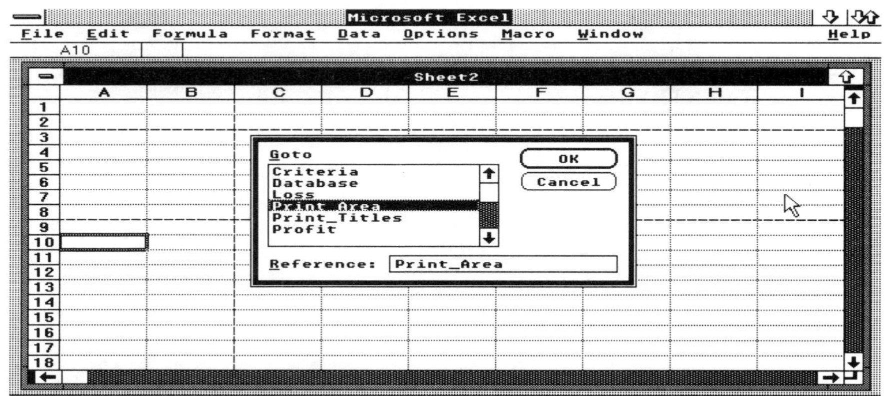

2.5 Trick: **Move the active cell around the worksheet quickly with the accelerator keys.**

Move the active cell quickly across the worksheet by holding the Ctrl (PC) or Command (Macintosh) key and pressing the arrow key for the direction you want to travel. If the active cell is on a filled cell, the cell travels in the direction of the arrow key until it encounters a blank cell. If the active cell is on a blank cell, the cell travels in the direction of the arrow until it encounters a filled cell.

2.6 Tip: **Select cells by pressing the Shift key as you move the cursor or as you click your mouse.**

Hold down the Shift key as you move with the arrow keys to select cells. With the mouse, click on the cell at one corner and then hold down Shift and click on the diagonally opposite corner to select the range between the corners. Use the Shift key in combination with other movement keys to select cells as you move the active cell.

Using Shift in combination with other movement keys is a fast way of selecting cells. Hold down Shift and click between distant cells as a quick method of selecting large areas with the mouse.

2.7 Tip: **Use keystrokes to select rows, columns, or the entire worksheet.**

In addition to clicking on row or column headings, you can select the row(s) of the active cell or range by pressing Shift+space bar. Select the column(s) of the active cell or range with Ctrl+space bar (PC) or Command+space bar (Macintosh).

2.8 Tip: **To format all cells at one time, select the entire worksheet quickly.**

Selecting the entire worksheet is a useful way to apply a format to the entire worksheet. Select the entire worksheet with the mouse by clicking in the blank box at the intersection of the row and column heading. Select the entire worksheet from the keyboard by pressing Shift+Ctrl+space bar (PC) or Shift+Command+space bar or Command+A (Macintosh).

2.9 Tip: **Select adjacent cells with the accelerator key.**

You can select adjacent filled cells or adjacent unfilled cells quickly by pressing Shift+Ctrl+arrow key (PC) or Shift+Command+arrow (Macintosh). In figure 2.3 the active cell is B8. Pressing Shift+Ctrl+right arrow (PC) or Shift+right arrow (Macintosh) selects cells B8:F8.

You can select large databases, sort areas, or print ranges using the Shift+Ctrl+arrow (PC) or Shift+Command+arrow (Macintosh) key combination by starting with the active cell at the top left and then pressing

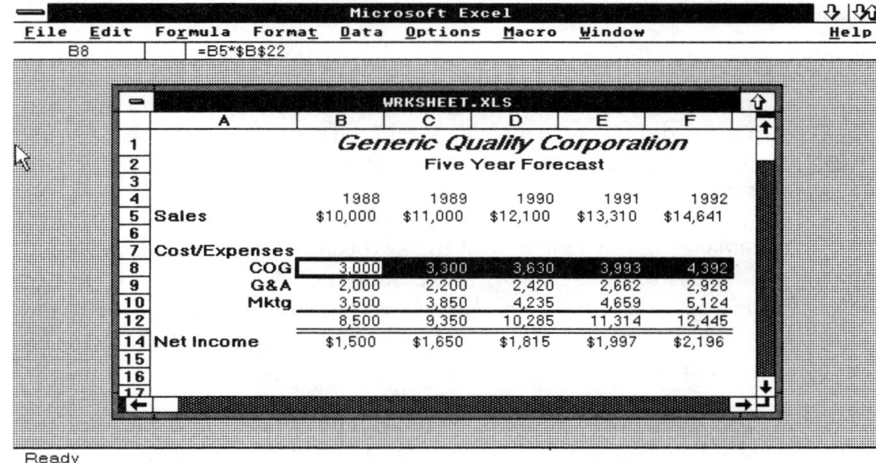

Fig. 2.3. Adjacent cells selected with the accelerator key.

Shift+Ctrl+down arrow (PC) or Shift+Command+down arrow (Macintosh). Then press Shift+Ctrl+right arrow (PC) or Shift+Command+right arrow (Macintosh). Beware that if a blank cell is met before the end of the range is reached, only part of the range you want is selected.

2.10 Tip: **To select or format several data-entry areas, select noncontiguous ranges, rows, or columns.**

You can select noncontiguous cells, rows, or columns with either the mouse or the keyboard, as in figure 2.4. This powerful feature is unavailable in other major spreadsheets. With this capability, you can select several data-entry areas, or you can format separate, but similar, areas of the worksheet with one command.

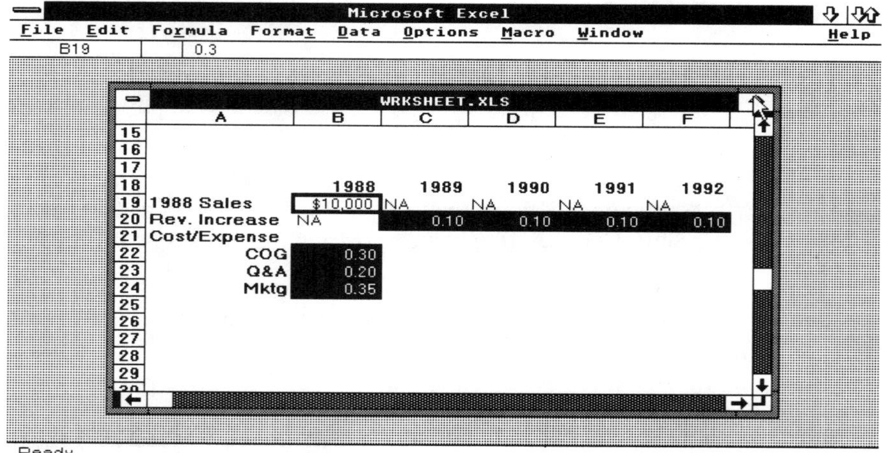

Fig. 2.4. Selecting noncontiguous areas of a worksheet.

To select noncontiguous ranges with the mouse, select the first area and then hold down the Ctrl (PC) or Command (Macintosh) key as you drag across each subsequent area. Clicking on any cell without holding the Ctrl (PC) or Command (Macintosh) key unselects all selected areas.

To select noncontiguous ranges with the keyboard, select the first range and then press Shift+F8. ADD appears at the bottom of the screen. Move to one corner of the next range to select. Hold down the Shift key and move to the diagonally opposite corner. The ADD indicator disappears. Press Shift+F8 again to retain the selected ranges and select another range.

To select noncontiguous rows or columns with the mouse, press Ctrl (PC) or Command (Macintosh) and click on each row or column heading.

2.11 Tip: Select large ranges with the Goto key or the mouse.

You select a range of cells when you want to change an area of cells with a single command or when you want to define a space in which to enter data. If the range is large, selecting the range by scrolling from one corner to another takes a long time. Instead, you can use a quick method to select a large range.

To select a large range with the keyboard, select one corner of the range, press the Goto key—F5 on the PC, Command+G on the Macintosh. Type the address of the diagonally opposite corner in the **R**eference box and then hold down the Shift key as you select OK.

To select a large range with the mouse, click on one corner of the range and use the mouse to scroll to the diagonally opposite corner. Then hold down the Shift key as you click on the opposite corner.

2.12 Tip: Select related or groups of cells with Formula Select Special.

When checking for errors or formatting, it is convenient to select all cells of a certain type within an area. To select related cells, use the Fo**r**mula **S**elect Special command. The Fo**r**mula **S**elect Special command has numerous options, as shown in table 2.1

Table 2.1
Formula Select Special Options

Item	*Option*
Notes	**N**otes
Constants	**C**onstants
Formulas (different types)	Fo**r**mulas (and type)
Blanks	**B**lanks
Rectangle range of touching cells	Current Regi**o**n
Cells that belong to an array	Current **A**rray

If you want to select special cells from the entire worksheet, select only one cell before choosing the command. To select special cells within an area, select the area and then choose the command. The use of Fo**r**mula **S**elect Special in debugging is described in Chapter 6.

2.13 Tip: **To see all corners of a large selected range, use Ctrl+. (period) for PC Excel or control+. (period) for Macintosh Excel.**

When you print large areas or select large databases, you may want to see all the corners of the range to make sure that they are correct. To see all corners of a large selected range quickly, PC users press Ctrl+. (period); Macintosh users press control+. (period). Each corner is activated in turn.

2.14 Tip: **Move any corner of a selection with a shortcut key.**

To move any corner in a selected range, press Ctrl+. (period) on the PC or control+. (period) on the Macintosh until the active cell is diagonally opposite the corner you want to move. Move the corner opposite the active cell by holding down the Shift key and pressing the arrow keys, or by holding down the Shift key and clicking at the new corner. To see the corner you are moving, scroll the window so that the corner opposite the active cell is visible.

Using Range Names

Range names help to make your worksheets more readable. Instead of cell references appearing in formulas, you can enter English-like names. Range names are also important when building worksheets you use with macros. If you change the worksheet, a macro that uses cell references may not be able to find the correct location, but a macro that uses range names will.

2.15 Tip: **Use range names to move to and select areas quickly.**

Range names turn cell references into English-like names. For example, instead of referring to the range as B12:G45, you can refer to the range as MONTHLY_REPORT. This name makes formulas easier to read and worksheets easier to operate.

You can name ranges with the Formula **D**efine Name command. For instance, figure 2.5 shows naming a range Data Entry. When you want to reselect these same cells, select the Fo**r**mula **G**oto command or press F5 (PC) or Command+G (Macintosh) and then choose the name you want. This feature is useful for reselecting a frequently used data-entry area.

You can name areas you use frequently such as sort ranges or print areas so that you don't have to select them manually. For example, you may have a

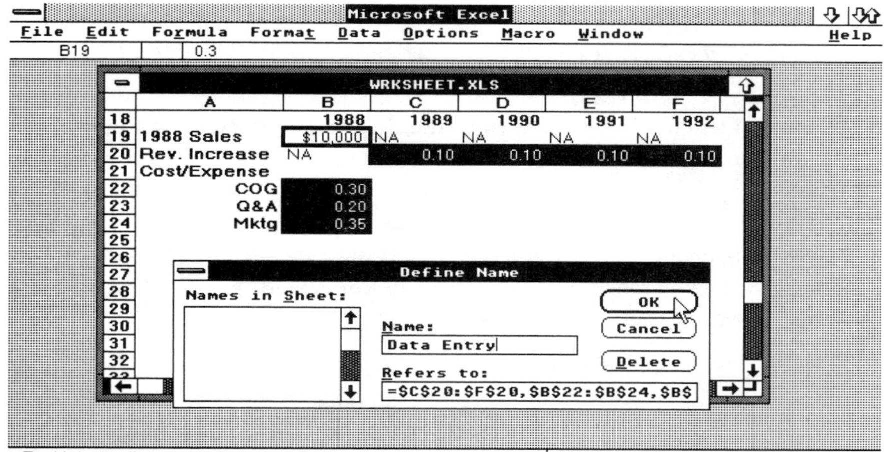

Fig. 2.5. Naming nonadjacent ranges.

multipage report that spans three noncontiguous ranges, A1:H89, L120:P240, and S300:W350. Rather than select and print these ranges manually each month, select all three ranges at once by holding down the Ctrl (PC) or Command (Macintosh) key and dragging over the ranges. This action selects all three at one time. Now choose Fo**r**mula **D**efine name, type the name **MO_REPORT** in the **N**ame box, and choose OK.

Next month when you want to print these same three ranges, press F5 (PC) or Command+G (Macintosh). Then choose MO_REPORT from the list of names. Choose **O**ptions Set Print **A**rea and print with **F**ile **P**rint.

2.16 Tip: Name ranges and cell references if you will use these references in macros.

Macros exist in one or more sheets separate from the worksheet. If you change a worksheet by inserting or deleting rows or columns, macros will not adjust to reference where an item in the worksheet has moved.

You can solve this problem by using names to reference ranges in the worksheet. Even if you change the worksheet, the macro still can find the named range.

2.17 Tip: Follow specific rules when entering range names.

Range names can be up to 255 characters in length. Using shorter names leaves you more room in formulas. Type names in upper- or lowercase; Excel refers to the same name in either case. Do not use spaces or hyphens in names.

Where you need a space, use an underline. Do not use names that look like cell references such as B13 or R1C12.

2.18 Trap: **Be careful when moving, inserting, and deleting within named ranges.**

Named ranges change the cells they reference when you insert or delete rows and columns or when you move the entire range. You must understand how names will change if you edit your worksheet. In nearly all cases, Excel adjusts the named range to refer to the cells you intended. The following rules define when a named range moves with cells that are moved.

If you move all cells that enclose a named range, the named range moves with the cells. If you move a range of cells that contains two corners on the same side of the named range, the two corners of the named range move, and the named range is redefined to include those corners. Commands that can make these moves include Edit Cu**t** and **P**aste; Edit **I**nsert cells, rows, or column; and Edit **D**elete cells, rows, or columns. If you move a single corner of the named range, the named range is not redefined. Edit Cu**t** and **P**aste is the only command that moves a single corner.

Inserting rows at the top row of a range moves the range down. Inserting columns at the left column of a range moves the range left. Deleting a row or column that contains two corners of a range reduces the size of the range as you would expect. The range name is not destroyed as it is in Lotus 1-2-3.

If you are unsure of a range name's new location, choose the Fo**r**mula **G**oto command, select the name, and see the cells it defines.

2.19 Tip: **Name values and formulas to make formulas easy to read.**

You can store values and formulas in range names to make formulas easier to read. Putting values and formulas in range names also reduces clutter because constants and formulas aren't in the worksheet. The disadvantage to this technique is that the values and formulas are not readily apparent. This process is not the same as naming a cell and its contents. You are actually storing a constant or formula in the name.

Figure 2.6 shows the Define Name dialog box with a formula in the **R**efers to: box. The name for the result of this formula is Sales_Inc. You enter the formula in the **R**efers to: box just as you enter one in the formula bar. Enter the absolute references $C$20 and $B$5 by clicking on the cells in the worksheet. (If a cell is not visible behind the Define Name box, use the scroll bars to move the worksheet or drag the dialog box with its title bar.) Clicking on a cell

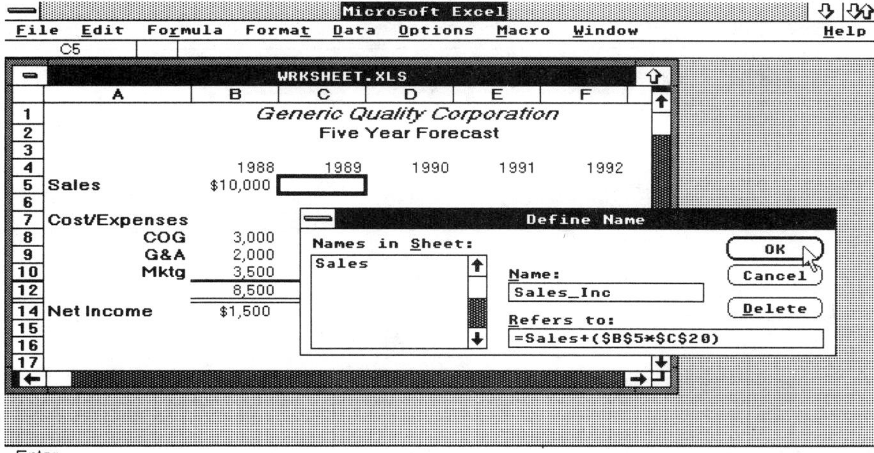

Fig. 2.6. *The Define Name box.*

produces an absolute reference. After naming a formula, enter it in a cell by typing the equal sign and its name, such as **=Sales_Inc**.

This named formula is the same as an absolute reference formula; the range does not adjust to new locations to which it is copied. For this reason, if you enter Sales_Inc in C5, it will not give correct results when copied to D5:F5.

2.20 Tip: **Change named formulas to relative reference for copying.**

You normally build named ranges with absolute references. The named formula refers only to the specific cells named by the absolute references. In some cases, you will want a relative reference-named formula that you can use in different locations in the worksheet.

To build a relative named formula, select the cell in which you would put the named formula if you were typing it into a cell. Choose the Fo**r**mula **D**efine Name command. Enter the formula by typing or clicking on worksheet cells. Use F4 (PC) or Command+T (Macintosh) to change cell references from absolute to relative where needed. In figure 2.7, $C$20 will stay "absolutely" the same when copied, but B5 will change "relative" to its copied location. Choose OK. The name Sales_Inc_Rel contains the formula.

In figure 2.7, the named formula has been made into a relative formula. If you enter this formula in cell C5 as **=Sales_Inc_Rel**, the formula gives correct results if you copy it into D5:F5. Be careful when copying relative reference-named formulas. Because you cannot see how the cell reference has adjusted relative to a new location, troubleshooting may be more difficult.

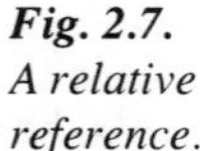

Fig. 2.7.
A relative reference.

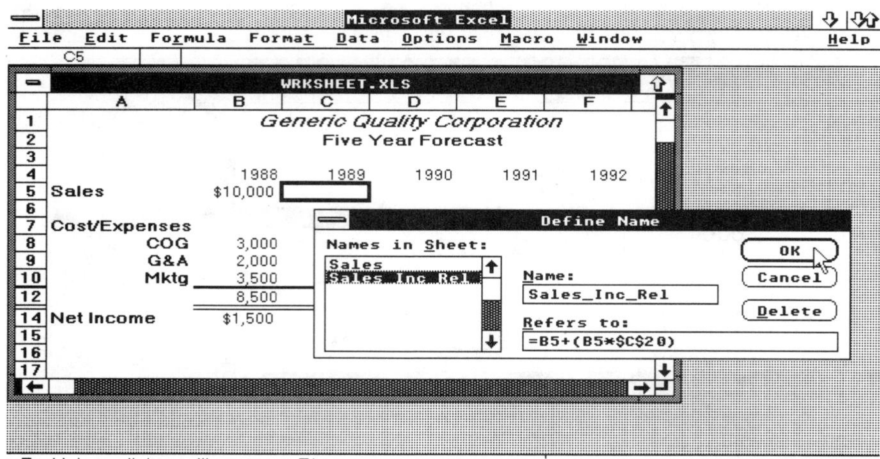

2.21 Tip: **Use range names to save typing and memory when entering long formulas.**

If you have one or more formulas that involve a frequently used, but lengthy term, save typing time and memory by assigning a name to the lengthy term in your formula. To do so, use the Formula Define Name command. Using the English-like name in your formulas instead of the actual term saves typing, makes the formula more readable, and allows you to type longer formulas in the formula bar. Be careful with this feature—you may create complex formulas that are difficult for somebody not familiar with that worksheet to review and understand.

2.22 Tip: **Create a list of all range names and what they represent with the Formula Paste Name command.**

Document what range names represent by making a list of names with the Formula Paste Name command. Select a cell in a clear area of your worksheet (preferably an area you reserve for documentation). Choose the Formula Paste Name command. Choose the Paste List button. A two-column list is pasted into your worksheet. Each row in the list contains the range name and the cell reference, value, or formula that the name represents.

Entering Data

Once you build your worksheet, you or your associates will spend most of the time entering data. You can use shortcuts for entering data.

2.23 Tip: **Don't wait for recalculations as you enter data.**

You do not need to wait for recalculations to finish as you enter data. Pressing a key or clicking the mouse stops the calculation. When you pause during data entry for a few seconds, Excel resumes recalculating and includes the changes you made.

2.24 Tip: **Turn off recalculation when entering data in a large worksheet.**

Another way to enter data and not wait for recalculation is to choose the **O**ptions **C**alculation **M**anual command. This command stops all recalculation until you order Excel to recalculate the worksheet.

2.25 Trap: **If Calculate displays on-screen, be sure to recalculate the worksheet; otherwise, results may be incorrect.**

The word Calculate appears at the bottom of the worksheet if the worksheet results need recalculation. To recalculate all sheets, use the **O**ptions **C**alculate **N**ow command or press F9. To calculate only the active worksheet, use Shift+**O**ptions **C**alculate **D**ocument or press Shift+F9.

Recalculating only the active worksheet is faster than calculating all worksheets. If your worksheet contains results that are linked to dependent calculations in other worksheets, you should recalculate all worksheets.

2.26 Tip: **To enter numbers, use the 10-key numeric keypad.**

If your computer has a combined 10-key arrow and numeric pad, you can use it to enter numbers quickly. Press the NumLock key. A NUM indicator appears at the bottom of the screen. Then use the numeric keypad to enter numbers. When you want to use the numeric key pad to move the active cell, hold down the Shift key and press the arrow keys. Release the Shift key to return to numeric entry.

2.27 Tip: **Use the Options Workspace Fixed Decimal command to have Excel enter the decimal point for you.**

If you want Excel to enter the decimal point for you during numeric data entry, check the **O**ptions **W**orkspace **F**ixed Decimal command. When **F**ixed Decimal is selected, you can enter a number in the worksheet, and Excel places the decimal point. Enter the number of decimal places you want in the **P**laces text box shown in figure 2.8.

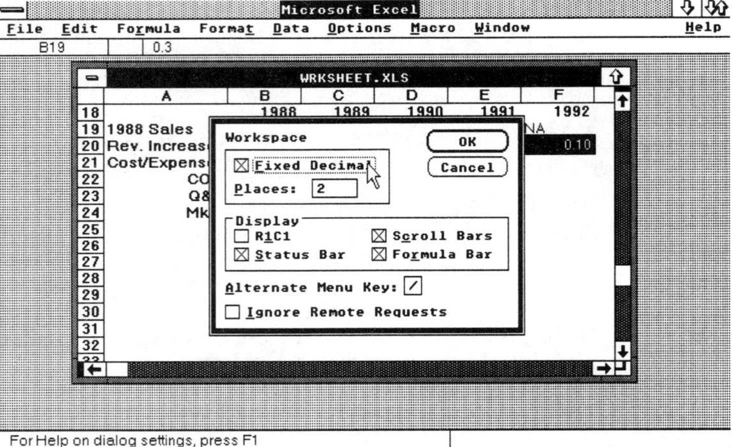

Fig. 2.8. *Setting up Excel to enter decimal points automatically.*

If you want to enter a number with a different number of decimal places than you entered in the **P**laces box, enter the decimal point manually. Your entry overrides the automatic decimal.

2.28 Tip: **To enter nonkeyboard characters with PC Excel, use ANSI or IBM Extended Character sets. With the Macintosh, use Option or Shift+Option.**

You can type nonkeyboard characters in an Excel worksheet when you need to enter characters such as the copyright symbol © or registered trademark ®. These characters are located in an extended character set beyond the characters used on the keyboard. Your computer may contain one or more sets of extended characters.

In PC Excel, two standard sets of characters understood by most MS-DOS computers and printers are the ANSI set and the IBM PC Extended Character set. The characters display on-screen if your computer contains that character set.

To type an ANSI character in the formula bar, press the NumLock key so that NUM appears at the bottom of the screen. Hold down the Alt key and type the four-number combination that matches the ANSI character you want. You must type the four numbers on the numeric keypad.

When you release the Alt key, the character appears at the cursor location in the formula bar. You can find a full list of ANSI characters in *Using Microsoft Windows* published by Que Corporation or in your computer manual. Figure 2.9 shows some ANSI characters on the Excel screen.

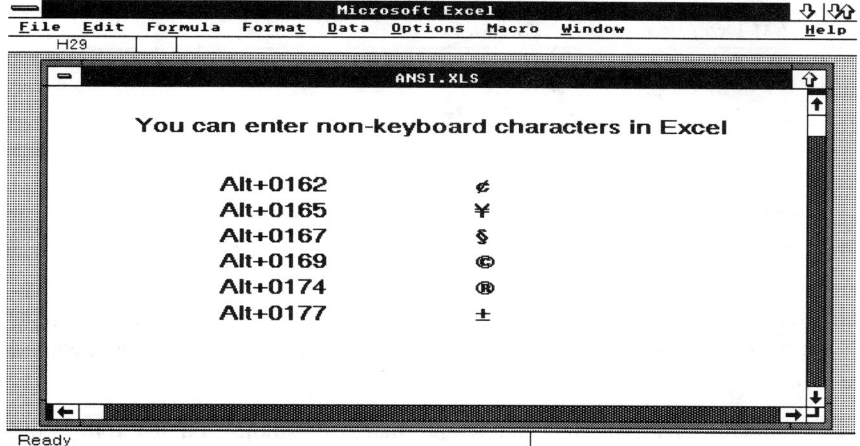

Fig. 2.9. ANSI characters on-screen in an Excel worksheet.

Enter characters from the IBM PC Extended Character set with the same procedure using the appropriate number. As before, make sure that you use the numeric keypad to enter the numbers.

Although your screen may display a character, the character prints only if your printer contains the same character set. Some dot-matrix printers can switch between different character sets. If you use a laser printer with soft fonts or font cartridges, your character set changes depending on the soft font or cartridge. The characters associated with each are listed in the documentation that came with the software or cartridge. If you are unsure what characters will print, try different character code numbers from 127 to 255 until you find the character you want.

Some of the characters and their codes for the ANSI and IBM Extended Character set are shown in table 2.2.

Table 2.2
Some ANSI and IBM Extended Characters

ANSI Code	*Character*
0162	¢
0163	£
0165	¥
0169	©
0174	®
0177	¶
IBM Extended Code	*Character*
155	¢
156	£
157	¥
227	¶

In Macintosh Excel, enter nonkeyboard characters by holding down either Option or Shift+Option as you type a keyboard character. The nonkeyboard character appears on-screen and prints.

The available symbols and characters change depending on the font being used. To see the symbols and characters and the key with which the character is associated, pull down the Apple menu and choose Key Caps. The screen shows a keyboard. Select the font you want to use. The keyboard letters change to match the font.

Press the Option key or Shift+Option to see which characters are available. Find the symbol or character you want and its associated keys. Close the Key Caps menu to return to Excel.

In Excel, type the symbol or character by holding down Option or Shift+Option and pressing the letter that provides the symbol or character you want.

2.29 Tip: **If you want data entered in only specific cells, restrict the data-entry area.**

Excel can restrict data entry to selected cells. Figure 2.10 shows the cells selected for data entry. You can select these cells manually each time, give them a name, and use Formula Goto. Or you can record a macro to select the cells. Typing data and pressing the Enter or Tab key enters the data and moves to the next cell. Excel even remembers the order in which cells are selected and repeats that order during data entry.

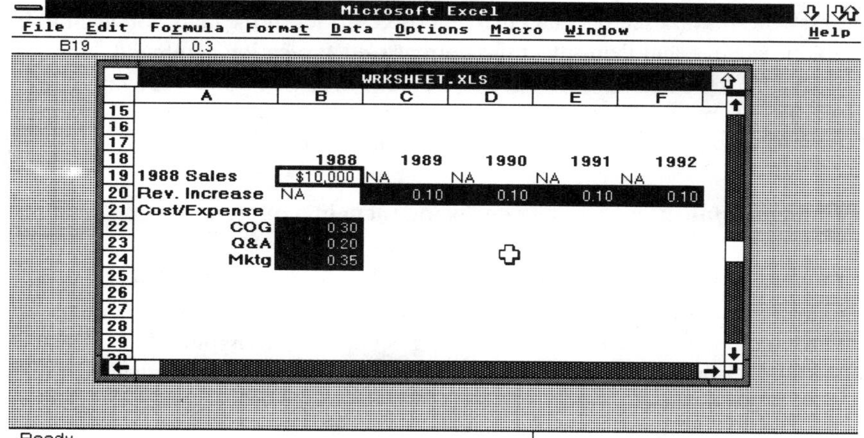

Fig. 2.8. *Cells selected for data entry.*

To select multiple cells, hold down the Ctrl (PC) or Command (Macintosh) key as you drag or click on the cells you want selected. Begin with the second cell in which you want data, proceed through the other cells in the order in which you want data entered. Click on the cell that will be first during data entry.

As you enter the data, you move in a specific direction depending on the key you press. For instance, press Enter to move down; press Shift+Enter to move up; press Tab to move right; and press Shift+Tab to move left.

In Macintosh Excel, you can choose the **O**ptions **W**orkspace command and select **M**ove Selection After Return if you want the active cell to always move down after pressing Enter.

2.30 Tip: **Turn on worksheet protection to protect cells from accidental changes.**

To protect cells from accidental changes, turn on worksheet protection by choosing the **O**ptions **P**rotect Document command and pressing Enter. This command locks all cells in the worksheet and prevents them from being changed.

You can format specific cells so that you can make changes even while the document is protected. To format specific cells, first remove worksheet protection if it is on by selecting **O**ptions Un**p**rotect Document, enter the password if you used one, and then choose OK. Select the cells you want to be able to change and then select the Forma**t** Cell **P**rotection command. Unselect **L**ocked. When **L**ocked is unselected, a cell is unprotected even though worksheet protection is on. Now select the **O**ptions **P**rotect Document command to protect all other cells in the worksheet.

2.31 Tip: **Change numbers into text by enclosing them in a quoted formula.**

In most cases, such as in the use of string (text) formulas, Excel automatically converts numbers to text. Should you find a case where text numbers are needed, you can create them. Enter numbers as text by typing a space before the number or by entering the number as a text string. Use a text string formula such as the following:

="95409"

Entering Dates and Times

Dates and times in Excel can be powerful. You can do math with dates and times to calculate such things as the number of hours worked or the number of days an account receivable is overdue. This section discusses tips, tricks, and traps for working with dates and times.

2.32 Tip: **Use quick keys to enter the date and time in your worksheet.**

You can enter the date and time set in the computer into an Excel worksheet quickly. To enter the current date in PC Excel, press Ctrl+; (Ctrl+semicolon). To enter the current time, press Ctrl+: (Ctrl+colon).

To enter the current time in Macintosh Excel, press Command+; (Command+semicolon). To enter the current date, press Command+- (Command+hyphen).

Unless formatted otherwise, the date appears in the format MM/DD/YY (3/27/89), and the time appears in the format HH:MM:SS AM/PM (9:10:15 AM).

2.33 Tip: **Date and time stamp your worksheets or printouts.**

You can have Excel automatically date and time stamp your worksheet if you need to provide an audit trail. In the cell where you want the time, date, or both, enter the NOW( ) function. You don't include any arguments within the parentheses.

NOW( ) produces the serial date and time set in your computer's clock—such as 32605.75. The fractional part of the serial date number is the time, a fractional part of 24 hours. Use a date or time format to convert a serial date such as 32605.75 into an understandable date and time.

This function updates whenever you open the file and whenever you recalculate. Permanently stamp the time by converting the NOW( ) function into a constant. To do so, select the cell, select the entire formula, and press F9 (PC) or Command+= (Macintosh).

Chapter 8 describes how to date and time stamp the header or footer on each page of a printout.

2.34 Tip: **Let Excel format date and time entries.**

If you type a date or time in a format that Excel recognizes, Excel automatically formats the cell to match that date and time. To see the date and time formats that Excel recognizes, select the Forma**t** **N**umber command and scroll through the Format **N**umber list box. Excel recognizes many date and time variations that are similar but not exactly like the formats in the list box. For example, Excel recognizes and formats the entry March 31, 1989 even though it does not appear in the list box.

Dates or times that Excel does not recognize are entered as text. For example, 31 March, 1989 enters as text. If the date you enter does not appear in the formula bar in the format MM/DD/YYYY, Excel did not recognize its format.

2.35 Tip: **To save time typing dates, enter just the month and the day—Excel enters the year for you.**

Type dates in the current year using just the month and day. Excel enters the year for you. For example, typing **5-14** enters and formats as 14-May. If you type a month and year, Excel enters the date as the first of that month. For example, typing **Nov 50** enters and formats as Nov-50. You see the actual dates 5/14/89 and 11/1/1950, respectively, in the formula bar.

2.36 Trap: **Enter accurate dates; otherwise, you might enter a date you don't want.**

Make sure that your dates are valid before you type them. For example, entering 2/30 in an unformatted cell enters 2/1/1930. February has only 28 or 29 days; therefore, Excel assumes that you have entered a month and year and enters the date as the first of the month.

2.37 Trap: **Dates entered in previously formatted cells may not display as numbers.**

Excel automatically formats dates when entered if the cell is in General format. If the cell is not in General format, Excel recognizes the entry as a date, calculates the serial date number, but displays the serial date number in the cell's current format. This date can produce some unusual results.

The worksheet in figure 2.11 illustrates how the dates displayed in column B appear if they are entered in column D, which has a General format and if entered in column F, which has a variety of numeric formats. For example, F7

Fig. 2.11. Date and numeric formats.

Microsoft Excel

File Edit Formula Format Data Options Macro Window Help

D18

DATEFRMT.XLS

Dates Entered in Formatted Cells
May Not Display Correctly

Date Entered	Entered in General Formatted Cell	Entered in Formatted Cell	Col. F Cell Format
5/14/90	5/14/90	$33,007	$#,##0
Aug 6, 90	6-Aug-90	3.31E+04	0.00E +00
3 Aug	3-Aug	32723	0
12/24	24-Dec	12/24/89 0:00	m/d/yy h:mm

Ready

has the format shown in G7 for currency. When you type the date shown in B7 into F7, the date appears as currency because of F7's existing format.

To change the incorrectly formatted dates back to a date display, use Format Numbers to reformat the cells with the correct date format.

2.38 Tip: **Use date calculations to figure the number of days between dates and future dates.**

Date calculations are important to many types of series analysis, from aging accounts receivables to analyzing the growth rates of animal populations. Excel has the capability to work with dates as easily as it does with numbers. For instance, businesses often need to calculate a future payment date or calculate the days since the last payment. With Excel, this calculation is done as easily as any simple math formula.

Although Excel appears to accept dates as you type them, it really converts the date into a serial date number. This number is the number of days from the beginning of the century or the beginning of 1904. Most computer programs use a serial date calculated from the beginning of the century. You can see the serial date number by reformatting a date cell to General format.

Figure 2.12 shows how to calculate the number of days between dates and how to calculate a future date. Excel formats cells B8, B9, and E8 when you enter the dates.

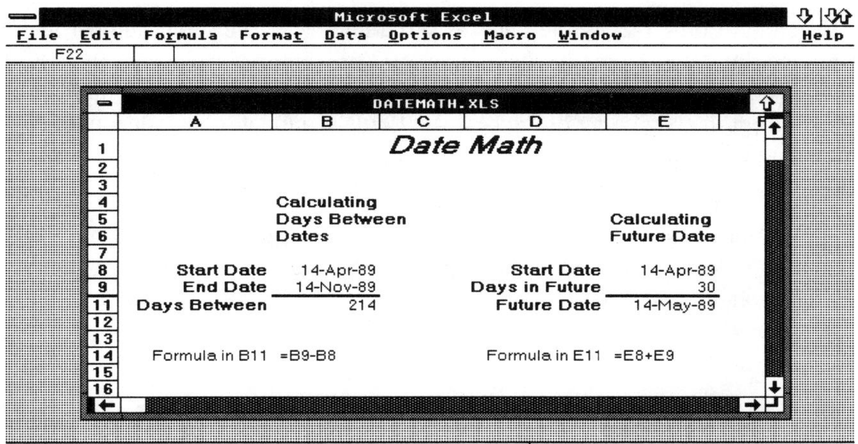

Fig. 2.12. Using date calculations.

The following formula, in cell B11 in the worksheet, calculates the number of days between the date in B9 and B8:

=B9–B8

The following formula, in cell E11, calculates the date 30 days in the future from 14-Apr-89:

=E8+E9

The formula in cell E11 produces a serial date number, 32642, when first entered. Change the serial date number to a date display by formatting it with the Forma**t** **N**umber command.

2.39 Tip: Use the 1904 Date System command to make sure that PC Excel and Macintosh Excel dates are the same.

Worksheets transported between PC Excel and Macintosh Excel may have date discrepancies. Older Macintosh Excel worksheets calculated the serial date number from 1904. Newer PC and Macintosh Excel worksheets can calculate serial date numbers from 1900 or 1904. To resolve discrepancies, make sure that the two systems use the same serial date calculation by choosing the **O**ptions **C**alculations command and selecting the 1904 **D**ate System command. This setting applies only to the currently active worksheet. The worksheet retains this setting when you save the file.

2.40 Trap: If you export Excel serial dates to other applications, check them. Excel's dates may be one day off.

Excel and Lotus 1-2-3 store dates as serial numbers. The serial number is the number of days from the beginning of this century. However, the 1-2-3 worksheet was originally built with an error that miscalculated the number of days from the beginning of the century. Lotus serial dates have one extra day. To maintain compatibility, Excel has continued this convention.

This convention may cause discrepancies if you export Excel serial dates to applications that correctly calculate the serial date. If data imported from Excel appears to be one day off, return to the worksheet, create formulas that subtract a day from the serial date, and repeat the export.

Entering a Series of Numbers or Dates

Surveys have revealed that 80 to 85 percent of the uses for electronic worksheets are in budgeting and forecasting. In both of these areas, you need to enter a series of dates and sometimes a series of numbers. Excel can perform this task for you. With the **D**ate Se**r**ies command you can enter a sequence of ascending or descending numbers, dates, or times that increment by the amount you specify.

2.41 Tip: **Enter numeric or date sequences with the Data Series command.**

The **D**ata Se**r**ies command saves time and prevents errors when you need to enter a series of numbers or dates. This command can even enter date sequences that involve months or weekdays. For instance, you might want to enter a series of months for a loan payment schedule.

Figure 2.13 shows the **D**ata Se**r**ies dialog box. The entries specify numeric data that increase in positive increments of 2 until the selected cells are filled. Notice that the first cell in the selected range, B15, must contain the starting value. The range to be filled is B15:H15. Row 17 shows the results of this series.

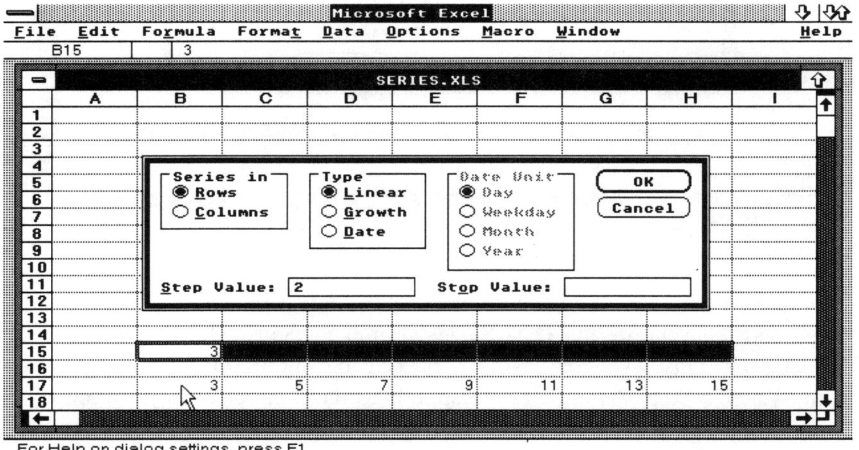

Fig. 2.13. Entering a series of numbers with the ***Data Series*** *command.*

2.42 Tip: **Enter a decreasing sequence with the Data Series command.**

To create a decreasing sequence or series, enter the starting value in the first cell of the selected range and then enter a negative value in the **S**tep Value box. If you enter a Sto**p** Value, it must be smaller than the starting value.

2.43 Tip: **Enter a series of dates with the Data Series command.**

Use the **D**ata Se**r**ies command to enter a variety of date sequences. Figure 2.14 shows an example of a date sequence. Notice that the starting date is in the first of the selected cells in the row. Date series fill from the left across a row or down columns. When you choose the OK button in figure 2.14, row 15 will appear the same as row 17.

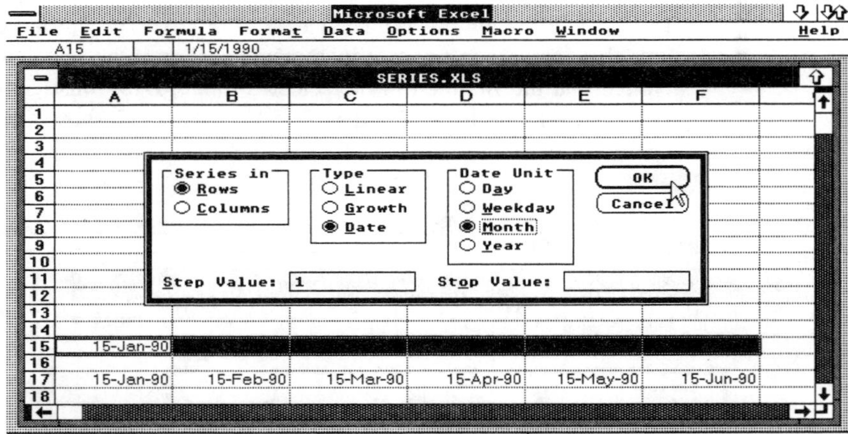

Fig. 2.14. Entering a series of dates with the ***D****ata Se****r****ies command.*

To create a date sequence, select the starting date and row or column to be filled and then choose the **D**ata Se**r**ies command. Select the **D**ate command. Select either D**a**y, **W**eekday, **M**onth, or **Y**ear depending on the sequence you want. Enter a **S**tep Value that corresponds to the number of days, weekdays, months, or years until the next date in the sequence. Date sequences that change by month keep the same day; date sequences that change by year keep the same month.

2.44 Tip: **Use a Stop Value to stop a series on a selected date.**

You can stop a date series at a specific date. This feature is useful if you're not sure how many cells will be used for the series. Begin by selecting more cells than the series will contain. Stop the extra cells in the range from filling with dates by entering a Stop Value in the **D**ata Ser**i**es dialog box. The St**o**p Value for a date sequence must be a date that Excel recognizes, such as 8/6/99 or 6-Aug-99. Figure 2.15 shows a date series that stops the sequence on April 15, 1990. Notice that the date formats do not have to match.

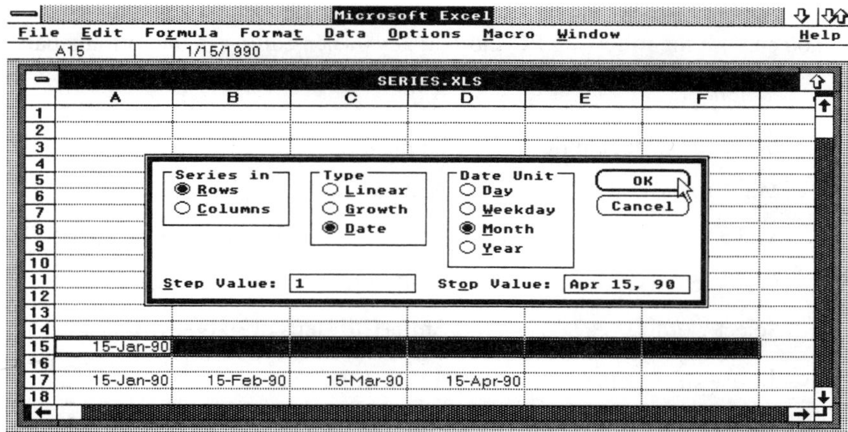

Fig. 2.15. Specifying a final date in a series.

2.45 Trick: **Use the Data Series command to enter a series of times.**

The **D**ata Ser**i**es dialog box does not have options available for a time series, but with a little knowledge you can create a time series or date-time series. Enter and format the starting time in the first cell of the range. Select the row or column range of cells that will contain the sequence and then select the **D**ata Ser**i**es command with the **L**inear type. Enter the **S**tep Value as a decimal percentage of a 24-hour day. For example, .041666667 (1/24) is an hour expressed as a decimal part of a day. Press Enter. You can generate series of 6-hour increments for example, using a **S**tep Value of .25.

Editing Data

You may find yourself using the mouse to position the cursor in the formula bar and to select characters to replace or delete. If you're a touch-typist, you may prefer making selections and changes from the keyboard. Whichever way you like to edit, use the shortcuts in this section to make the process faster. Until you learn these shortcuts for editing, you may want to write them down on a 3-by-5 card and put them by your computer screen.

2.46 Tip: **Use PC shortcut keys in the formula bar.**

You can use the following PC shortcut keys when editing in the formula bar:

Action	*Key*
Move to the beginning	Home key
Move to the end	End key
Move by word	Ctrl+left- or right-arrow key
Select letter(s)	Shift+left- or right-arrow key
Select word(s)	Shift+Ctrl+left- or right-arrow key

2.47 Tip: **Use mouse shortcuts when editing in the formula bar.**

With both PC and Macintosh Excel, you can use the following mouse shortcuts to edit text or formulas in the formula bar:

Result	*Mouse Action*
Select characters	Drag across character
Select word or reference	Double-click on word or reference
Select words or references	Double-click on word or reference and then drag the mouse
Select extensive characters	Click before first character; Shift+click after last character

Copying and Moving Cell Contents

If you had to enter every formula, building a worksheet would take considerable time. Instead, you can use commands to cut and paste or copy and paste formulas.

2.48 Tip: **Save time when you build similar formulas by cutting, copying, and pasting elements in the formula bar.**

Save time when building complicated formulas that are similar. Instead of retyping terms that are the same, copy the parts of the formulas you want from other cells. Use the cut, copy, and paste features of Excel in the formula bar to move pieces of the formula the same way you move cells or ranges.

To cut or copy from the formula bar, select the part of the formula you want. Choose the **E**dit Cu**t** or **E**dit **C**opy command. Move the cursor to a new location in the same formula bar or select a new cell's formula bar. If you cut from a formula, be careful that you don't cut out a needed part. Before you choose a new cell's formula bar, select X or press Esc to preserve the original formula and exit the cell. Choose the **E**dit **P**aste command. You can continue to paste until you cut or copy again.

2.49 Tip: **Use a shortcut key to duplicate a formula or format.**

On the PC, press Ctrl+' (apostrophe) to copy an exact duplicate of the formula or value above the active cell. Cell references do not adjust for their new locations. Press Ctrl+" to copy the value and format from the cell above. The formula is converted to a value.

On the Macintosh, when working in the formula bar, press Command+' (apostrophe) to copy the value of the cell above into the formula bar.

2.50 Tip: **Always examine copied formulas for correctness.**

Original formulas that are correct, but that copy incorrectly usually require an absolute or mixed reference address in the original before copying. Absolute addressing, such as $B$24, fixes a row or column address so that it will not change when copied. The $ sign precedes the row or column you want to remain unchanged. When you copy a formula, check to be sure that the references are correct.

2.51 Tip: **To change quickly between absolute and relative reference, use the F4 (PC) or Command+T (Macintosh) key.**

You can change quickly between relative, mixed, and absolute references in formulas. Move the insertion point in the formula bar next to the address you want to change. Then press F4 (PC) or Command+T (Macintosh). Each press of F4 or Command+T produces a new combination of $ signs in the address.

2.52 Tip: **Use R1C1 cell references for ex-Multiplan users and macros; use A1 references for ex-1-2-3 users.**

Excel uses either A1 or R1C1 cell addressing. A1 cell references use column headings from A through IV and row numbers from 1 to 16,384. R1C1 cell references display column headings as numbers 1–25,650; both row and column positions are given by a number such as R12C25 (row 12, column 25).

Use the method you prefer. Some macro programming is easier in R1C1 addressing. Change between methods by choosing the **O**ptions **W**orkspace command and then selecting either **R**1C1 or A**1**. Worksheet addresses automatically adjust.

2.53 Tip: **Use Ctrl+Enter (PC) or Command+Enter (Macintosh) to enter multiple items or formulas with a single keystroke.**

Excel makes it easy to copy a formula or text into a range of cells as you enter it in one cell. First, select the range of cells to receive the entry. Figure 2.16 shows a worksheet with the range B8:F8 selected. Next, enter the formula, **=B5*$B$22**, into the formula bar. To copy the formula to all cells in the selected range, press Ctrl+Enter (PC) or Command+Enter (Macintosh). This action enters the formula and copies it to all cells in the range. Copied formulas adjust their relative cell references just as they would with a copy or fill command.

2.54 Tip: **Enter information quickly with the Edit Fill command.**

Edit Fill Rig**h**t and **E**dit Fill Do**w**n fill a formula right or down into a range of cells. These commands are much quicker than the copy and paste commands.

To fill a formula or value into a range to the left or to a range above, hold down the Shift key as you select the **E**dit command. Two new commands appear, Fill Left (**h**) and Fill Up (**w**). These commands fill a range with the formula or value in the rightmost cell. Or they fill upward with the formula in the bottom cell.

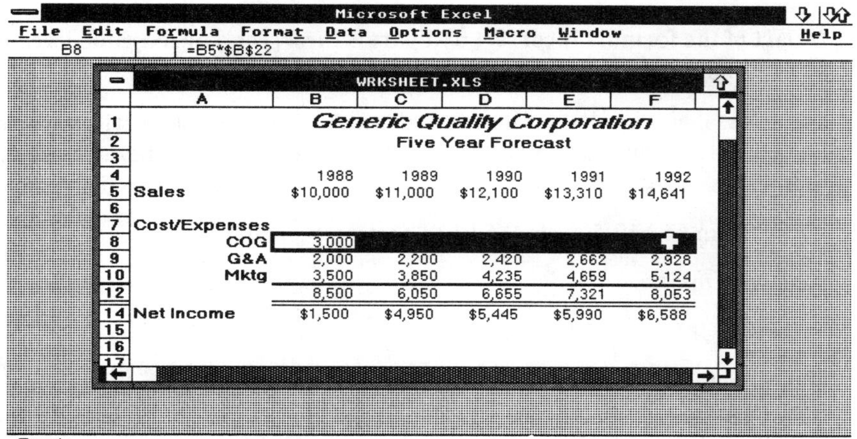

Fig. 2.16. Copying a formula to a range.

Working with Formulas

The foundation of any worksheet is its formulas. In this section, you learn tips for working with formulas.

2.55 Tip: Enter formulas in lowercase to proofread them.

Type formulas in lowercase letters, as in the following example:

=sim(b6:b12)/d50

If you enter the formula without typographical errors, Excel converts functions and cell references to uppercase letters. Incorrect terms or misused terms remain in lowercase so that you can more easily catch mistakes. The preceding formula enters as the following:

=sim(B6:B12)/D50

A #NAME? error appears in the cell. You quickly can catch the error by looking for text that remained in lowercase—in this case, sim. Change sim to sum and recheck the formula.

Note that range names you create in lowercase remain in lowercase when you use them in formulas.

2.56 Trap: **If part of the formula is correct and part is incorrect, you may not receive an error message.**

Formulas that calculate differently depending on logical tests may not immediately produce an error when entered. For example, when you enter the following

=if(sum(b6:b12)500,sim(b6:b12),"Order too small")

it converts to

=IF(SUM(B6:B12)500,sim(B6:B12),"Order too small")

Notice that sim should be SUM in the second half of the test. If the sum of B6:B12 is less than or equal to 500, Excel misses this error because the FALSE portion of the IF function, "Order too small," is evaluated. Only when SUM(B6:B12) is greater than 500 will Excel see you've made an error. You can catch the error by entering the formula in lowercase. You then see the errors in lowercase letters.

2.57 Tip: **To operate on all cells in a row or column, specify only the entire row or column.**

If you want a formula or function to operate on all cells in a row or column, specify only the row or column for a range. For example, to sum all the cells in column B, use the following formula:

=SUM(B:B)

To find the average of all the cells in rows 5 through 12, use the following formula:

=AVERAGE(5:12)

2.58 Tip: **To enter the results of a calculation, convert the formula into a number.**

If you need to calculate an entry value and then enter it in a cell, save time by doing the calculation in the formula bar and entering the result. For example, to calculate a tax and enter the result, type the following:

=.06*550.00

Then calculate the result by pressing F9 or choosing **O**ptions Calculate **N**ow. Press Enter to enter the result.

2.59 Tip: **To freeze a range of formulas so that they do not recalculate, change formulas in cells into values.**

Change formulas in cells into values when you need to freeze a range of formulas so that they do not recalculate. To change formulas into values, select the range that contains the formulas and then choose the **E**dit **C**opy command.

If you want to replace the formulas with their results, leave the active cell where it is. But, if you want to keep the formulas intact, make a copy of the values to another part of the worksheet. To do so, move the active cell to the top left corner of the range where you want the values to appear. Choose the **E**dit Paste **S**pecial command. From the Paste **S**pecial dialog box, select the **V**alues and N**o**ne options to paste the values (see fig. 2.17). Then choose OK.

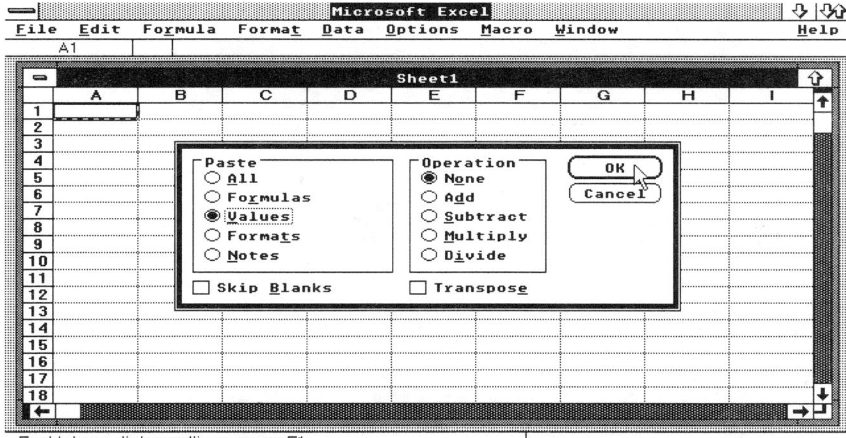

Fig. 2.17. The Paste Special dialog box.

If you move to a new location, you should repeat the **E**dit Paste **S**pecial command in the same location and paste the formats over the values so that they appear with the same format as the originals.

To change formulas in the formula bar to values, select the entire formula and choose the **O**ptions Calculate **N**ow command or press F9.

2.60 Trick: **Change named formulas or values throughout a worksheet with the Formula Replace command.**

If you use a named formula in multiple locations in your worksheet, you can make changes to the range name easily. You need only change the definition of the named formula to update the multiple locations that use the formula.

Choose the Formula **D**efine Name command, select the name of the formula, and change its formula in the **R**efers to: box. When you choose OK, all references to that formula are updated.

3

Formatting Worksheets

Excel's formatting capabilities are impressive. You can use many predefined numeric and date formats, draw lines, and shade cells. You also can go beyond the standard formats by creating custom formats and adding colors. Custom formats can include text, date separators, date text, foreign characters, and numeric precisions. Excel gives you virtually unlimited formatting ability. You can print the results of your work so that they appear as if they came from a typesetter.

Using Formatting Shortcut Keys

Excel recognizes many numeric and date formats automatically. When you type an entry, Excel automatically formats the cell to match the closest predefined format. Sometimes you will need to change the format of an existing cell's content. The following tips can save you time.

3.1 Tip: **Save time with formatting shortcut keys.**

To save time when formatting, use the keystrokes in table 3.1.

Table 3.1
Formatting Shortcut Keys

Number/Date Formats	*PC Key*	*Macintosh Key*
General	Ctrl+~	Command+Option+~
0.00	Ctrl+!	Command+Option+!
h:mm AM/PM	Ctrl+@	Command+Option+@
d-mmm-yy	Ctrl+#	Command+Option+#
$#,##0.00;($#,##0.00)	Ctrl+$	Command+Option+$
0%	Ctrl+%	Command+Option+%
0.00E+00	Ctrl+^	Command+Option+^

If you frequently need a formatting shortcut key different from these, create the shortcut using the macro recorder.

You also can use the following key combinations to format Macintosh Excel borders:

Outlined	Command+Option+0
Left	Command+Option+left-arrow key
Right	Command+Option+right-arrow key
Top	Command+Option+up-arrow key
Bottom	Command+Option+down-arrow key

3.2 Tip: **Use the Edit Repeat command to repeat formatting.**

You can use the **E**dit **R**epeat command to repeat the previous formatting command. This command can save you time if you are entering many similar formats.

Formatting Rows, Columns, or the Entire Worksheet

You don't have to format your worksheet a few cells at a time. The tips in this section show you how to format entire rows or columns at one time so that you save time as well as memory.

3.3 Tip: **Set the initial worksheet font before you start.**

In PC Excel, Font 1 designates the default font used for row and column headings and for unformatted cells. Use the Forma**t** **F**ont command to set Font 1.

In Macintosh Excel, use the **O**ptions **S**tandard Font command to select the default font used throughout the worksheet. This font will be used for the row and column headings and for all cells unless you change selected cells or ranges with the Forma**t** **F**ont command.

3.4 Tip: **Use a large global font when displaying worksheets for a group.**

If you are displaying worksheets from the screen for a group, increase the readability by substituting Font 1 for a larger font using the Forma**t** **F**ont F**o**nts> option with PC Excel. For Macintosh Excel, increase the standard font size by choosing **O**ptions **S**tandard Font. This action increases row and column headings as well as cell contents (see fig. 3.1). The contents of the formula bar

Microsoft Excel - UNDERLN.XLS

File Edit Formula Format Data Options Macro Window Help

	A	B	C	D	E
1			Generic Quality Corporatio		
2			Five Year Forecast		
3					
4		1988	1989	1990	19
5	Sales	$10,000	$11,000	$12,100	$13,31
6					
7	Cost/Expenses				
8	COG	3,000	3,300	3,630	3,99
9	G&A	2,000	2,200	2,420	2,66
10	Mktg	3,500	3,850	4,235	4,65
12		8,500	9,350	10,285	11,31
13					

Fig. 3.1. Using a large global font for group presentations.

are not made larger. For more display area, use the **O**ptions **W**orkspace command to turn off the status and formula bars.

3.5 Tip: **Set global worksheet formats before you start working.**

Some of your worksheets will have a dominant format you will want to set before you begin work. Setting this global format saves you time that would be needed to format many cells or ranges individually.

To select such formats as row height, column width, numeric formats or alignments, begin by selecting the entire worksheet. With the mouse, click on the blank square at the intersection of the row and column headings as shown in figure 3.2. (The mouse cursor is the thick plus sign in figure 3.2.) From the keyboard, press Shift+Ctrl+space bar in PC Excel or Command+A in Macintosh Excel to select the entire worksheet.

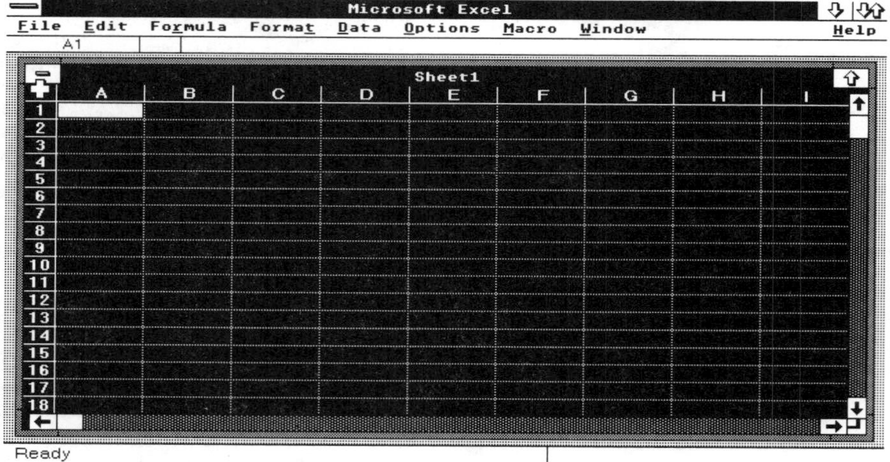

Fig. 3.2. Selecting the entire worksheet with the mouse.

Once you select the entire worksheet, choose formats that apply to most of your work. For example, you may want most numeric formats with alignment right, a column width of 12, and this format: $#,##0 ;($#,##0).

3.6 Tip: **Change multiple row heights or column widths at one time.**

You can change multiple row heights or column widths at one time by selecting the rows or columns and then dragging to a new location the divider below a row heading or the divider to the right of a column heading. You can select adjacent or nonadjacent rows and columns.

With the mouse, select adjacent columns by holding down the Shift key and dragging the mouse pointer across the column headings. Select noncontiguous columns by holding down the Ctrl (PC) or Command (Macintosh) key as you click each column heading. Figure 3.3 shows noncontiguous columns selected.

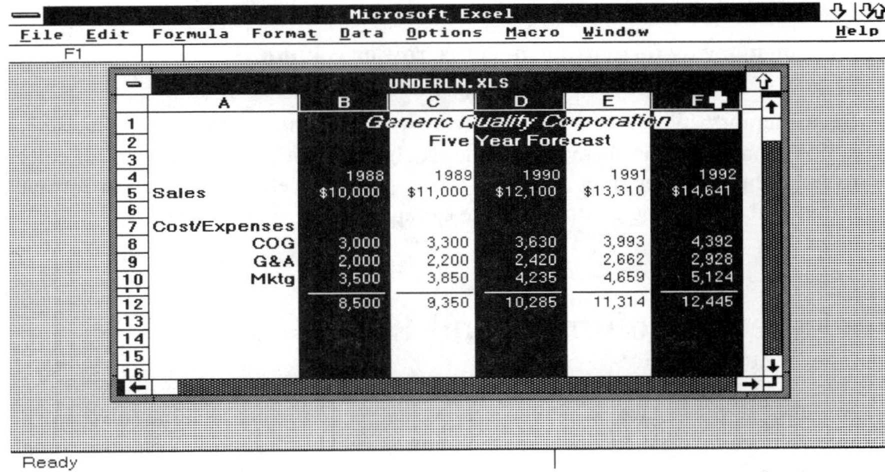

Fig. 3.3. *Selecting noncontiguous columns of a worksheet.*

Once the columns are selected, move the mouse pointer to the right divider between the column headings of one of the selected columns. The pointer changes to a two-headed arrow. Drag the columns to a new width.

From the keyboard, select multiple columns by moving the active cell into the column and pressing Ctrl+space bar. Once one column is selected, hold down the Shift key and press the right- or left-arrow key to select multiple columns. Then use the Format Column Width command to enter a new column width.

Select adjacent rows by holding down the Shift key and dragging the mouse pointer across the row headings. To select nonadjacent rows, hold down the Ctrl (PC) or Command (Macintosh) key as you click on each row heading. To change the height of selected rows, move the mouse pointer to the divider below a row heading until the pointer becomes a two-headed arrow. Then drag the divider to a new location.

To select adjacent rows from the keyboard, move the active cell into the first row and then press Shift+space bar. Hold down the Shift key and press the up-

or down-arrow key to select multiple rows. Then use the Forma**t** **R**ow Height command to change the row height.

3.7 Tip: **Widen the column when ### appears in a cell.**

If a cell fills with ###, the column is not wide enough to display a number, formula result, date, or custom text format. Widen the column to see the cell's contents using the Forma**t** **C**olumn Width command.

3.8 Tip: **Save memory by formatting an entire row or column.**

Save memory by selecting the entire row or column when formatting. This action stores a single formatting code, such as $#,##0, that applies to all cells in the column rather than storing a format in each cell. You then can format individual cells in the column that are exceptions.

Hiding Worksheets, Columns, and Rows

A cluttered workspace on-screen can be just as confusing as a cluttered work area on your desk. With the techniques in this section, you can hide worksheets from view, but still maintain cell links. You can redisplay the hidden worksheets almost instantly. You also can hide rows or columns selectively within worksheets to protect proprietary information from displaying on-screen or from printing.

3.9 Tip: **Hide worksheets to reduce clutter.**

Hide worksheets to reduce clutter on-screen and to hide calculations the user doesn't need to see. Hide the active worksheet with the **W**indow **H**ide command. Unhide a worksheet with **W**indow **U**nhide.

3.10 Tip: **Hide rows and columns you don't want seen or printed.**

To hide rows and columns you do not want to display or print, reduce the row height or column width to zero. Hide a column with the mouse by dragging the column-heading divider to the left until the mouse pointer passes the next left divider. This action makes the column width zero.

Hide a row by dragging up the bottom of a row-heading divider until it passes the bottom divider above it.

Use the Forma**t** **R**ow Height or Forma**t** **C**olumn Width to set zero height or width from the keyboard.

3.11 Tip: Use one of three ways to unhide rows and columns.

You can use one of three ways to display hidden rows or columns:

Use the Goto key, F5 (PC) or Command+G (Macintosh), to go to a cell in the hidden row or column. Then use the Forma**t** **R**ow Height or Forma**t** **C**olumn Width command to change the height/width from zero.

Or select columns or rows on both sides of the hidden column or row and then enter a positive height or width.

Or use the mouse pointer to pull a hidden row or column open. Figure 3.4 shows the pointer correctly positioned to drag open a hidden column F. The pointer is the double-headed arrow between the E and G column headings. With the left tip of the pointer on the column divider, you can drag column F open by dragging to the right.

Drag open hidden rows by using the upper tip of the double-headed arrow to drag the hidden row down.

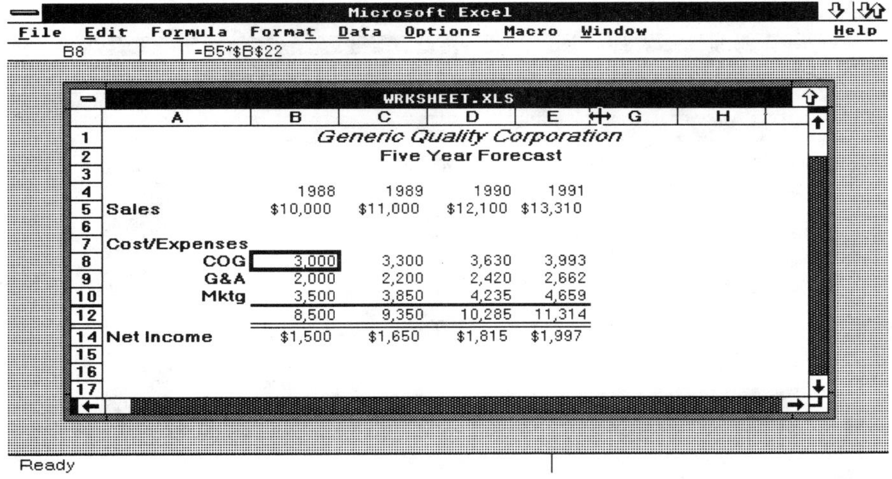

Fig. 3.4. Opening a hidden column.

Formatting and Creating Custom Formats

Although Excel has many predefined numeric and date formats, you'll want to use the custom formatting features to create numeric, date, and even text formats that fit your exact needs. The following section describes how to create custom formats and how to push them to their limit by adding nonkeyboard characters, by adding color, or by making cell contents disappear.

3.12 Trap: **Displayed numbers may not be the number used in calculations; if this causes problems, use the Precision as Displayed option or the ROUND function.**

Formatted numbers present a serious danger in any electronic worksheet. The formatted number you see and print may not be the number used in calculations. Some financial institutions, when first using electronic spreadsheets, calculated payments in error on the order of hundreds of thousands of dollars before realizing that a discrepancy had occurred. Many electronic spreadsheet users still aren't aware of the problem.

Figure 3.5 shows a simple example: The calculated total in cell E12 does not appear to be correct. The discrepancy occurs because Excel adds the actual numbers in the cells, not the formatted numbers that are displayed. The actual unformatted numbers with their full precision are shown in column D.

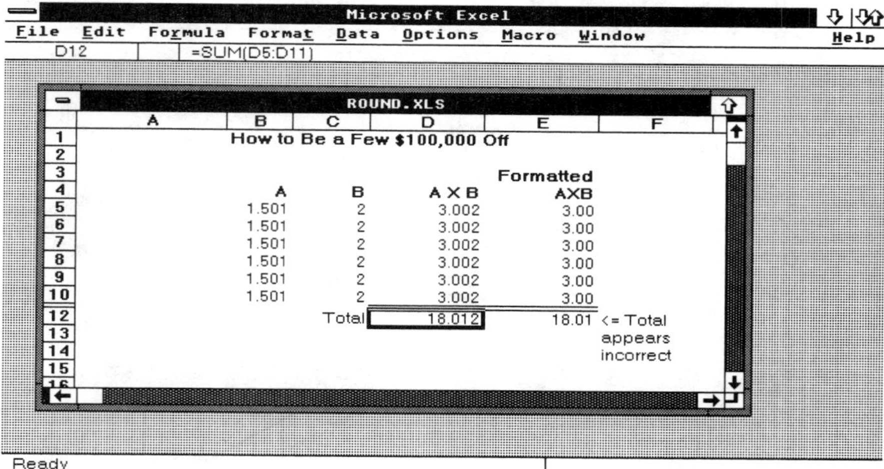

Fig. 3.5. Formatted numbers that appear to give incorrect results.

Excel is built to take care of this discrepancy in two ways; you can adjust individual cells or adjust the entire worksheet. Adjust individual cells so that the number used in calculations matches the format used in the ROUND function. For example, the following command rounds the number or formula results in D5 to two decimal places:

=ROUND(D5,2)

You usually nest a formula inside the ROUND function to calculate a formula and round it in the same cell. You might use the following example in cell E5:

=ROUND(A5*B5,2)

To adjust the entire worksheet so that the number displayed is the same as the number used in calculations, choose the **O**ptions **C**alculation command and select **P**recision as Displayed.

Note that when you choose **P**recision as Displayed, constant numbers in the worksheet permanently round to the precision that matches their format. Should you later unselect **P**recision as Displayed, these constant numbers do not return to their full precision. Formula results do return to full precision.

3.13 Tip: **Create custom number and date formats for a variety of entries—phone numbers, foreign currencies, text dates, and others.**

With Excel's capability to create custom number and date formats, you can create formats to display a variety of numbers and dates:

- Colors for error-checking numbers
- Colored text for presentations
- Text warnings based on results of logical functions
- The decimal precision you need
- ANSI characters such as yen or copyright symbols
- Phone number formats
- Mixed text and numbers for parts and serial numbers

To enter a custom numeric or date format, select the cell(s) you want changed and choose the Forma**t** **N**umber command. Type the custom format in the **F**ormat text box shown in figure 3.6. If a predefined format is similar to the custom format you need, select it from the Format **N**umber list box, modify the format in the **F**ormat text box, and then choose OK.

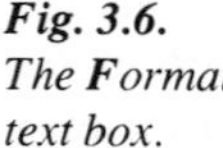

Fig. 3.6.
*The **F**ormat text box.*

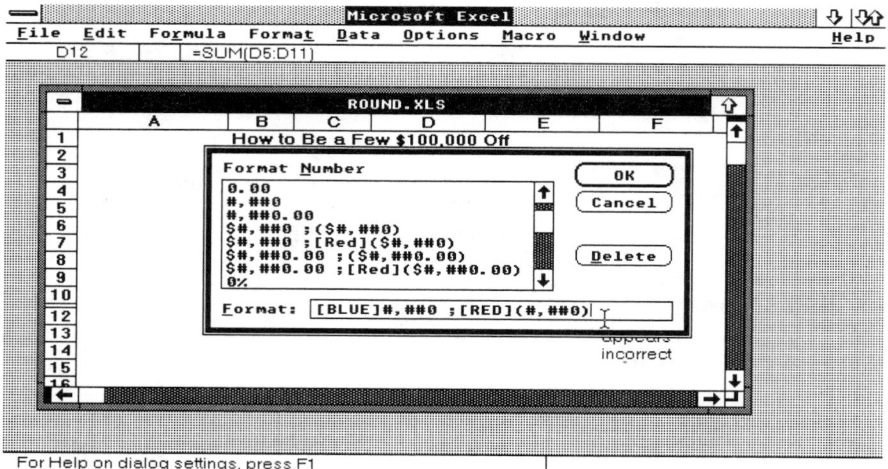

Custom formats are divided into four segments by three semicolons (;). Each segment can have a different format. The segments define the format according to their numeric sign or text:

positive_number;negative_number;zero;text

For example, a format such as the following gives positive numbers a dollar currency format with two decimal places and a trailing space:

$#,##0.00 ;[Red]#,##0.00;0;[Blue]

The trailing space keeps positive numbers aligned in columns with negative numbers. The negative format, after the first semicolon, displays negative numbers in red. Negative numbers are assigned a dollar currency format and two decimal places and are enclosed in brackets. The zero format, after the second semicolon, displays zero results as 0. Text entered in a cell with this format appears in blue.

Table 3.2 shows some of the symbols you can use for custom numeric formatting.

Table 3.2
Custom Numeric Formatting Symbols

Symbol	*Result*
0	Places holder for zeros and numbers. A zero appears if a number is not entered at that location.
#	Places holder for numbers. Zeros do not display if a number is absent. Decimal numbers are rounded to the decimal places prescribed with #.
.	Marks the decimal place.
,	Marks the thousands. You need to place only the first one.
%	Multiplies the number by a 100 and follows it with a percent sign.
E- E+ e- e+	Scientific notation. Uses 0's and #'s to the right of the E or e to indicate the exponent's size.
: $ - + ( ) space	Displays that character in the location shown.
\	Displays the character following the backslash. Does not show the backslash. Similar to quotation marks for a single character.
"text"	Displays the text or special character within quotations marks.
*	Fills the remaining column width with the character following the asterisk (one asterisk per format).
@	Text typed into the cell appears at the location specified by @. You can use this option only with text entries.

Figure 3.7 shows some custom numeric formats you might need during calculations. Figure 3.8 shows custom numeric formats used for such purposes as part numbers, telephone numbers, dot leaders, page numbers, and error checking.

Fig. 3.7. Custom numeric formats for calculations.

Microsoft Excel - NUMFONTS.XLS

File Edit Formula Format Data Options Macro Window Help

D25

	A	B	C	D
1		*Custom Numeric Formats*		
2				
3		**Custom Format**	**Entry**	**Display**
4	**Numeric**	0.0000;	0.34	0.3400
5		0.0000;	0	0.0000
6		0.0000;	-0.34	
7				
8		#.0000;-#.0000;.0000	0.34	.3400
9		#.0000;-#.0000;.0000	0	.0000
10		#.0000;-#.0000;.0000	-0.34	-.3400
11				
12	**Currency, Aligned**	$#,##0 ;($#,##0);0 ;	4356.67	$4,357
13		$#,##0 ;($#,##0);0 ;	-4356.67	($4,357)
14				
15	**Accounting**	[BLUE]#,##0.00 "Db";[Red](#,##0.00) "Cr"	-64.35	(64.35) Cr
16		[BLUE]#,##0.00 "Db";[Red](#,##0.00) "Cr"	99.95	99.95 Dt
17				
18	**Measurements**	0.0000 E+000 "Ang."	5296	5.2960 E+003 Ang.
19		0.0000 E+000 "Parsecs"	0.5296	5.2960 E-001 Parsecs
20				

Ready

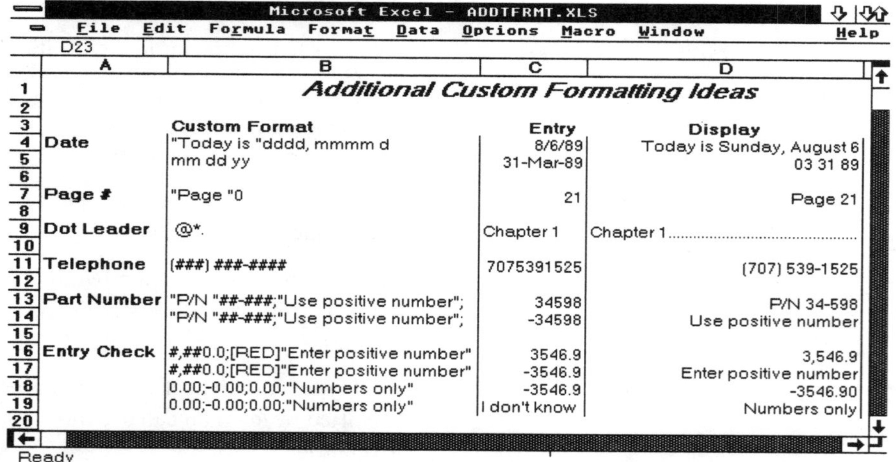

Microsoft Excel - ADDTFRMT.XLS

File Edit Formula Format Data Options Macro Window Help

D23

	A	B	C	D
1		*Additional Custom Formatting Ideas*		
2				
3		**Custom Format**	**Entry**	**Display**
4	**Date**	"Today is "dddd, mmmm d	8/6/89	Today is Sunday, August 6
5		mm dd yy	31-Mar-89	03 31 89
6				
7	**Page #**	"Page "0	21	Page 21
8				
9	**Dot Leader**	@*.	Chapter 1	Chapter 1....................................
10				
11	**Telephone**	(###) ###-####	7075391525	(707) 539-1525
12				
13	**Part Number**	"P/N "##-###;"Use positive number";	34598	P/N 34-598
14		"P/N "##-###;"Use positive number";	-34598	Use positive number
15				
16	**Entry Check**	#,##0.0;[RED]"Enter positive number"	3546.9	3,546.9
17		#,##0.0;[RED]"Enter positive number"	-3546.9	Enter positive number
18		0.00;-0.00;0.00;"Numbers only"	-3546.9	-3546.90
19		0.00;-0.00;0.00;"Numbers only"	I don't know	Numbers only
20				

Ready

Fig. 3.8. Other custom numeric and text formats.

3.14 Tip: **Find custom formats in the list box quickly with the End key.**

Excel places custom formats at the bottom of the Format Number list box. In PC Excel with the Format list box active, go quickly to the custom formats by pressing the End key.

3.15 Trick: **Create a style library of custom formats.**

You can transfer custom formats to other worksheets by selecting a cell with the custom format and choosing **E**dit **C**opy. Activate the worksheet to which you want to transfer the custom format, select an appropriate cell, and then choose the **E**dit Paste **S**pecial command with Forma**t**s and N**o**ne. The format transfers between worksheets. You see the custom format in the bottom section of the receiving worksheet's Forma**t** **N**umber list box.

You can create a library of custom format styles by creating one worksheet that contains many different formats. Label the formats in column A and format the adjacent cell in column B. You then can open this library worksheet alongside your normal worksheets and then copy the custom formats you want.

3.16 Tip: **For a neat appearance, align positive and negative numbers in a column.**

Negative formats that enclose the number in brackets or parentheses may throw a column of positive and negative numbers out of alignment. You can align the right edge of positive numbers with negative numbers with an adjustment to the positive format. To do so, define positive numeric formats that include a space to the right of the positive number. For example, the following format misaligns positive and negative numbers in a column:

```
$#,##0;($#,##0)
```

However, the trailing space in the following format accounts for the last parenthesis in the negative number, keeping positive and negative numbers in alignment:

```
$#,##0 ;($#,##0)
```

3.17 Tip: **Align dates and numbers just like text.**

Use the Forma**t** **A**lign command to align numbers and dates in a worksheet the same way you align text. Because dates are really numbers, they cannot exceed the cell's width.

3.18 Tip: **Prevent zeros from being displayed using one of three methods.**

You can use one of three ways to hide zeros in your worksheets. To hide zeros throughout the entire worksheet, choose the **O**ptions **D**isplay command and unselect the **Z**ero Values option. Or use a formula such as =IF(A1*B1=0,"",A1*B1). In this equation, if the result of A1*B1 equals nothing, "", appears in the cell; otherwise, the result of A1*B1 appears.

As the third option, format the number with a semicolon to mark the zero format position, but do not enter a zero format, as in the following example:

$#,##0;($#,##0);

3.19 Tip: **Hide text or positive, negative, or zero numbers using custom formats.**

If you don't include a format between semicolons in a custom format, nothing displays. You can hide text or positive, negative, or zero numbers. For example, the following format hides negative numbers:

#.00;;0

This custom format hides zeros:

#.00;-#.00;;

3.20 Tip: **Format numbers, dates, or text in color for error checking and appearance.**

You can format numbers, dates, and text to improve appearance and to check for errors. Formatting positive numbers in black (no format color specified) or in blue makes them easier to distinguish from negative numbers formatted in red. A format code for this might appear as the following:

[BLUE]$#,##0;[RED]($#,##0);[GREEN]0;[MAGENTA]

This command formats positive numbers as blue, negative numbers as red, zeros as green, and text as magenta.

You can use the following colors: black, white, red, green, blue, yellow, magenta, and cyan. Enclose the color in square brackets.

3.21 Tip: **Display text warnings using custom color formats.**

Data-entry checking and warnings are easier to see when in color. For example, the following IF function in cell D10 checks that the value in cell C10 is greater than 12:

=IF(C10>12,0,–1)

If C10 is not greater than 12, the formula produces a result of –1. You can use this negative sign to display a text message and color that are predefined in cell D10's custom format.

Suppose that, for instance, the IF function in D10 is formatted with the following:

;[RED]"Enter a value more than 12";

A red text warning appears in D10 whenever the entry in C10 is 12 or less. Because you did not specify a positive format or zero format, positive and zero numbers in D10 are hidden.

3.22 Tip: **Include ANSI characters in numeric and date formats.**

In PC Excel, if you need to use symbols, such as the Japanese yen or British pound, you can insert them in your worksheet by using ANSI or extended character sets.

For example, the following code inserts a yen symbol:

¥#,##0 ;(¥#,##0)

You create this format like any other custom numeric code. To insert the yen symbol, press Alt and type **0165** on the numeric keypad. This format produces a yen symbol in the Courier, Helvetica, and System screen fonts. A different symbol may print depending on the character sets available with your printer. Test the different numeric codes to find the code that will print the symbol you want.

For Macintosh Excel, press Option+Y to access the yen symbol and then follow the standard formatting procedure. For other non-U.S. currency symbols, use the Key Caps Desk Accessory to determine what combination of keys will produce the symbol you want. Enter the key combination whenever you want a custom character in a custom format.

3.23 Tip: **If you work with non-U.S. date and currency formats, customize Excel to display international dates and currency.**

If you normally work with non-U.S. date and currency formats, you can customize Excel to display most international date, time, and currency formats. When PC Excel is customized using the Control Panel, all the numeric and date formats in the Forma**t** **N**umber list box reflect the formats for the country you choose.

In PC Excel, choose the Application Control menu by clicking on the box icon to the left of Excel title or pressing Alt+space bar. Then select the **Run** command. Select the Control **Panel** and then choose OK. When the Control Panel appears, choose **Preferences** **Country** Settings. The dialog box in figure 3.9 is displayed.

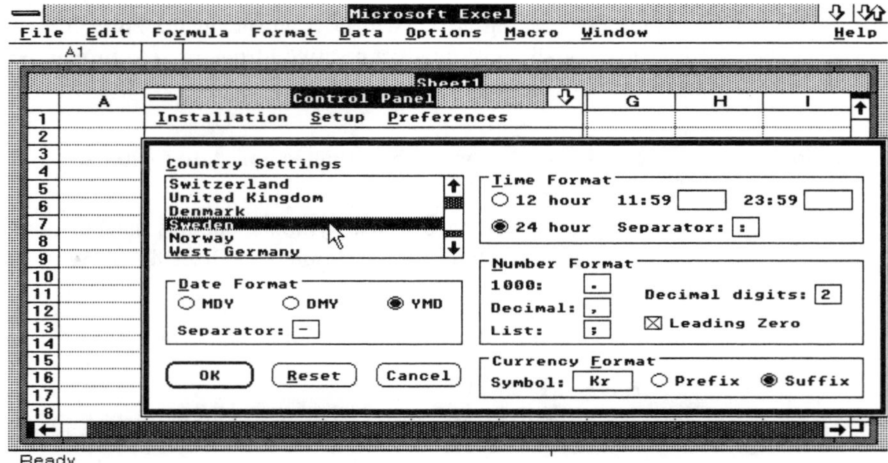

Fig. 3.9. Selecting international date, time, number, and currency formats.

From the list box, select the country you want and then check that other options have changed to reflect the standard formats for date, time, number, and currency you want. Customize the ones you want to appear differently and choose OK. Press Alt+F4 to close the Control **Panel**. Close Excel and Windows. When you restart Excel, the numeric and date formats for the country selected appear in the Forma**t** **N**umber list box.

Note that PC Excel 2.1 contains a bug that prevents this feature from working for the yen symbol. You can create a custom ANSI character manually as described in Tip 3.21.

3.24 Tip: **If you use a different date and time format from the ones Excel offers, create custom date and time formats.**

If you don't find a date or time format you want, you easily can create your own. Select Forma**t** **N**umber and use the symbols in table 3.3 to type a date format in the **F**ormat text. You may want to first select an existing date format and modify it.

Table 3.3
Date Format Symbols

Symbol	*Result*	*Example*
d	Day	5
dd	Two-digit day	05
ddd	Three-letter abbreviation	Tue
dddd	Full-text day	Tuesday
m	Month	6
mm	Two-digit month	06
mmm	Three-letter abbreviation	Jun
mmmm	Full-text month	June
yy	Two-digit year	92
yyyy	Four-digit year	1992
h	Hour	0 to 24
hh	Two-digit hour	00 to 24
m	Minute	0 to 59
mm	Two-digit minute	00 to 59
s	Second	0 to 59
ss	Two-digit second	00 to 59
AM/PM am/pm A/P a/p	Display with 12-hour clock time	
- / :	Dividers	7/3/90

3.25 Tip: **Format dates to show both the text day, date, and month.**

You can repeat date formats within the same format. This option helps when creating calendars, appointment databases, project scheduling worksheets, or tickler files. For example, entering the date 5/14/92 and formatting it with the custom format dddd, dd mmmm produces this date:

Thursday, 14 May

3.26 Tip: **If you want text to appear in the same cell as a number, combine text with custom numeric and date formatting.**

When you want text to appear in the same cell as a number, use a custom numeric format. You can use this format with numbers such as part, service, telephone, and employee numbers.

Remember to enter the number as a normal number or date. Typing dashes or text causes Excel to think that you are typing text; the number will not receive its custom format.

You can enter telephone numbers with a format such as the following:

"Ph."(###) ###-####;"Enter without a leading dash";;"Enter only the number"

The following shows entries and results of using this format:

Entry	*Displayed Result*
5391525	Ph. () 539-1525
7075391525	Ph. (707) 539-1525
-539-1525	Enter without a leading dash
0	(blank)
539-1525	Enter only the number

One drawback to this technique is that columns that contain the entry must be wide enough to display the entire text and numeric/date content. If the column is not wide enough, ### fills the cell.

3.27 Tip: **Combine text, numbers, and dates with & for better formatting.**

You will encounter problems with the preceding tip if the display is wider than the column. The result cannot be aligned if it exceeds the column width.

If you want to use a date or number as you do text or if you want to create titles that include changing dates and numbers, use a formula like the following:

="Report for month ending "& TEXT (A12,"MMMM D, YYYY")

If A12 contains 8/6/90, the formula produces the following text result:

Report for month ending August 6, 1990

This text can exceed the column width and can be formatted and aligned as normal text.

3.28 Tip: **Don't enter dashes in a numeric format.**

Entering a number for a custom format and including the dashes normally entered by the formatting can cause a confusing entry. Excel may interpret the numbers and dashes as a date. Date entries produce a serial date number to which Excel then applies the custom format. Look at the following examples:

Entry	*Format*	*Display*
0301	"Code "0#-0#	Code 03-01
03-01	"Code "0#-0#	Code 325-68

In the second example, instead of 03-01, Excel enters a serial date number, 325-68, for 3/1/89.

Formatting with Lines and Shades

With Excel, you can print true solid underlines. You don't have to use dashes or equal signs as substitutes for solid lines or double lines. You can use the lines and shades in Excel for everything from creating simple flow charts, to enhancing a balance sheet, to creating business forms. Some businesses are even typing information directly into a high-quality Excel form and doing away with the need for preprinted forms.

3.29 Tip: **To format your worksheet, create single and double underlines.**

You can include underlines in your worksheet, for example, to set off totals. Create single underlines by selecting the cell or range of cells to be underlined. Then choose the Forma**t** **B**order command, select **B**ottom, and choose OK.

Create double-underlines by selecting the cell or range of cells where you want the double-underline. Then choose the Forma**t** **B**order command, select **T**op and **B**ottom, and choose OK. This sequence of commands produces lines at the top and bottom of the selected cells. Close the distance between the top and bottom lines by shrinking the row height. To do this, drag up the row-heading divider below the row. From the keyboard, select a cell in that row and then choose Forma**t** **R**ow Height. Enter a height of approximately 3 points and then choose OK. The exact amount of space you need between double-underlines may vary slightly among printers.

3.30 Tip: Include the underline cell in SUM functions.

Always include the cell that contains the underline as an end point of a SUM or range function. This line prevents inexperienced users from inserting a new data row at the bottom of a column that is outside the SUM range. If you underline the bottom cell, users will insert rows above the underline and stay within the SUM range. Figure 3.10 shows an example of the end point of a SUM function; the hidden row 11 is used to create a solid underline.

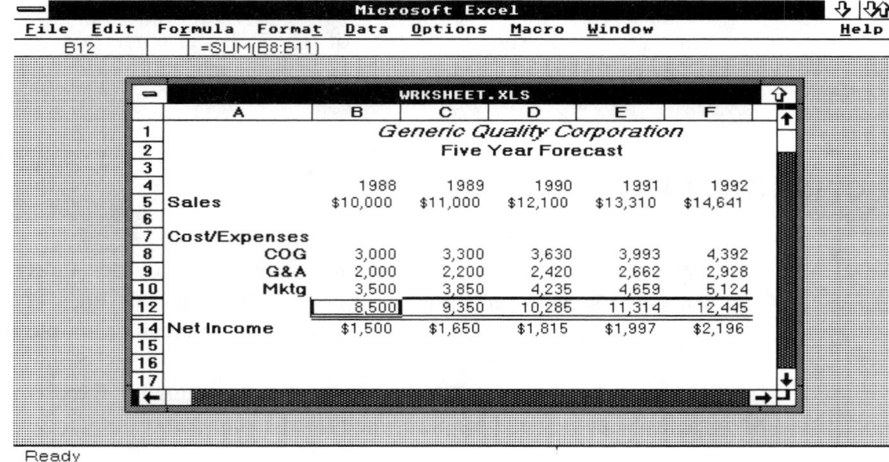

Fig. 3.10. Using the cell with the underline as the end point of the SUM function.

To prevent inserting rows incorrectly at the top of a range, you may want to include a header cell. In this case, use the following SUM formula:

```
=SUM(B7:B11)
```

3.31 Trick: To separate underlines between cells, use one of two methods.

When using bottom borders to underline cells, the underlines touch, making it difficult to read totals. To separate underlines at the bottom of columns, use one of the following methods.

In the first method, insert blank columns between columns and narrow these columns to create a space between the totals.

A second method uses two Excel functions to calculate and place the appropriate number of underline characters. Figure 3.11 shows the underlining formula in the formula bar and the resulting underlines in row 11.

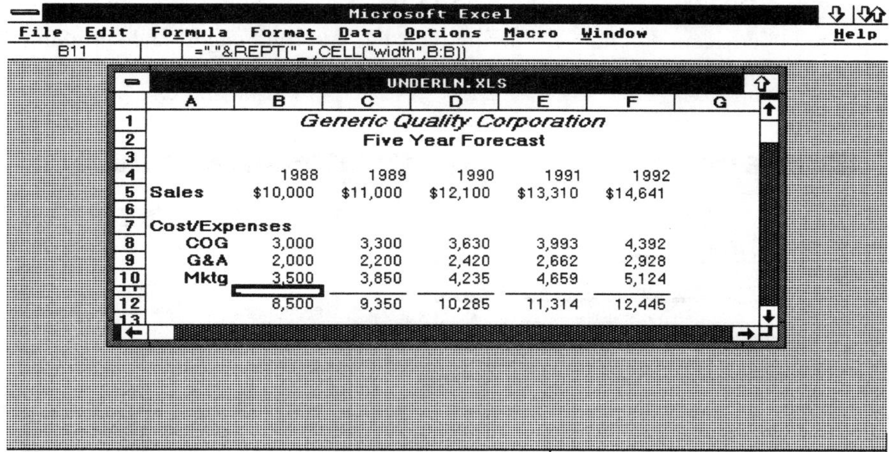

Fig. 3.11. *Using Excel functions to make underlined totals more readable.*

The following formula is entered in cell B11:

=REPT("_",CELL("width",B:B))

Copy this formula to C11:F11 to create separated underlines. Then reduce the vertical height of row 11 to shrink the space over the underline character. You can create a double-underline using two rows of this formula and reducing the height of each row.

In the formula, the CELL function calculates the width of column B. This width then is used to calculate the number of underline characters, "_", that will be repeated in the cell.

The underlines normally leave a small leading and trailing space. If you want to add more leading or trailing spaces, insert concatenated space characters and reduce the number of repetitions:

=" "&REPT("_",CELL("width",B:B)–2)&" "

3.32 Tip: **Use adjacent rows and columns to enter thick lines.**

Enter thick horizontal lines by selecting multiple adjacent rows and then choosing the Forma**t** **B**order command. Select **T**op and **B**ottom and choose OK. This command applies to all selected rows. Now compress the row heights of the selected rows so that they are each 1 point tall. Your result is thick lines like those shown in figure 3.12. Thick vertical lines are produced by selecting adjacent columns, bordering their left and right edges, and shrinking the column widths to a fractional unit such as .1.

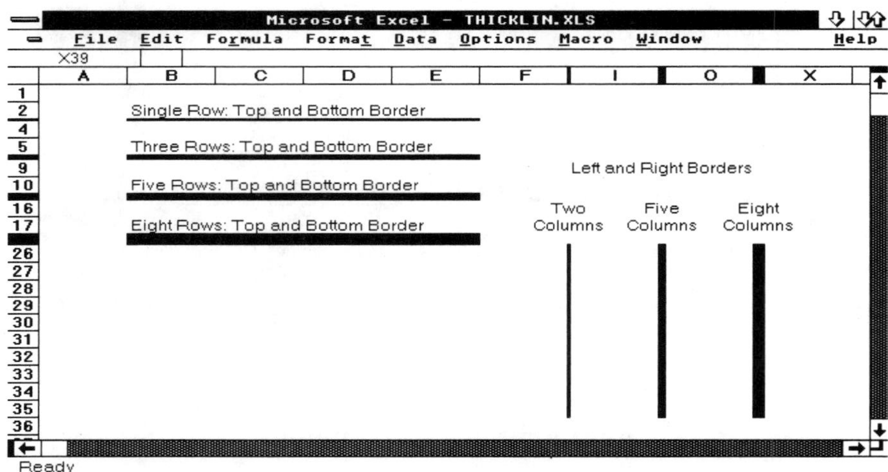

Fig. 3.12. *Creating thick horizontal and vertical lines.*

3.33 Tip: **Create shadow boxes to set off titles and results.**

Use shadow boxes to set off titles or special information. Create shadow boxes by drawing thick lines as described in the preceding tip. Offset the lower lines by one cell to the right and offset the vertical lines by one cell down. Figure 3.13 shows an example of using shadow boxes.

3.34 Trap: **Check row and column widths if your borders disappear.**

Borders may disappear if there is not enough room to display them or if the cell contains hidden characters. If borders do not appear on the top, check that the row is tall enough. If borders do not appear on a left or right edge, widen

Microsoft Excel - PRESENTN.XLS

File Edit Formula Format Data Options Macro Window Help

PC Productivity Pointers ©

Excel - Part of a Strategic Software Direction

- o **Power available to more levels of user**
- o **Maximizes new H/W, S/W and training investment**
- o **Preserves existing office H/W and S/W investment**
- o **Dynamic data exchange between applications**
- o **Learning transfers to other progams**

Ron Person & Co.

San Francisco and Santa Rosa CA, 707-539-1525

Microsoft Windows and OS/2 Software Training Nationwide

Fig. 3.13. *Shadowed boxes.*

the column. In narrow columns, displaying the cell's contents takes precedence over displaying left and right borders.

Left or right borders also may disappear if an adjacent cell contains a space and if the range that includes the space and the bordered cell are formatted with **F**ill alignment. To check for this, select the cell with incorrect borders and choose the Forma**t** **A**lignment command. If the **F**ill option is selected, select any other option and choose OK.

4

Calculating with Functions, Tables, and Arrays

While you can use electronic spreadsheets to do repetitive math, some of their greatest power comes in how quickly spreadsheets calculate complex formulas and equations and analyze databases. One of the advantages of using Excel is its extensive list of functions. Functions are prebuilt equations and formulas provided for your use. For example, you don't have to know the equation to calculate a mortgage payment—all you need to know is the data that goes into the equation. Excel even prompts you for the data. Excel also will enter the function in a cell or formula if you want.

If you work with much data that you need to analyze, Excel can reduce hours or days of manual work down to seconds or minutes of calculation time. Some of the ways in which you can use database analysis include to study surveys, total ledgers by account codes, or cross-tabulate receivables by account and time. This chapter covers tips, tricks, and traps to use to speed calculations.

Entering Functions

Excel uses a few techniques to help you enter functions without mistakes. Use these techniques whenever you're not sure how to type the function.

4.1 Tip: **Reduce mistakes by selecting functions and pasting arguments in formulas.**

Let Excel help you enter functions and arguments whenever you are unsure. Select the cell in which you want a function, or position the cursor in an equation already in the formula bar. Then choose the Formula Paste Function command. Excel displays a Paste Function list box from which you can select a function (see fig. 4.1).

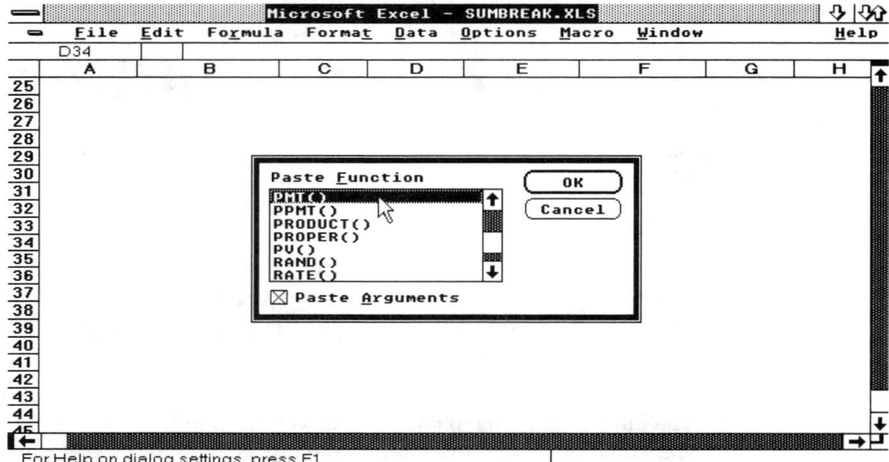

Fig. 4.1. The Paste Function list box.

A quick way to select from the list box is to select anything in the box and then type the first letter of the function you want. Continue to type that letter or scroll down until the function you want is selected.

Select the Paste Arguments check box if you want Excel to paste in prompts for the arguments between parentheses. Then choose OK. The Paste Arguments option inserts the text to show the required items and their order in the parentheses.

Some functions have more than one set of arguments. When this occurs, Excel presents a list box from which you must choose the set of arguments to be pasted. The Excel reference manual defines arguments in detail.

4.2 Trick: **Select function arguments and then replace them.**

When you paste a function with the Paste Arguments option selected, the function appears in the formula bar with text prompts between parentheses:

=PMT(*rate*, *nper*, *pv*, *fv*, *type*)

When pasted the first argument prompt, *rate*, is selected. To replace this argument, type or click on a cell address or value.

To select and replace other arguments quickly with the mouse, double-click on the argument prompt to select it. Double-clicking on an argument selects everything between two commas. Once selected, you can type an entry or click on a cell to enter a cell reference. For example, in the preceding PMT( ) function, double-clicking on the *p* in *nper* selects the entire argument. Typing **360** replaces *nper*. Double-click and drag to select multiple arguments.

To select and replace arguments quickly using a PC's keyboard, move the insertion point to the left of the argument you want replaced. Hold down the Shift key and press Ctrl+right arrow to select from the current insertion point past the next comma. Type the new argument and a comma. Repeat the process for other arguments.

4.3 Tip: **Use pasted argument names as range names.**

You can use the text prompts that Excel pastes into a function as range names just as though you had typed the range name. For example, if you paste the following function and press Enter, you get a #NAME? error because Excel thinks that the text prompts are names:

=PMT(*rate*, *nper*, *pv*, *fv*, *type*)

If you now name the appropriate cells with the same names as the prompts, the function will calculate. You can name the appropriate ranges either before or after you paste the function, but the spelling must be the same. Also, you must name cells for all arguments or delete the arguments not used.

This trick is especially useful when you are analyzing a database with database functions such as DSUM( ), DCOUNT( ), and DAVERAGE( ). These functions use the format

database function(*database*, *field*, *criteria*)

If you have already set the database and criteria with the **D**ata Set Data**b**ase and **D**ata Set **C**riteria commands, the names database and criteria are already defined. All you need to do is paste the function and then replace the field argument with the top cell in the column you want analyzed.

4.4 Tip: **Include extra cells at the ends of ranges used in functions.**

Many functions—for example, SUM( )— act on a range of cells. All the functions that act on a range can develop a problem when a novice user inserts cells or rows for additional data.

An example of such a problem is illustrated in figure 4.2. In this worksheet, the SUM( ) function in cell C11 is

=SUM(C6:C10)

Fig. 4.2. *A SUM( ) formula.*

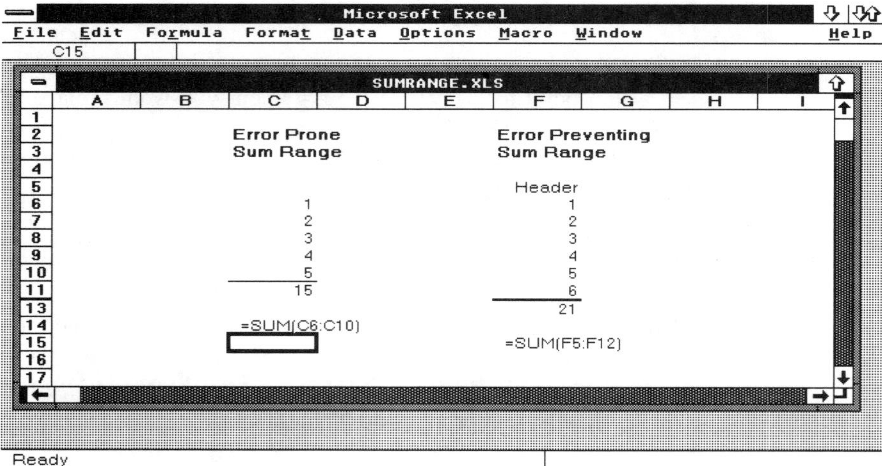

This function sums the cells from C6 to C10. If a user attempts to insert additional cells at the top, C6, or at the SUM cell, C11, the SUM( ) function does not adjust to include the additional cells. The result can be numbers in a range that appear to be totaled, but are not.

To insert cells correctly in such a case, you must insert rows or cells through the middle of the range—between the range end points—to keep the range intact. For example, inserting a cell at C9 moves the rest of the column down, and the SUM( ) function changes to the following:

=SUM(C6:C11)

A better solution, and one that prevents errors, is to build function ranges like that in column F. In cell F13 the formula is

=SUM(F5:F12)

This function sums from a text header down to a hidden line in row 12. The user can insert rows at any obvious location, and the insertion will still be between the range ends. And the sum will be accurate.

4.5 Trick: **Separate multiple ranges in arguments with a comma.**

Some functions such as SUM( ) can operate on more than one argument or range at a time. For these functions, use a comma to separate the ranges. For example, the following function totals the cells in both ranges and cell F5:

=SUM(B5:B12,D5:D12,F5)

Working with Functions

Functions are premade formulas that perform calculations for you. Rather than entering long and complex equations, you have to enter only the data input that the formula uses. The functions do all the calculations for you, without errors. Excel performs these calculations much faster than a worksheet-built formula.

Excel has more functions than other worksheets. Make sure that you scan through the Excel reference manual to see what functions are available.

4.6 Tip: **Use the ROUND( ) function to round cell contents to any precision.**

Excel and other worksheets calculate with the full precision of the number stored in a cell, even if the display format shows the number as rounded to a smaller number of decimals. In Excel, you can choose the **O**ptions **C**alculations Precision as Displayed command to round the number used for calculation to the same precision as the number used in the display. In some cases, however, you will want to round the number in just one cell. To do so, use the ROUND( ) function.

The ROUND( ) function rounds off the contents of the formula, number, or cell reference in the first argument to the precision of the second argument, using this format:

ROUND(*number*, *number_of_digits*)

The *number_of_digits* can be positive, negative, or zero. If positive, the number is rounded to that many decimal places to the right of the decimal. If zero, the number is rounded to a whole number. If negative, the number is rounded to the left of the zero. The following show examples of the function. In these examples, A1 contains 2 and B1 contains 1400.028.

=ROUND(A1*B1,2) is 2800.06
=ROUND(A1*B1,0) is 2800
=ROUND(A1*B1,–3) is 3000

4.7 Trick: **Round off to any number with the ROUND( ) function.**

If you need to round off to the nickel or if you work for the federal government and need to round off to even millions, you will find this trick useful. To round a number in cell B2 to the nearest 50 cents (or .50), use the following formula:

=ROUND(B2/.5,0)*.5

You can round to any value by substituting that value for the .5 in the formula.

4.8 Tip: **Use lookup functions to retrieve information from lists or tables.**

Do you have to look up a number from a table, chart, or book before you can do a calculation? If so, you should consider using lookup tables. Excel contains more than one function to help you look up information in tables. The following example uses VLOOKUP( ) to look up information related to a vertical list. Other types of lookup functions in Excel include LOOKUP( ), HLOOKUP( ), and INDEX( ).

In figure 4.3 the range C10:F15 contains a commission table where the commission depends on the product class and the amount of the sale. The amount of sale is entered in cell D3, and the product class is entered in D4. From these two entries, a VLOOKUP( ) function in D5 can look up the commission rate so that cell D6 can calculate the commission in dollars.

The VLOOKUP arguments are

=VLOOKUP(*lookup_value*,*table*,*col_index*)

The formula in cell D5 is

=VLOOKUP(D3,C11:F15,D4+1)

The VLOOKUP( ) function uses the amount in D3 as the *lookup_value* to go down the first column in the *table* until it finds a value equal to D3. If it can't

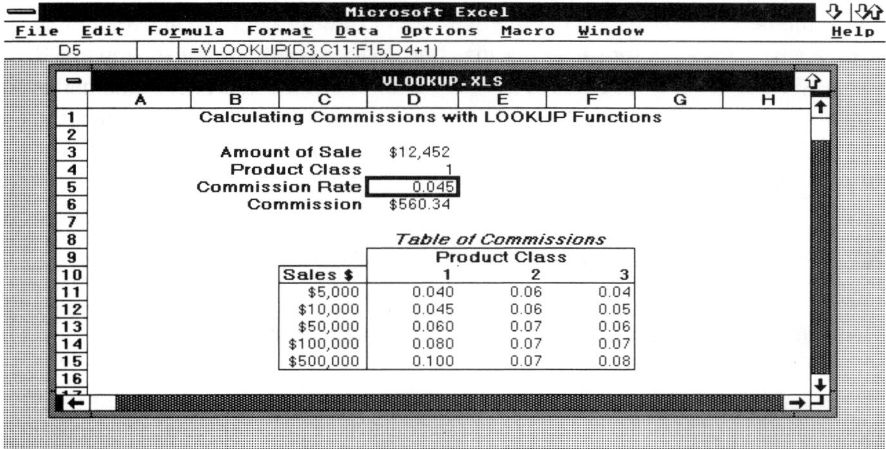

Fig. 4.3. Using VLOOKUP to look up a value.

find a value equal to D3, the function uses the next highest value that doesn't exceed D3. The values in the first column of the table can be text, numbers, or logical values. These entries must be in ascending order.

Once Excel finds the row containing the *lookup_value*, it looks across that row to the cell indicated by *col_index. col_index* is the number of the column that contains the necessary information. Column tables start their column numbering at 1. Because the formula uses D4+1, the product class of 1, 2, or 3 aligns the lookup with columns containing commission rates.

In the example, the VLOOKUP( ) function looks down the first column for a match to $12,452 until it finds $50,000 in the fourth row of the table (counting the heading). This amount is larger than the sale; therefore, the third row is used. The VLOOKUP( ) function then looks across the table in the third row to column 2. Column 2 is used because the product class is 1, and 1 is added to that in the formula. The intersect of the third row and the second column in the table is 0.045 or a sales commission of 4.5 percent.

4.9 Tip: Use MIRR( ) rather than IRR( ) for investment analysis.

Excel contains many more worksheet functions than other spreadsheets such as Lotus 1-2-3 Release 3. These Excel functions give you the ability to use more accurate and up-to-date financial analysis methods. For example, you may have used the internal rate of return, IRR( ), function with Lotus 1-2-3. While IRR( ) is also available in Excel, you may want to use the more accurate modified internal rate of return function, MIRR( ), with Excel.

As figure 4.4 demonstrates, the internal rate of return overestimates the return that a cash flow will return to the investor. IRR( ) results in an overestimate because it reinvests positive cash flows at the same rate as the finally calculated internal rate of return. In reality, the smaller and short-term cash flows from an investment rarely get the same higher return as the large initial investment.

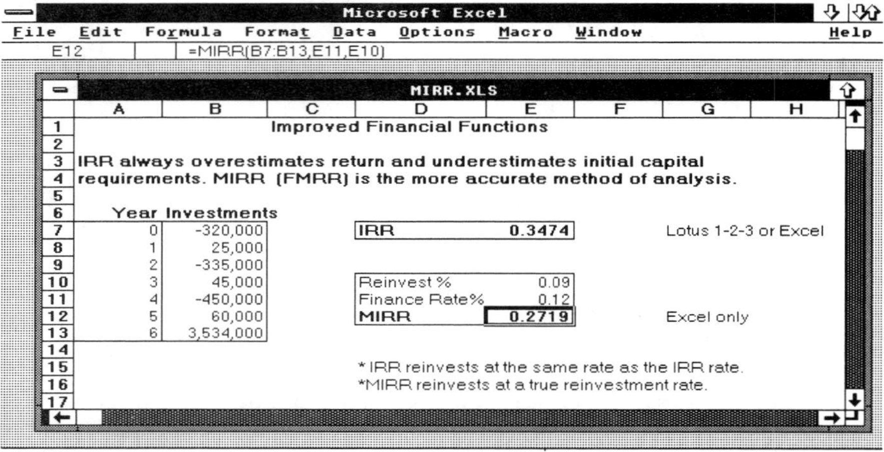

Fig. 4.4. Comparing the MIRR( ) and IRR( ) functions.

For this reason, you should use the modified internal rate of return when calculating what an investment might return. The modified internal rate of return reinvests positive cash flows at a reinvestment rate or safe rate that you specify.

In figure 4.4, the MIRR( ) function uses as arguments the evenly timed cash flows listed in B7:B13. These cash flows must be in the order they occur. The negative cash flow at year 0 is the initial investment. Other negative cash flows are amounts put into the investment. The $3,534,000 is the return at the end of year 6. The reinvestment rate or rate at which you saved your positive cash flows is an annual rate in cell E10. The finance rate in cell E11 is the rate at which you finance money borrowed for the negative cash flow.

Working with Text Formulas

Text formulas in Excel enable you to manipulate text, pull out phrases, separate or combine text, and even combine numbers and text for use in worksheet headings or text. You can use text formulas and functions to extend Excel's capability. If you need to do something with text and it doesn't seem possible, look through the text functions, rethink the problem, and you'll probably find a solution.

4.10 Tip: **Combine text with formulas.**

With the ampersand (&), you can join text. For example, if A1 contains Think and B1 contains Globally, the following formula in C1 results in Think Globally:

=A1&" "&B1

Notice that a space had to be placed between the two text contents of the cell. The cells did not contain a space. If the space, in quotation marks, where not there, the result would have been this:

ThinkGlobally

Explicit text in the formula but not in a cell must be enclosed in quotation marks. Using these same cell contents, the following formula produces Think Globally - Act Locally:

=A1&" "&B1&" - Act Locally"

Figure 4.5 shows other examples of concatenating text.

4.11 Trick: **Use text functions to extract data for form letters or new database columns.**

If you've created database fields that contain the information you need to sort or search, but you can't get to the information, don't give up. In many cases you can use text, date, or math functions to calculate the data you need.

For example in figure 4.5, rows 3 and 4 simulate a database. The data in E4 contains the city, state, and ZIP code as a single entry. With the use of text functions, you can extract data you need from the existing data in the database.

In the example, you could extract names, titles, or amounts for use in a simple form letter that concatenates (joins) the database information with text in the letter. Cells B7, B9, B13 and B15 show different examples of how to do this.

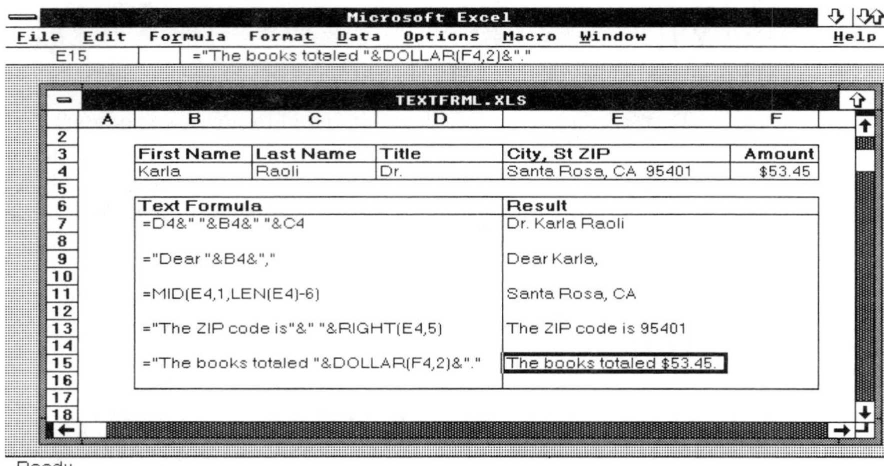

Fig. 4.5. Concatenating text.

If you need to sort or search on data that isn't readily available in the database, you can sometimes pull the data out with the use of text functions. For example, the city, state abbreviation, and ZIP code are in a single cell or database column in figure 4.5. You can use text functions in a new column to pull out the state or ZIP code. You can use this new column to sort or search on in a database.

To find the ZIP code, use a RIGHT( ) function. Cell B13 illustrates the RIGHT( ) function used to extract a ZIP code. This function pulled the right five characters from cell E4.

If you want to convert the text formulas permanently into characters, copy the cells containing the functions and then paste them back over themselves with the **E**dit Paste **S**pecial command with **V**alues selected.

4.12 Trick: Create lists of special PC characters (ANSI) using the CHAR( ) function.

If you aren't sure which special ANSI characters your computer uses on-screen or how these characters correspond to printed characters, you may want to build a table of all characters. This trick shows you how.

Use the **D**ata Se**r**ies command to create a list of numbers from 127 to 255. As figure 4.6 illustrates you don't have to create a continuous list. In fact, you can more easily print if the list is not continuous.

Microsoft Excel - ANSICHAR.XLS

File Edit Formula Format Data Options Macro Window Help

I9 =CHAR(H9)

	Num.	Char.	Num.	Char.	Num.	Char.	Num.	Char.
3	161	¡	178	²	195	Ã	212	Ô
4	162	¢	179	³	196	Ä	213	Õ
5	163	£	180	´	197	Å	214	Ö
6	164	¤	181	µ	198	Æ	215	×
7	165	¥	182	¶	199	Ç	216	Ø
8	166	¦	183	·	200	È	217	Ù
9	167	§	184	¸	201	É	218	Ú
10	168	¨	185	¹	202	Ê	219	Û
11	169	©	186	º	203	Ë	220	Ü
12	170	ª	187	»	204	Ì	221	Ý
13	171	«	188	¼	205	Í	222	Þ
14	172	¬	189	½	206	Î	223	ß
15	173	-	190	¾	207	Ï	224	à
16	174	®	191	¿	208	Ð	225	á
17	175	¯	192	À	209	Ñ	226	â

Ready

Fig. 4.6. *ANSI characters.*

In the cell adjacent to each number, enter the function =CHAR( ) using the reference of the cell to the left as shown in figure 4.6. For example, cell I9 contains the formula =CHAR(H9).

Although you can see a character on-screen, it may not print the same way on your printer. To see the corresponding characters for your printer, print the worksheet. Compare the printed list to the screen list. If your printer uses font cartridges or soft fonts, you may want to change fonts and reprint. Some font sets use different characters for the characters from 127–256.

In PC Excel, you can enter these ANSI characters by holding down the Alt key as you type a zero followed by the three-number ANSI code. Use only the numeric keypad to enter the numbers. The character will appear on-screen when you release the Alt key. On the Macintosh, access the characters using the Option and Shift keys. Use the Key Caps desk accessory for a layout of these characters.

Preparing Reports with Totals and Subtotals

This section provides simple solutions to the problems of creating running totals or subtotals when a field's contents change. Use these techniques to enhance reports you extract from Excel or dBASE databases extracted with Q+E.

4.13 Tip: Create running totals with a SUM( ) function and mixed references.

Running totals produce a cumulative total so that you can see how an amount is building. These totals are easy to produce once you learn how to mix absolute and relative reference addressing.

Figure 4.7 shows a running total created to the right of an extract from a database. The running total in column E was created by entering the following formula in cell E8:

=SUM($D$7:D8)

This function totals from D7, which is zero because it is text, down to D8, the first entry. After entering this formula, copy it down the column with the **E**dit Fill Down command. Notice that the $D$7 portion of the SUM range stays absolutely fixed in each formula because the reference is absolute. The D8 portion changes relative to its new location because it is a relative reference. The result is that each formula sums from the top down to its own row.

Fig. 4.7. Running totals.

Microsoft Excel

File Edit Formula Format Data Options Macro Window Help

E8 =SUM($D$7:D8)

SUMTOTAL.XLS

	A	B	C	D	E	F	G
6		Extract Range					
7		Firm	Acct_ID	Amount	Running Total		
8		XYZ Tech.	1030	$85.00	$85.00		
9		Xanthic Dev.	1030	$67.90	$152.90		
10		RPC and Co.	1030	$5.09	$157.99		
11		Mountain Time	1030	$66.67	$224.66		
12		XYZ Tech.	1035	$12.00	$236.66		
13		Corpae Co.	1035	$32.76	$269.42		
14		Chang Dist.	1035	$43.00	$312.42		
15		RPC and Co.	1040	$67.43	$379.85		
16		Wing Tech.	1040	$3.00	$382.85		
17		NueronLink	1040	$11.00	$393.85		
18		HiFlyers, Inc.	1040	$10.50	$404.35		
19		Xanthic Dev.	1050	$3.50	$407.85		
20		Mountain Time	1050	$67.89	$475.74		
21		Chang Dist.	1050	$15.35	$491.09		
22		RPC and Co.	1050	$23.00	$514.09		
23							

Ready

4.14 Tip: Create totals on breakfields with the IF( ) and SUM( ) functions.

Displaying subtotals only when a database category changes produces a cleaner, easier-to-read report. One simple method that doesn't involve macros is shown in figure 4.8.

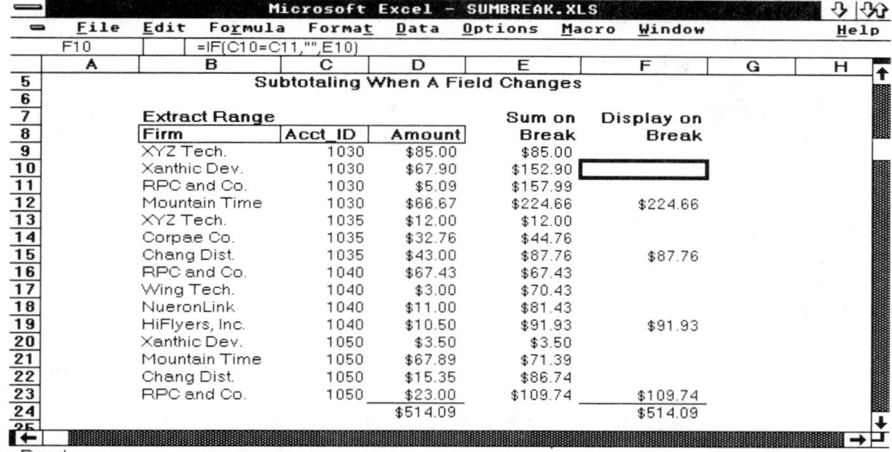
Microsoft Excel - SUMBREAK.XLS

File Edit Formula Format Data Options Macro Window Help

F10 =IF(C10=C11,"",E10)

	A	B	C	D	E	F	G	H
5		Subtotaling When A Field Changes						
6								
7		Extract Range			Sum on	Display on		
8		Firm	Acct_ID	Amount	Break	Break		
9		XYZ Tech.	1030	$85.00	$85.00			
10		Xanthic Dev.	1030	$67.90	$152.90			
11		RPC and Co.	1030	$5.09	$157.99			
12		Mountain Time	1030	$66.67	$224.66	$224.66		
13		XYZ Tech.	1035	$12.00	$12.00			
14		Corpae Co.	1035	$32.76	$44.76			
15		Chang Dist.	1035	$43.00	$87.76	$87.76		
16		RPC and Co.	1040	$67.43	$67.43			
17		Wing Tech.	1040	$3.00	$70.43			
18		NueronLink	1040	$11.00	$81.43			
19		HiFlyers, Inc.	1040	$10.50	$91.93	$91.93		
20		Xanthic Dev.	1050	$3.50	$3.50			
21		Mountain Time	1050	$67.89	$71.39			
22		Chang Dist.	1050	$15.35	$86.74			
23		RPC and Co.	1050	$23.00	$109.74	$109.74		
24				$514.09		$514.09		

Ready

Fig. 4.8. Subtotaling by account number.

Figure 4.8 again shows an extract from a database. Column E contains running totals that start over whenever the Acct_ID number changes. These totals are used to produce the displayed subtotals in column F. If you do not want to see the totals in column E, you can shrink the column width to zero with the Forma**t** **C**olumn Width command or put the range E7:E23 in a different location that isn't visible or that won't print. The range E7:E23 is necessary for the calculations, but doesn't have to show in the final results.

This method of producing subtotals when a field changes requires three formulas. To bring the first amount into column E, cell E9 contains

=D9

The following function, in cell E10, compares the current row's Acct_ID with the Acct_ID in the preceding row:

=IF(C10=C9,D10+E9,D10)

If the Acct_IDs are the same, the current amount and the previous subtotal are added together. If the Acct_IDs are not the same, it means a break has occurred. In this case, the current amount is displayed, and the function restarts the subtotal for a new Acct_ID.

Notice that column E contains all the subtotals needed. However, the extraneous running totals for each account also are displayed. Formulas in column F selectively display the running subtotals from E only when the Acct_ID changes. Cell F9 contains the following formula:

=IF(C9=C10,"",E9)

This formula checks to see whether the current row's Acct_ID matches the Acct_ID in the next row. If the two match, nothing, "", is displayed. If the two are different, the Acct_ID is about to change; therefore, the subtotal in E9 is displayed. Copy the formula in cell F9 down column F.

Checking Data for Accuracy

Functions are extremely useful for cross-checking data as it is entered. You can put cross-check formulas into worksheets next to a data-entry cell, into a database entry range, and even into a macro to check data coming from a macro controlled input box.

4.15 Tip: **Use IF( ) and AND( ) functions to check numeric ranges.**

Figure 4.9 shows how the AND( ) function when used inside an IF( ) function can check an entered number against a range. The example shown in the formula bar checks to see whether the entry in cell D4 is greater than 0 AND less than 11. If both of these conditions are true, Ok displays in the IF( ) function cell, E4. If either condition is false, the entire AND( ) function returns false, and the text prompt Enter between 1 and 10 appears in cell E4.

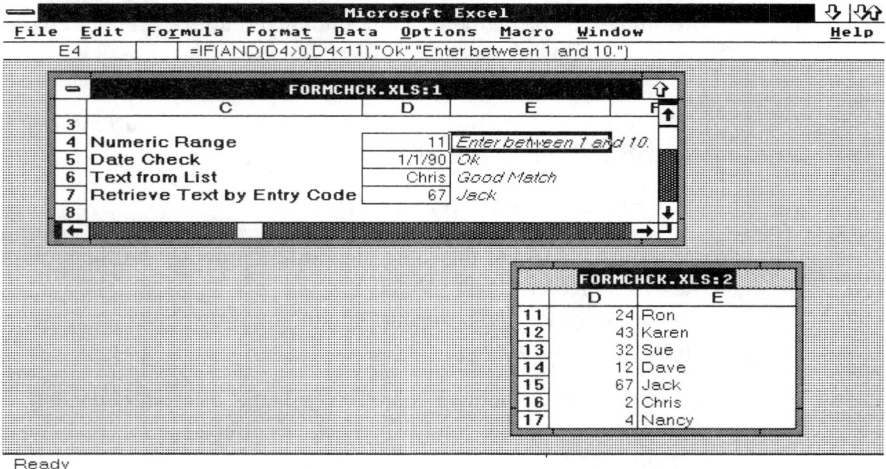

Fig. 4.9. Checking numeric ranges.

4.16 Tip: **Use IF( ) and DATEVALUE( ) functions to check valid date entries.**

Figure 4.10 is similar to the previous numeric range check except that a range of dates is used to verify the date entered in cell D5. The DATEVALUE( ) function calculates the serial date number for the dates inside the parentheses. Once these date serial numbers are calculated for 1/1/1990 and 12/31/1990, the numbers are used to compare against the date serial number in cell D5. The process works the same as the numeric entry range check in the preceding tip.

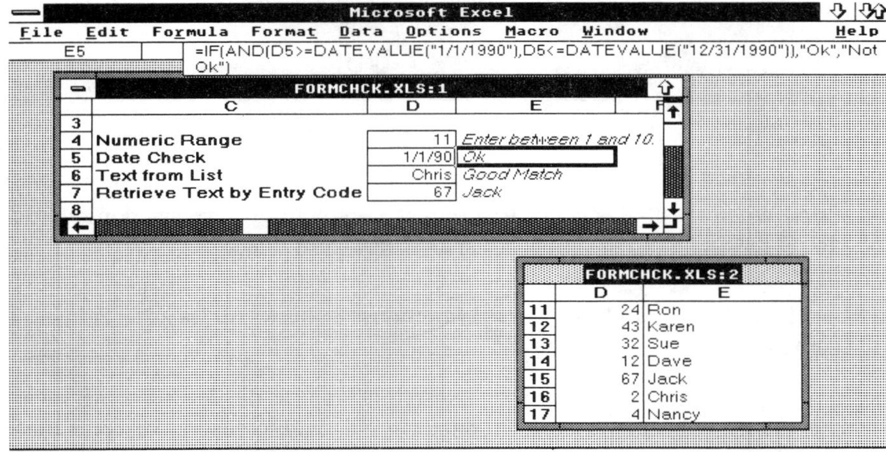

Fig. 4.10. Checking date entries.

4.17 Tip: **Use IF( ), ISNA( ), and MATCH( ) functions to check entries against a list.**

This tip is especially useful for cross-checking entries against a list to ensure that the entry is spelled correctly and that the entry is a valid item on an approved list.

Figure 4.11 shows a name typed into cell D6. The adjacent cell, E6, displays Good Match to show that Chris is in the list in the range E11:E17. The list in E11:E17 can be in any order.

The MATCH( ) function compares the text in cell D6 against the contents of the range E11:E17. The third argument is 0 which means that the match must be exact. If an exact match is found, its location in the list is returned. In this example, the number 6 is returned. Because 6 is returned, the ISNA( ) function returns FALSE, causing the IF( ) function to display Good Match.

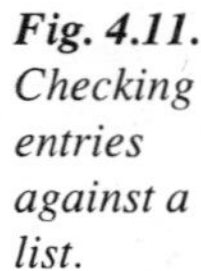

Fig. 4.11. Checking entries against a list.

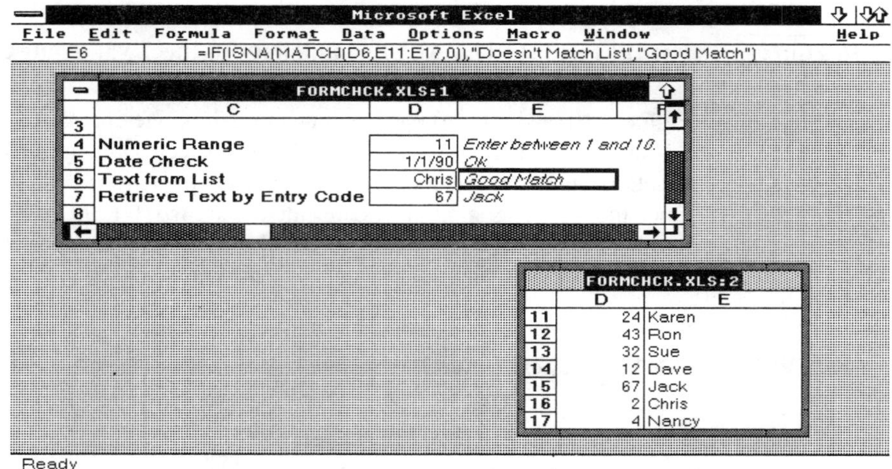

If MATCH( ) cannot find an exact match in the list, it returns the error value #N/A. When the ISNA( ) function sees the #N/A result, the function returns TRUE, making the IF( ) function display Doesn't Match List.

4.18 Tip: Use the INDEX( ) and MATCH( ) functions to check entries and reduce typing.

In figure 4.12 the number 67 typed into cell D7 returns the desired name, Jack. You can use this entry method to reduce typing and to ensure correct entries instead of typing frequently used names, part descriptions, and so on. If the number is not in the list in the range E11:D17, #N/A appears in cell E7. The numeric list in E11:D17 does not have to be in sorted order.

This combination of functions works because the MATCH( ) function begins by looking down the list in range D11:D17 until it finds an exact match to the number entered in cell D7. When it finds that match, the function returns the numeric position in the list—in this case, the number 7.

The INDEX( ) function returns the item located at the seventh row and the second column in the range D11:E17. That item is the name Jack.

4.19 Trick: Use an array formula to check valid entries against a list.

Array formulas are a powerful feature available to Excel. In figure 4.13, cell C7 contains an array formula that uses the sum of an IF( ) function to determine whether the entry in cell C7 is in the list E7:E11.

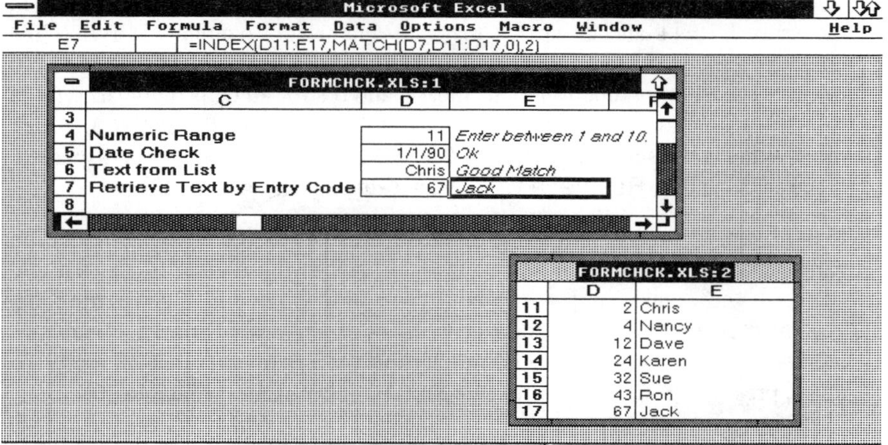

Fig. 4.12. Using INDEX( ) and MATCH( ) to check entries.

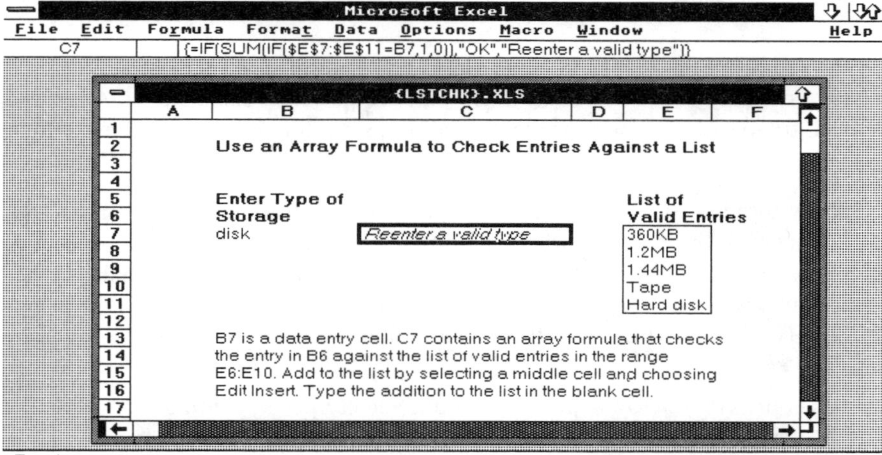

Fig. 4.13. Using an array formula to check entries against a list.

While array formulas look similar to normal formulas and functions, they act on all the cells in the array. This array formula checks each cell in the array E7:E11 against cell B7.

The data in the range E7:E11 is entered normally, but the formula in cell C7 is not. You must enter array formulas by pressing Shift+Ctrl+Enter (PC) or Shift+Control+Enter (Macintosh). If entered correctly, the formula appears within braces in the formula bar. These braces are shown in figure 4.13.

The array formula works because the IF( ) function goes through each cell in the array E7:E11 and compares that cell against the contents of B7. If the contents are equal, the value 1 is the result. If the contents are not equal, 0 results. The SUM( ) function totals the 1's and 0's for all cells in the array. The first IF( ) function in the formula checks to see whether the SUM( ) is 1 or more—this is the same as TRUE. If the SUM( ) is 1 or more, OK is displayed. If the SUM( ) is 0, Reenter a valid type is displayed.

If the list of valid entries is in the same worksheet as the array formula, you can add to the list by inserting additional cells in the middle of the list and typing the new entries in those cells. If you add to either end of an existing list, you must change the range address specified in the array formula. When you reenter the array formula after editing it, don't forget to enter it as an array. To do so, press Shift+Ctrl+Enter (PC) or Shift+Control+Enter (Macintosh).

Working with Arrays

Formulas or constants entered as arrays are a powerful Excel feature that can save memory in your worksheet and produce powerful calculations. An *array* is a group of formulas or values stored in a series of cells, or a reference to a series of cells.

Array formulas or constants appear in the formula bar enclosed in braces { }. Do not type these braces when entering the array. Instead begin by selecting the cell or range of cells to contain the array, type the values or formulas in the formula bar, and then enter the array into the selected cells by pressing Shift+Ctrl+Enter (PC) or Shift+Control+Enter (Macintosh).

4.20 Tip: **Select arrays quickly with the Formula Select Special command.**

Select an entire array quickly by selecting a single cell in the array and then choosing Formula Select Special with the Current Array option selected. An even faster method is to select a cell in the array and then press Ctrl+/ (forward slash).

4.21 Tip: **Edit all array formulas at one time.**

You cannot change a single cell within an array. You must change the entire array. To do this, select the entire array using the procedure from the preceding tip; then press F2 or click in the formula bar. Edit the formula or values.

Reenter the array by pressing Shift+Ctrl+Enter (PC) or Shift+Control+Enter (Macintosh).

4.22 Tip: **Save memory and space with array math.**

You can do in one cell with an array formula what takes many cells and much memory with a regular method. For example, figure 4.14 shows how to produce the sum of numerous multiplications. One method is shown in cells D4:D10. Each number in column B is multiplied by the number in column C, and the result is placed in column D. The result is then totaled by the SUM( ) function in D10.

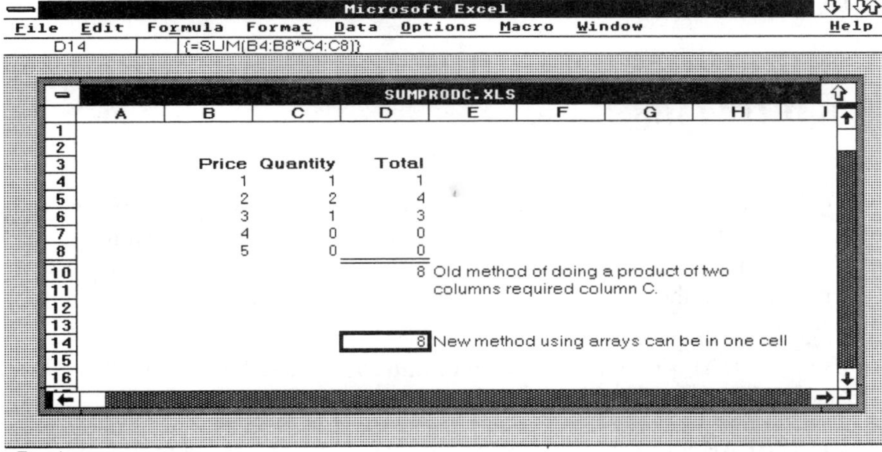

Fig. 4.14. Using array math.

An array can do all this in a single cell. The array formula in cell C14 is

{=SUM(B4:B8*C4:C8)}

This formula takes the array sum of the ranges B4:B8 times C4:C8. This formula is the same as multiplying each cell of B4:B8 times the corresponding cell in C4:C8. The SUM( ) function totals all the individual results. Remember that you must enter this as an array formula, not a normal formula.

4.23 Tip: **Turn off automatic recalculation if array formulas slow data entry.**

Like data tables, large array formulas or many array formulas used to analyze a database may slow calculation time. Prevent this by switching to manual recalculation. You cannot selectively turn off array formulas.

4.24 Tip: **Check for other array tips and tricks in this chapter.**

Other areas of this chapter describe powerful methods of using formula arrays. The section on checking data entry with functions describes how to check data against a list with the use of array formulas. A later section in this chapter on database analysis shows how to use a single array formula to do the work of a DSUM( ) function and criteria range.

Asking "What If" Questions

You don't have to sit back, relax, and sip a hot steaming mug of coffee as you type one number at a time into the worksheet and then write down the result. You can make Excel do all the plugging of "what if" numbers for you. Excel will plug in all the values at once and build tables that show the results.

4.25 Tip: **Use the GOALSEEK.XLM macro to find the answer for "what if" questions.**

The LIBRARY directory or folder contains numerous ready-to-run macros, one of which is GOALSEEK.XLM. Use GOALSEEK to do multiple "what if" analysis when you need to find the exact cell input that will produce an exact output. For example, you may want to find out how many units you need to sell at $100 per unit to generate $45,000 in gross profit, assuming that you get 36 percent profit on each unit. You can use this macro to calculate the number of units.

Start GOALSEEK.XLM by opening the file. When you open the file, the command Goal Seek is added to the bottom of your Formula menu, and GOALSEEK's macro sheet is hidden.

To find a solution using GOALSEEK, click on the cell in which you want to find a solution. This is known as the target cell. Choose the Formula Goal Seek command. The first dialog box opens showing the reference for the target cell. Choose OK. When the second dialog box appears, enter the value you want as a goal for the target cell. Choose OK.

In the third dialog box, enter the address of the input cell in which you would type values to change the target cell's results. If that cell is not visible, scroll the worksheet behind the dialog box or move the dialog box by dragging its title bar. Then click on the cell or point to the cell you want. The macro begins calculating. When it stops, a dialog box displays the input value that produces the target's goal.

4.26 Trick: Solve insolvable problems with multiple approximations.

Figure 4.15 demonstrates a type of problem found occasionally in business and frequently in science. In this type of problem, there is no exact answer. Instead, a close approximation of an answer is made through multiple calculations or iterations.

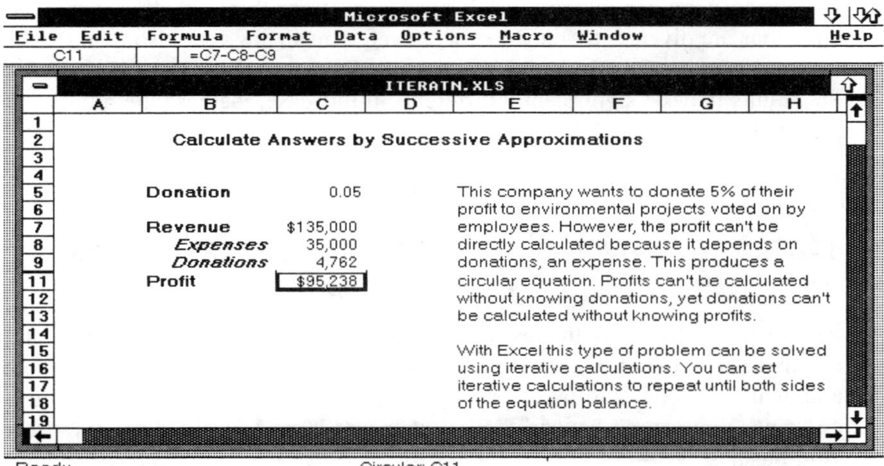

Fig. 4.15. Calculating an answer through iteration.

In figure 4.15 the company is donating 5 percent of profit to global environmental projects. However, this donation is an expense that reduces profit. Because profit is reduced, the donation amount which depends on profit must be recalculated. This circular process of recalculation must be done many times to approximate a profit and a donation that balance.

In the example, the only two equations are the profit in C11

=C7–C8–C9

and the donation in C9

=C11*C5

Notice how the two formulas depend on each other. If you enter this example, you will get a circular reference error box.

To let Excel recalculate the two equations until they balance, choose the **O**ptions **C**alculation command. Select the **I**teration option. Then choose OK.

In some cases you may want to change the maximum iterations and maximum change. Maximum It**e**rations specifies how many times Excel recalculates the worksheet before it quits. The default is 100. Maximum **C**hange determines how precise the answer will be. Recalculation stops when either the maximum number of calculations have been performed or when the largest change on the worksheet from the previous calculation is less than Maximum **C**hange.

If your answers explode and get further away from the correct answer, your equations are divergent—they do not converge on an answer. Also, you should test your iterations using both even and odd numbers of iterations. Sometimes the results may be significantly different. In this case, increase the number of iterations and recalculate.

Analyzing Databases with Functions and Data Tables

Excel's database is both easy to use with the automatic data form and extensive with the Q+E external database. Yet you can use Excel's worksheet and analytical power to take apart a database and find out the information it contains. You can go beyond the raw data and learn how the data will affect your business.

4.27 Trick: **Retrieve data selectively from a database or data table with intersecting named ranges.**

You can easily retrieve cell contents from a database or data table if you set up the database or data table correctly and use this trick. This trick enables you to retrieve a cell of information from the database or table if you know the field heading (column heading) and row heading (left label) for that cell. Suppose that a parts inventory database contains the following field names:

QNTY_ON_HAND
BACK_ORDER

And suppose that the left column of the database or data table contains unique part names for each row, such as

FUEL_GASKET

You could retrieve the number of fuel gaskets on hand with the following equation:

=FUEL_GASKET QNTY_ON_HAND

Or you could retrieve the number on back order with this equation:

=FUEL_GASKET BACK_ORDER

To accomplish this, assign the field name to each column in the database and the text name in the left column to each row in the database or data table. The intersect of a named column and named row is a specific cell. In Excel the intersect operator is a space character. The preceding equations are the two names separated by a space character.

You also can perform a math or text function on the cell contents returned this way. For example, if each gasket costs $55.50, the value of the fuel gaskets currently on hand is calculated with this equation:

=55.50*(FUEL_GASKET QNTY_ON_HAND)

To name all the rows and columns quickly, first ensure that you have valid text names along the top and left borders of your data. Names cannot begin with a number and cannot contain certain symbols.

Next select the database or data table and include the top row of headings and the left column of text names. If the range is named, such as Database, use the Goto key to select it. If the range is not named but is surrounded by blank cells, use the Fo**r**mula **S**elect Special command with the Current Regi**o**n option to select a rectangle of cells surrounded by blanks.

With the range selected, choose the Fo**r**mula **C**reate Names command and select the **T**op Row and **L**eft Column options; then choose OK. This command sequence names the columns in the selection with the top row headings and names the rows in the selection with the text in the left column.

4.28 Trick: Analyze databases or lists with IF( ) functions entered as arrays.

Arrays can be useful for analyzing databases. In a single cell, an array formula can do the work of a DSUM( ) function and its criteria range. Figure 4.16 shows how to total the amounts corresponding to a list of regions. The array formulas that perform this calculation are in cells E6:E9.

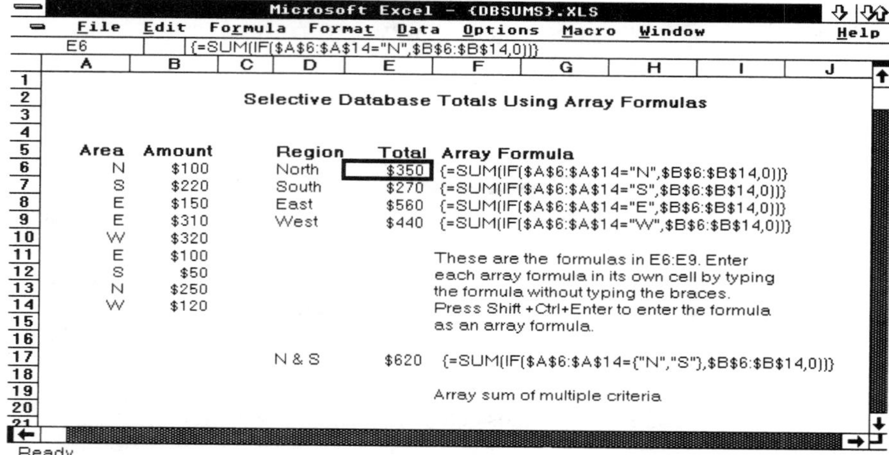

Fig. 4.16. Using array formulas with databases.

The array formula in cell E6 compares each cell's contents in the range A6:A14 against the value N. When a cell in A6:A14 contains N, the condition is TRUE. For true conditions, the IF( ) function looks at its second argument and finds the corresponding array element in the range B6:B14—in this case, the amount on the same row where N is located. For example, finding N in cell A13 causes the IF( ) function to produce the amount $250 from column B. If the cell being examined in A6:A14 does not equal N, a FALSE condition results, and the IF( ) function produces a 0. The SUM( ) function totals all the amounts and zeros produced for each cell.

Remember that when entering array formulas like this example, do not type the braces that enclose the formula. Type the formula in the formula bar and then enter it by pressing Shift+Ctrl+Enter (PC) or Shift+Control+Enter (Macintosh).

4.29 Trick: **Do complex database analysis with array formulas entered in a single cell.**

In figure 4.16, cell E17 contains an array formula that also examines the list in the range A6:B14. However, this formula produces a total for both north and south regions. In the formula to the right of cell E17, you can see that the IF( ) function compares the range A6:A14 against a manually entered array of {"N","S"}. This tip works the same as the preceding tip, but instead of comparing the range against a single N value, the function compares each cell in the range against both N and S. This produces the sum of amounts for N and S.

To create this formula, type the formula and the braces, { }, that surround the "N","S" term. Do not type the braces that surround the entire formula. Enter the formula by pressing Shift+Ctrl+Enter (PC) or Shift+Control+Enter (Macintosh). The outside braces are entered when you enter the formula.

4.30 Tip: **Use database statistical functions to analyze your database.**

Excel contains database statistical functions that will help you analyze your database contents. The database functions analyze a database for records that meet criteria you specify. Then, using only those records that match the criteria, these functions total, average, count, calculate standard deviation, and perform other operations on the field you specify. If you have built a database in Excel, you will find the database functions of significant value, yet easy to use. The database functions all use the same format.

The following lists the functions, arguments, and use for three database functions:

DSUM(*database, field, criteria*)	Totals the field
DAVERAGE(*database, field,criteria*)	Averages the field
DCOUNT(*database, field,criteria*)	Counts the field

Figure 4.17 shows an example of using DSUM( ) to find the total of all amounts where the EXP CODE is 12. The DSUM( ) formula in cell E28 is

=DSUM(Database,5,Criteria)

Database is the range name given to cells A18:E24; the 5 indicates totaling the fifth column in the database; and Criteria is the range name for the cells B27:B28.

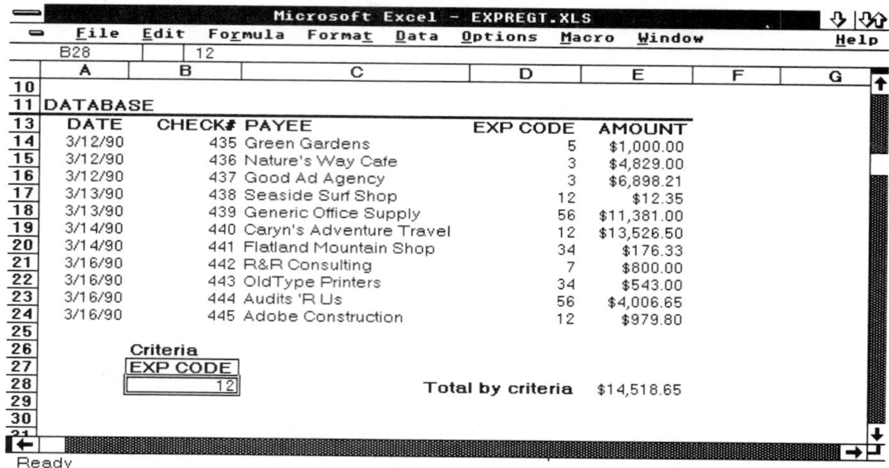

Fig. 4.17. Using the DSUM( ) function.

4.31 Tip: **Use database statistical functions on multiple databases and criteria at the same time.**

The database and criteria arguments within the database functions do not have to be the same database or criteria specified with **D**ata Set Data**b**ase or **D**ata Set **C**riteria. These ranges do not even have to be named. This means that you can analyze multiple databases with multiple criteria at the same time as long as the range names are unique or as long as cell references are used.

4.32 Trick: **Combine database functions and a data table for time-saving extensive database analysis.**

If you have much database analysis to do (which is the case if you are analyzing a mainframe download or you are tallying job-cost analysis figures), use this technique to save time. You can use database functions to do the database analysis, but use Excel's data table to repeat the analysis for each account code or item being analyzed.

In figure 4.18 the database in rows 13 through 24 is totaled by account code using the data table in B31:C37. (Some of the database records do not show on-screen.)

The data table inserts the expense codes in B32:B37 into the criteria in B28. As the data table automatically inserts each criteria in B28, the total of AMOUNT for records meeting that criteria is calculated and put in the appropriate cell in the range C32:C37. The DSUM( ) function used for the calculation is in cell C31.

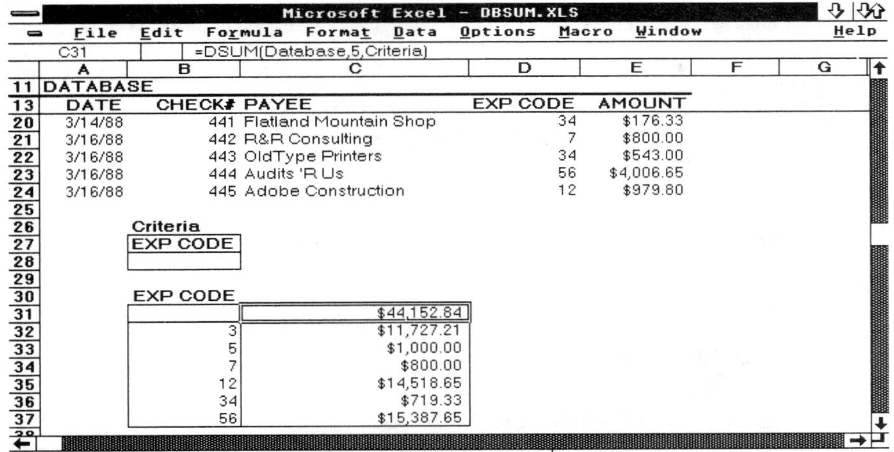

Fig. 4.18. Using database functions and a data table.

To create a data table that does this type of analysis, select an area for your data table and put a border around it for appearance and formatting. Leave the top left cell, B31 in the figure, blank. Put the database function you want to use for analysis into the cell to the right of the blank cell (cell C31 in figure 4.18). You do not have to use range names in the database function. You also can use cell references.

Down the left side of the table, cells B32:B37 in the figure, type the account codes to be automatically inserted in the criteria range.

Create the data table by selecting the range that includes the table, B31:C37 in the figure, and then choose **D**ata **T**able. The Table dialog box is displayed and asks where you want Excel to put the expense codes (see fig. 4.19). Because the expense codes are listed down the column of the table, select the **C**olumn Input Cell text box. Enter the cell reference of where in the criteria range you want the expense codes inserted. Either click on this location or type it. Figure 4.19 shows the completed box for this table. Choose OK.

The table will recalculate if you have **O**ptions **C**alculation set for automatic recalculation. If calculation is set for automatic except tables or for manual calculation, you must press F9 (PC) or Command+= (Macintosh) to recalculate.

4.33 Tip: **Use multiple data tables in Excel.**

You aren't limited to having one data table with Excel. You can have multiple data tables in a single worksheet. Each table can reference a different

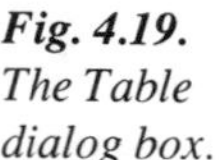

Fig. 4.19.
The Table dialog box.

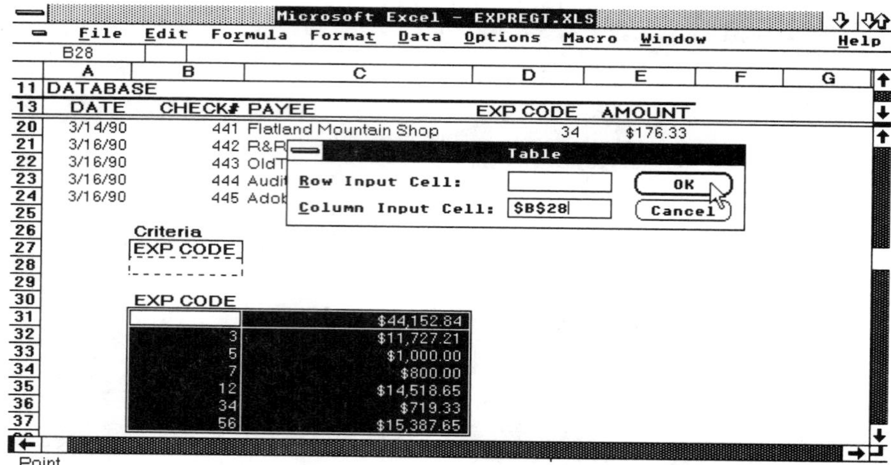

"database" and criteria. The tables are not limited to referencing the single database and criteria set with the **D**ata commands.

4.34 Tip: Analyze databases located in separate worksheets.

The database or worksheet you analyze with database functions do not have to have their criteria or database ranges in the same worksheet as the database function or the table using database functions. For example, the following function references the file GL.XLS within the WINDOWS\ACCTG subdirectory:

=DSUM('C:\WINDOWS\ACCTG\GL.XLS'!Database,5,Criteria)

4.35 Trap: Both database and analysis worksheets must be in memory for calculation.

If you use a database function or database function with a table to analyze a database in another worksheet, both worksheets must be open during the calculation. After you create the table, it can be opened by itself and still retain its calculated table by following these steps:

1. Choose **O**ptions **C**alculation **M**anual or Automatic except **T**ables. This command is available only when a worksheet is open. If one is not open, open a blank one and choose the command.

2. Open the worksheet containing the table.

3. When a dialog box requests Update references to unopened documents?, respond **N**o. This prevents the table from relinking with the worksheet on disk.

4. Do not recalculate the worksheet containing the table. If you do, all the tables that reference a database in another worksheet will change to #REF! errors. Use Shift+F9 to calculate the active worksheet if it is not the worksheet containing the table.

4.36 Trick: **Freeze large data tables or data tables that reference external databases to save time and prevent errors.**

You may not want to recalculate some data tables once they are complete. For example, a worksheet with large or numerous data tables can take a long time to recalculate. Waiting for the table can slow work. Also, if the data table references a database or criteria range in another worksheet, you won't want to recalculate. Recalculating the table produces #REF! errors. You can prevent both of these problems.

If your data table does not contain references to external databases or criteria, choose the **O**ptions **C**alculation Automatic except **T**ables command. This option lets you recalculate the worksheet without recalculating the table. The calculation shortcut keys (F9, PC and Command+=, Macintosh) also recalculate the tables. When you want to recalculate the tables, choose the **O**ptions **C**alculation **A**utomatic command.

If your data table contains references to external databases or criteria and you want to calculate it without having #REF! errors appear, you have two choices. The first choice is to load the worksheets that support the table. With the data table worksheet active, choose the **F**ile **L**inks command to load the worksheets that the table uses for external databases or external criteria. Once the files are open in memory, you can use the **O**ptions **C**alculation commands as described in the preceding text.

If you do not want to load the worksheets that support the data table, open the data table as described in the preceding tip so that the worksheet will not recalculate. Once the worksheet is open, use the **E**dit **C**opy command to copy the data table information you need. Leave the same range selected and choose **E**dit Paste **S**pecial with the **V**alues and N**o**ne options selected to paste unchanging values over the top of the table formulas. You must have the entire table selected for this method to work.

If you want to preserve your tables operation, save the frozen worksheet with another file name or do not paste over the table. Instead use the **E**dit Paste **S**pecial command to paste the values onto a new worksheet.

5

Working with Multiple Worksheets

One of Excel's powerful, yet easy-to-use features is the capability to display multiple worksheets on-screen and link the data among them. These links are more than just a static transfer of data. Every time a linked worksheet is opened, Excel refreshes the linked data.

In many cases, the links among worksheets are maintained even if a worksheet is still on disk. This gives you the opportunity to reduce memory requirements by linking smaller worksheets on-screen with large worksheets or databases on disk. You can even link Excel and Lotus 1-2-3 worksheets together.

Linked worksheets have many advantages. With linked worksheets you can design, build, and debug smaller worksheets. The advantage of small worksheets is that different individuals can work on separate worksheets. Also, you can more easily find and fix errors in small worksheets. And finally, small worksheets require less memory and recalculate faster. Each worksheet can operate within a functional area rather than address multiple areas. And when it comes time to improve or modify the worksheet system you have built, you don't have to tackle a giant behemoth. You can just change the smaller worksheets and relink them into the larger system.

Displaying Multiple Windows

One of Windows' significant advantages is its use of windows to display multiple applications. Within some Windows applications, such as Excel, you can display multiple files in multiple windows. In Excel, for example, you can display a worksheet and a macro sheet, each in their own window. This capability can be a great boon when debugging your worksheet or when entering data at one location and watching the result at another location.

5.1 Tip: **Open new windows in the same worksheet to get multiple views.**

If you want to view a separate section of the worksheet and splitting a window into panes doesn't work, open a new window in the same worksheet. Use this solution when you need to enter data into one location and see the results that display at a distant location. To open a new window, choose **W**indow **N**ew Window.

You can reposition and format the window separately from the original worksheet's window. Figure 5.1 shows one worksheet, MORTFRML.XLS, with a data-entry window and a results window, MORTFRML.XLS:2. Notice that each window has the file name in the title bar and a number indicating in what order the file was created.

The position and display of multiple windows are saved when you save the file. If you close all windows but one and then save the worksheet, the format and display used in that window are saved.

Fig. 5.1. A data-entry window and a results window.

Microsoft Excel

File Edit Formula Format Data Options Macro Window Help

B2 | 90000

MORTFRML.XLS:1

	A	B	C	D	E	F	G	H
14								
15		Worst					(inclds points)	
16	Periods	Rate/Yr	Balance	Pmt	IPmt	PPmt	AccumCost	AccumInte
24	7	0.0925	71,682.57	-590.02	-552.55	-37.47	-5,865.51	-4,070.6
25	8	0.0925	71,645.10	-590.02	-552.26			
26	9	0.0925	71,607.34	-590.02	-551.97			
27	10	0.0925	71,569.30	-590.02	-551.68			
28	11	0.0925	71,530.96	-590.02	-551.38			
29	12	0.1025	71,492.32	-640.64	-610.66			
30	13	0.1025	71,462.34	-640.64	-610.41			
31	14	0.1025	71,432.10	-640.64	-610.15			
32	15	0.1025	71,401.61	-640.64	-609.89			
33	16	0.1025	71,370.85	-640.64	-609.63			
34	17	0.1025	71,339.84	-640.64	-609.36			
35	18	0.1125	71,308.55	-692.59	-668.52			
36	19	0.1125	71,284.48	-692.59	-668.29			
37	20	0.1125	71,260.18	-692.59	-668.06			
38	21	0.1125	71,235.65	-692.59	-667.83			

MORTFRML.XLS:2

	A	B	
1	Loan Variables		
2	Value	$90,000	
3	Loan %	0.80	
4	Loan$	$72,000	
5			
6	Points	0.02	
7	Rate	0.0825	
8	RateDelta	0.01	
9	TimeDelta	6	mo.
10	Cap	0.135	
11	Term	30	
12			

Ready

Consolidating Data across Worksheets

Many companies use consolidations to roll together results from several divisions into a single consolidated result. You may need to consolidate monthly results into an annual consolidation, consolidate division results into a corporate consolidation, or consolidate product lines into a product mix consolidation.

Consolidating worksheets does not link worksheets together. Instead, consolidation uses the formulas or values from one worksheet to affect another. In its most common use, consolidation adds or subtracts values from one worksheet from the values in another worksheet.

5.2 Tip: **Use Edit Paste Special to consolidate data.**

Add values from one worksheet to another with the **E**dit Paste **S**pecial command. Figure 5.2 shows the results from two quarters—the first quarter, QTR1.XLS, and the second quarter, QTR2.XLS. To consolidate the results into the QTRCONS.XLS worksheet, use **E**dit Paste **S**pecial.

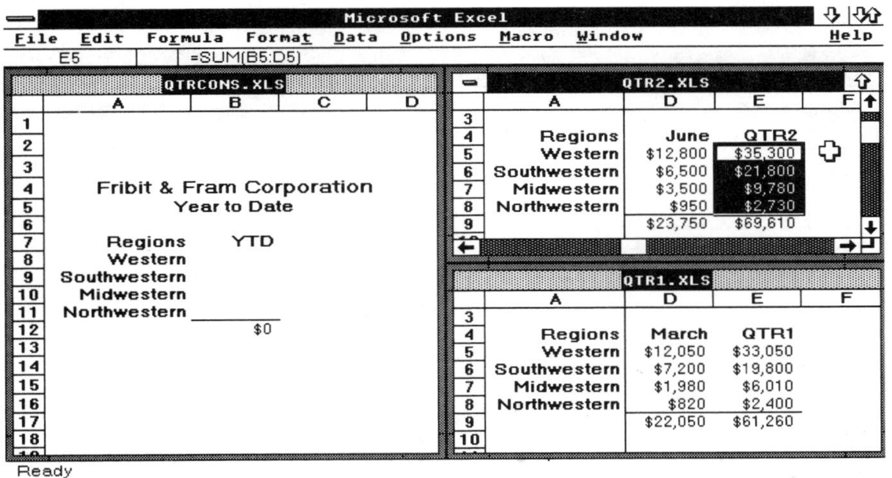

Fig. 5.2. Quarter results to be consolidated.

When you select **E**dit Paste **S**pecial, a dialog box appears (see fig. 5.3). Notice that the Operation group of buttons enables you to use the values or formulas in one worksheet to perform addition, subtraction, multiplication, or division on another worksheet.

Fig. 5.3. The Paste Special dialog box.

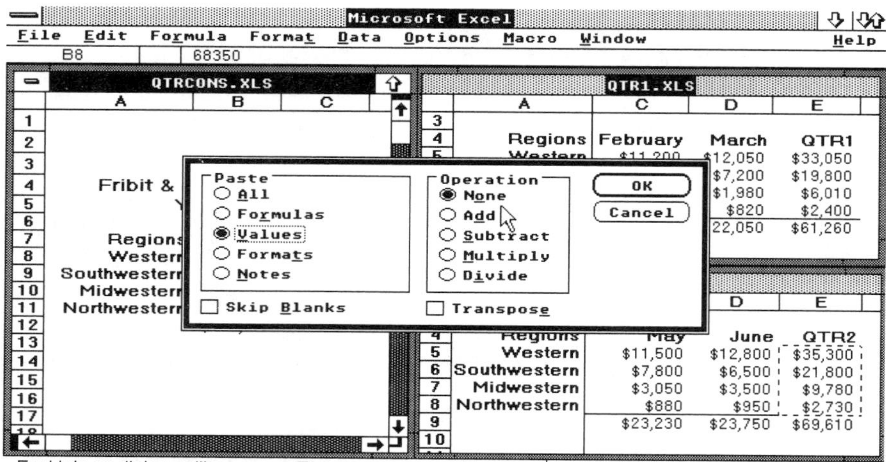

To transfer the first quarter data, copy the range E5:E8 from the QTR1.XLS worksheet with the **E**dit **C**opy command. Now position the cell pointer at B8 in the QTRCONS.XLS worksheet. Choose **E**dit Paste **S**pecial. To paste only the values into the consolidation worksheet, select Paste **V**alues and Operation N**o**ne and then choose OK. Only the values are transferred (see fig. 5.4).

Fig. 5.4. Pasting the QTR1 results.

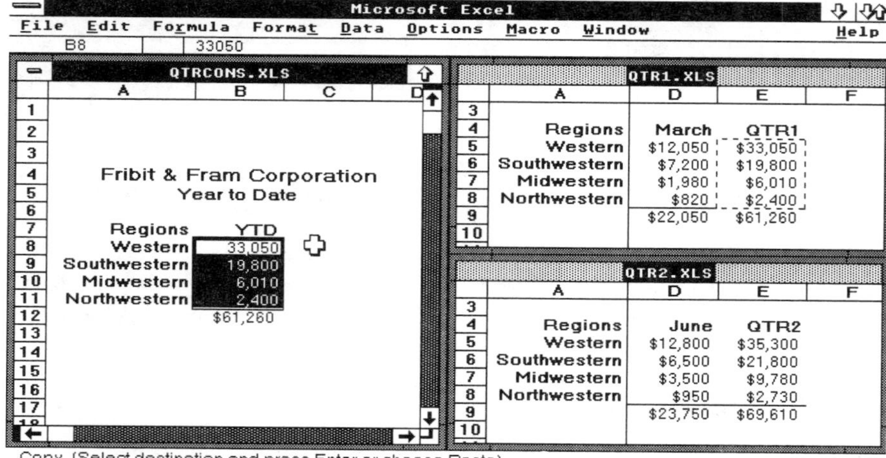

To add the values of the second quarter to the first quarter values in QTRCONS.XLS, select the range E5:E8 in the QTR2.XLS worksheet and choose the **E**dit **C**opy command. Now select cell B8 in QTRCONS.XLS.

Choose the **E**dit Paste **S**pecial command and select Paste **V**alues and Operation A**d**d. Choose OK. Figure 5.5 shows the finished consolidation. Notice in the formula bar that B8 contains a result of the values being added, not a formula.

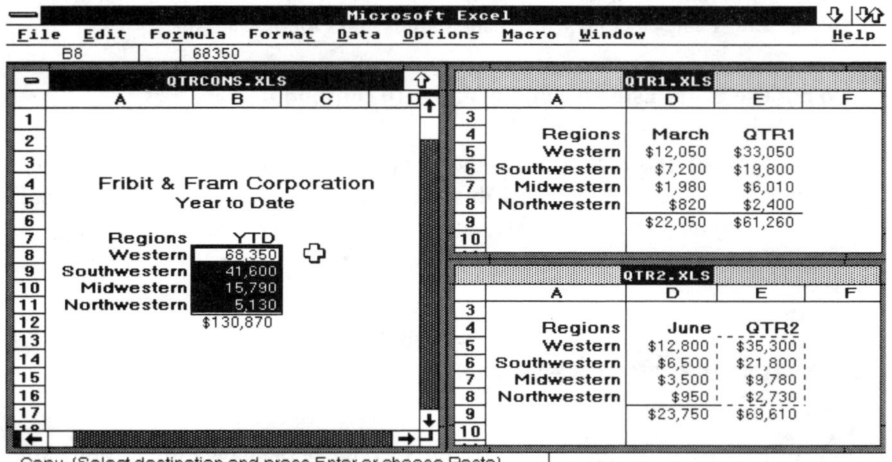

Fig. 5.5. The completed consolidation.

5.3 Trick: Use Edit Paste Special to remove errors in consolidations.

Consolidating values across worksheets with the **E**dit Paste **S**pecial command enables you to correct errors that are found later in the source worksheets easily.

When you find an error in one of the source worksheets, just redo the consolidation you did with the source worksheet, but use the opposite operation. For instance, if you added results, use the Operation **S**ubtract option of the **E**dit Paste **S**pecial command. This command subtracts from the consolidation all the values that were originally added. You then can correct the source worksheet and redo a correct consolidation with the Operation A**d**d option.

5.4 Trick: Paste twice with Edit Paste Special to include formats.

If you want to paste values and include formats from the original worksheet, keep the same range selected after the first paste and then select **E**dit Paste **S**pecial a second time using the Paste Forma**t**s option.

5.5 Trick: **Convert formulas to values with Edit Paste Special.**

Convert formulas to values in a worksheet when you want to save memory or prevent formula results from changing. To change formulas to values, select the formula and then choose **E**dit **C**opy. Without changing the selection, choose **E**dit Paste **S**pecial with Paste **V**alues and Operation N**o**ne.

5.6 Trap: **Do not use Edit Paste Special Formulas to consolidate data.**

Choosing **E**dit Paste **S**pecial with the Fo**r**mulas or **A**ll option does not consolidate or link data. Instead this command transfers a formula from one worksheet to another and adjusts the formula's relative references to the new location.

Linking Data across Worksheets

One of Excel's powerful and productive features is the capability to link cells and ranges across worksheets. Depending on the type of link, the worksheets can be in memory (on-screen) or on disk. When information in one linked worksheet changes, the link communicates that change to the other worksheet. While consolidation transfers values between worksheets, you must do the transfer manually or by a macro each time. Linked data differs—linked cells transfer values between worksheets immediately.

5.7 Tip: **Create and link small worksheets for the most advantageous use of Excel.**

You gain many advantages by creating smaller worksheets that are linked together:

- Systems require less memory because not all worksheets need to be open simultaneously.
- Different groups of users can build and then link worksheets together as long as the data being linked is planned and coordinated. This method improves programming productivity.
- You can update systems composed of worksheet modules more easily. The entire system doesn't have to change, just one worksheet within the system.

- Smaller linked worksheets calculate faster than large worksheets.
- You can link data-entry modules into a system so that users can enter data into a worksheet independently. That worksheet can then be linked or downloaded at a later time.
- Smaller linked worksheets are easier to debug and fix.
- With smaller worksheets, you reduce the chance of one worksheet corrupting another.
- If you use a linkage area (described later), you can examine the data being transferred.

5.8 Tip: **Create one of two types of external references: simple or complex.**

You can create two types of external references (or links). Simple external references can refer to information contained in a worksheet that is still on disk. Simple external references involve a single cell and do not include the external reference in a formula of any type.

Complex external references produce a result only when the supporting worksheet is open (in memory). Complex external references involve the external reference in a formula or use relative referencing. The following examples illustrate some simple and complex external references:

Simple	*Complex*
=QTR1.XLS!$B$5	=QTR1.XLS!B5 (B5 is a relative reference)
=QTR1.XLS!$B$5	=QTR1.XLS!$B$5*2 (Reference involved in a formula)
=QTR1.XLS!$B$5:$B$8	=SUM(QTR1.XLS!$B$5:$B$8) (Reference involved in a function)
=QTR1.XLS!Sales	=QTR1.XLS!Sales (Sales is a named formula or constant)

Notice that in the last example the name Sales can refer to a cell in the supporting worksheet and remain a simple external reference. If Sales is a named formula or constant, the external reference becomes complex.

5.9 Tip: **Produce simple external references with Edit Paste Link.**

If you copy and use the Edit Paste Link command to link a single cell or range of cells, the external reference is simple. If you edit the link so that it is part of a formula, the link becomes complex.

5.10 Tip: **Use simple external references to maintain flexibility.**

Simple external references enable you to keep the supporting worksheet on disk. When you open the linked worksheet, you are asked whether you want the links updated. Choosing OK updates the links from the information in the supporting worksheet; this worksheet remains on disk.

Keeping supporting worksheets on disk reduces memory requirements and speeds performance. You have a trade off, however, because it takes more work to create many individual simple external references than it does to link large arrays of cells.

5.11 Tip: **Keep the source worksheet open while you paste external references.**

Closing the source worksheet before you paste an external reference prevents the link from being pasted. When you choose the Edit Paste Link command, an alert box indicates that there is no link to paste. If the worksheets you want to link are too big to display simultaneously, type simple external references as described in the next tip.

5.12 Tip: **In large worksheets, type external references.**

Although it is easiest to use Edit Paste Special to create external references for worksheets, you may need to link worksheets that are too large to reside together in memory. To create external references for these worksheets, type the external reference. As a rule, remember to put single quotation marks around the file name of the worksheet to which you are linking.

The following shows some examples of correctly typed external references:

Simple External Reference	*Supporting Worksheet Location*
=QTR1.XLS!$E$5	Open, in memory
='QTR1.XLS'!$E$5	On disk, active directory
='C:\BUDGET\QTR1.XLS'!$E$5	On disk, different directory

5.13 Trick: **Enter multiple links quickly using relative external references.**

With this trick, you can create external references that link to cells in a relative location on the supporting worksheet. This trick can be handy if you need to link multiple cells and keep them in the same relative positions that they appear in the supporting worksheet. To create links with this method, both worksheets must be open.

Suppose that, for instance, you want to copy the values from one mortgage worksheet to another (see fig. 5.6). Start by copying the cell B2 of MORTFRML.XLS using **E**dit **C**opy. Then paste the contents into cell I10 on the mortgage analysis worksheet, MRTGANLY.XLS, using **E**dit Paste **L**ink. The resulting simple external reference in I10 is the following:

=MORTFRML.XLS!$B$2

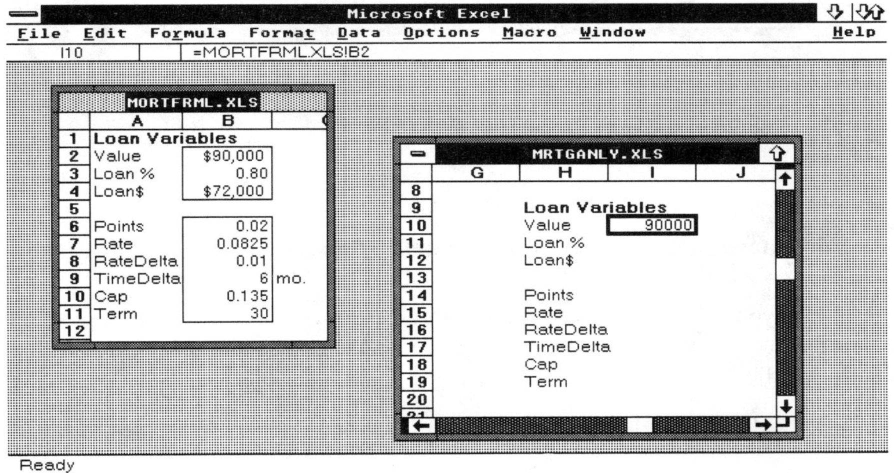

Fig. 5.6. Copying the cell B2.

Select the formula bar. Then press F4 (PC) or Command+T (Macintosh), or choose Formula Reference to change the $B$2 reference from an absolute to a relative reference. Press F4 or repeat the command until the formula appears as the following:

=MORTFRML.XLS!B2

Then reenter the formula in I10. You now have a complex external reference; the reference uses a relative reference address.

Using normal copying commands such as **E**dit **C**opy and **P**aste or **E**dit Fill Do**w**n, copy this formula into the cells below—I11:I12 and I14:I19. If you accidentally copy into extra cells, those cells reflect the contents of the same relative cell in the supporting worksheet, even if it is text. Your results should appear as those in figure 5.7. Because each of these external references is an individual reference, you can edit each individually. This makes it easy to include individual external references in formulas.

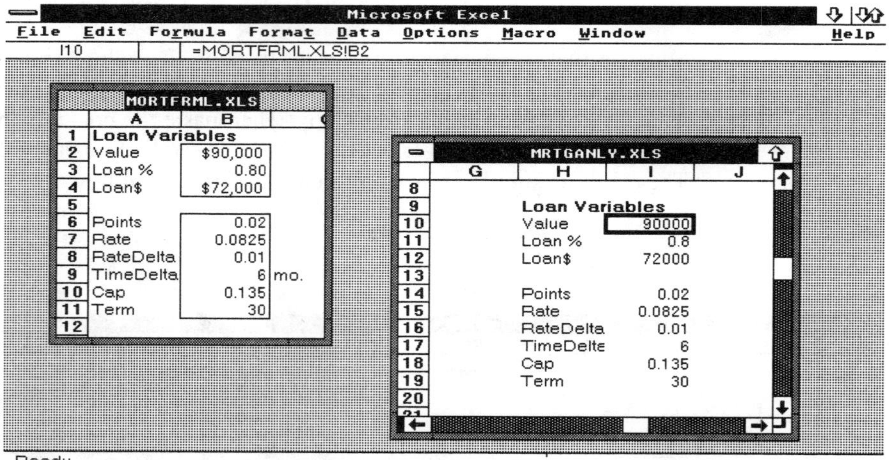

Fig. 5.7. The completed mortgage worksheet.

5.14 Trick: Edit external reference arrays to include a formula.

When you paste and link a range of cells, the result is a complex external reference that is an array. Each cell in the linked area contains a formula with a format like the following:

{=MORTFRML.XLS!$B$2:$B$4}

To change this external reference to a formula, you must change all the linked cells to include that same formula. Suppose that, for example, you want the cells in the dependent worksheet to reflect the following values in the supporting worksheet:

$B$2*2
$B$3*2
$B$4*2

You must select one cell within the linked area. Press F2 or select the formula bar. Notice that the { } brackets that indicate an array disappear. Edit the external reference to add the term *2. The external reference now appears in the formula bar:

=MORTFRML.XLS!$B$2:$B$4*2

You cannot press Enter to enter this formula. Because the formula is an array, you must reenter it as an array. To enter the formula and change all cells involved in the array, press Shift+Ctrl+Enter. All cells in the array now have the following formula:

{=MORTFRML.XLS!$B$2:$B$4*2}

5.15 Trick: Use single external references when each link uses a different formula.

In the preceding trick, you edited the complex external array so that all linked cells are multiplied by 2. In many cases you will want each link to have its own formula. When you want each linked cell to have a different formula, link each cell individually so that the cells are not arrays. This method enables you to edit each linked formula separately.

5.16 Trick: Link to Lotus 1-2-3 worksheets.

You can link Excel worksheets to Lotus 1-2-3 worksheets. These type of links are considered complex external references; therefore, both worksheets must be open. This capability is useful in office environments where some workers use 1-2-3, but others use Excel. You can create a worksheet, open it in Excel, and then link or consolidate data from the worksheet. This procedure is convenient when divisional offices use 1-2-3, but the corporate accounting office uses Excel. Divisional offices can submit 1-2-3 worksheets that can be linked with Excel.

5.17 Trick: **Link to dBASE databases.**

Use the Windows application Q+E to create links to dBASE databases that reside on disk.

5.18 Trick: **Do table look-ups or database work in other worksheets using links.**

Chapter 4, on functions and arrays, describes how to look up information in another worksheet or how to sum data from another worksheet selectively. Chapter 9, on databases, describes how to create a database so that the database, criteria, and extract range are each in separate worksheets, yet they pass information.

5.19 Trick: **Use range names to preserve external references.**

Use named ranges in external references when possible. Names preserve the link if you edit the supporting worksheet and move the referenced address. Suppose that, for instance, you create an external reference in the RATIOS.XLS worksheet:

=INCOME.XLS!$B$5

If you then insert rows or columns or move areas in the INCOME.XLS worksheet, the value in B5 may no longer reside in that cell—the value may appear in D12. The external reference in the RATIOS.XLS worksheet, however, still gets its information from B5 and will produce the wrong data.

Fix this problem by naming all cells that are used by external references in the supporting worksheet. Use the Fo**r**mula **D**efine Name command. The external reference then can use the name to refer to the supporting worksheet:

=INCOME.XLS!Net.Rev

Because names always adjust to any moves, inserts, or deletes, the external reference will still work.

Managing Linked Worksheets

Linked worksheets add a great deal of power and flexibility to electronic worksheets, but they also add a measure of responsibility. You can create a linked system of worksheets that is more difficult to understand and to keep up-to-date. This section discusses some tips on managing linked worksheets.

5.20 Tip: **Use the File Links command to open supporting worksheets.**

If you see #REF! in a worksheet that contains links, you may need to open the supporting worksheets. Opening the worksheets updates the complex external references that produced #REF!. To find and open supporting linked worksheets, choose the **F**ile **L**inks command (see fig. 5.8). Select the supporting worksheet you want opened and choose OK.

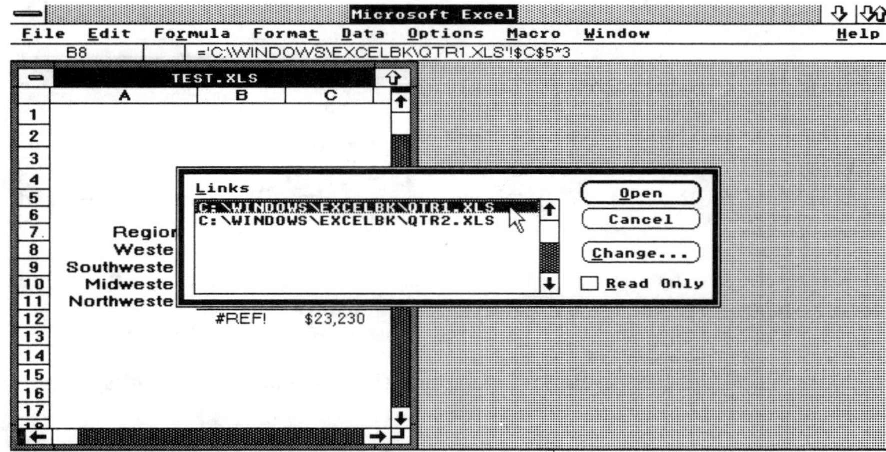

Fig. 5.8.
*The **L**inks dialog box.*

5.21 Tip: **Use the File Links Change command to relink "lost" worksheets.**

If you rename a supporting file or move it to a different directory, use the **F**ile **L**inks command to reconnect the file to the renamed or moved worksheets.

Find cells where the link has failed by choosing Fo**r**mula **S**elect Special, selecting the Formulas **E**rrors option, and then choosing OK. This command selects cells that contain errors. Check the selected cells for external references that may be causing the error.

If Excel cannot find all worksheets to establish a link, choose **F**ile **L**inks. Select from the **L**inks list box the file name that should contain the link. Then choose the **C**hange button. The Change Links dialog box shown in figure 5.9 appears with the name of the current supporting worksheet at the top. Use the

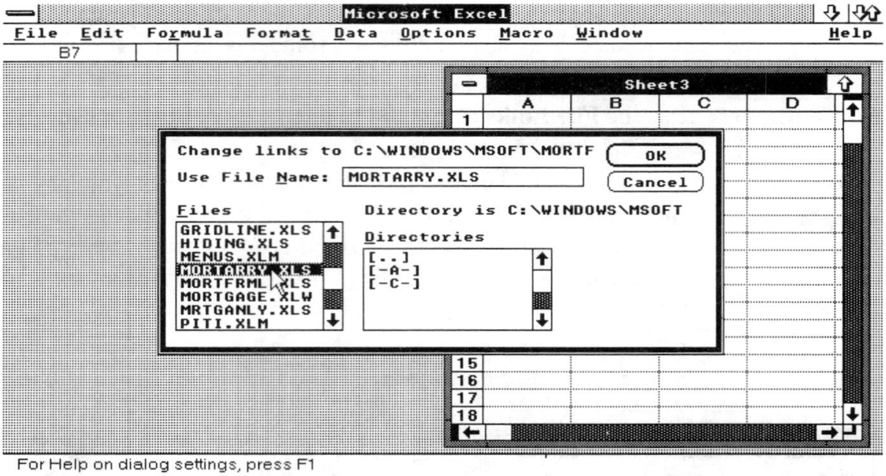

Fig. 5.9. The Change Links dialog box.

Directories list and scroll bars to find the new directory or the file's new name. Select the file or type the file's new name in the File **N**ame text box and choose OK.

All references to the supporting worksheet change to the directory and worksheet you select in the Change Links dialog box.

5.22 Trick: Make a linkage area so that all external references are simple links.

Make a linkage area in your worksheet for all external references. Cells within the worksheet that need data from an external reference then can refer to a cell within the linkage area.

The advantages of using a linkage area include the following:

- All external references in the linkage area are simple references because no formula is involved.
- All cells within the worksheet that need external data reference a cell in the linkage area, not an external reference. This method keeps all formulas free of external references.
- All incoming data from external references is visible, making debugging easier.
- All external references are located in one location; therefore, you can see a list of all linked files and their linked addresses or names.

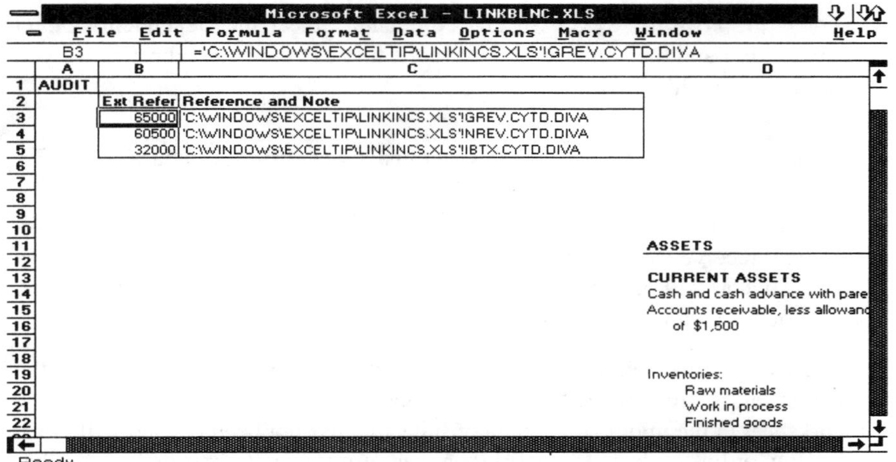

Fig. 5.10. The linkage area.

Figure 5.10 shows a simple example of a linkage area. The actual external references are located in cells B3:B5. Cells C3:C5 contain text copies of the external reference in column B. The balance sheet and ratio analyses located to the right of column D use the information linked into cells B3:B5.

In this example, all external references refer to the income statement worksheet, LINKINCS.XLS, located in the C:\WINDOWS\EXCELTIP directory. You can make the external references using range names in the LINKINCS.XLS worksheet. The descriptive range names use mnemonics so that you can find them easily. For example, NREV.CYTD.DIVA, means net revenue for the current year-to-date in division A. A table of range names in the LINKINCS.XLS worksheet would complete the documentation. Use the Formula **P**aste Name command with the Paste **L**ist option to paste a table of names and their addresses.

Make text copies of the external references in cells C3:C5 by copying the external references from column B. Then edit the copies to remove the equal sign (=) and reenter the references. Without the equal sign, the formula becomes text.

5.23 Trick: Use Formulas Select Special and the linkage area to display all formulas that require external data.

If you use a linkage area as described in the preceding trick, you gain the advantage of being able to find formulas that need external information easily. To display cells requiring external information, select one of the external references in the linkage area—for example, cell B4 in figure 5.10. Now choose the Formula Select **S**pecial command. Select the **D**ependents Di**r**ect Only option and then choose OK. All cells that use the external reference you selected are highlighted.

5.24 Tip: **Open linked worksheets in the correct order to get updated data.**

Worksheets that depend on links to worksheets that themselves contain links may not receive current updates unless you open the worksheets in the correct order. If you do not open the worksheets in the correct order, you may think that you have valid results when, in fact, they are not.

Because external references update the contents of cells only when the worksheet is first opened, a problem can occur. As a consequence, one worksheet in the middle of a chain of links that has not been opened will block the flow of linked data. This worksheet passes out-of-date information to other worksheets that depend on it.

Suppose that, for example, the FORECAST.XLS worksheet depends on the CONSOL.XLS worksheet. The CONSOL.XLS worksheet depends on the divisional EAST.XLS worksheet. If someone updates the data in the EAST.XLS worksheet, you won't see accurate data in FORECAST.XLS until CONSOL.XLS is opened and saved again. Opening CONSOL.XLS updates its external references with the data from EAST.XLS.

An alternative is to have all worksheets open at the same time. But this method is not always possible with large worksheets.

5.25 Trap: **Save newly linked worksheets in the correct order; otherwise, you will lose the link.**

It is important to save newly linked worksheets in the correct order. Saving in the correct order ensures that the external reference contains the correct file names for the files they reference.

Save newly linked files or files with new names by saving them from the lowest dependency to the highest. For example, if EAST.XLS feeds into CONSOL.XLS and CONSOL.XLS feeds into FORECAST.XLS, you should save EAST.XLS first, then CONSOL.XLS, and finally FORECAST.XLS. By saving in this order, the external reference always contains the current file name for the worksheet it references. If you don't change the file names or directories of linked worksheets, you don't need to worry about the order in which you save.

Separating Large Worksheets into Smaller Worksheets

In theory, you should plan your worksheets ahead of time and build them using small linked worksheets. In practice, you may find yourself working with large worksheets that have evolved over time. Figure 5.11 shows a map of such a worksheet that has had pieces added to it over time. The result is a large worksheet that is difficult to maintain, has poor performance, and can no longer be enhanced.

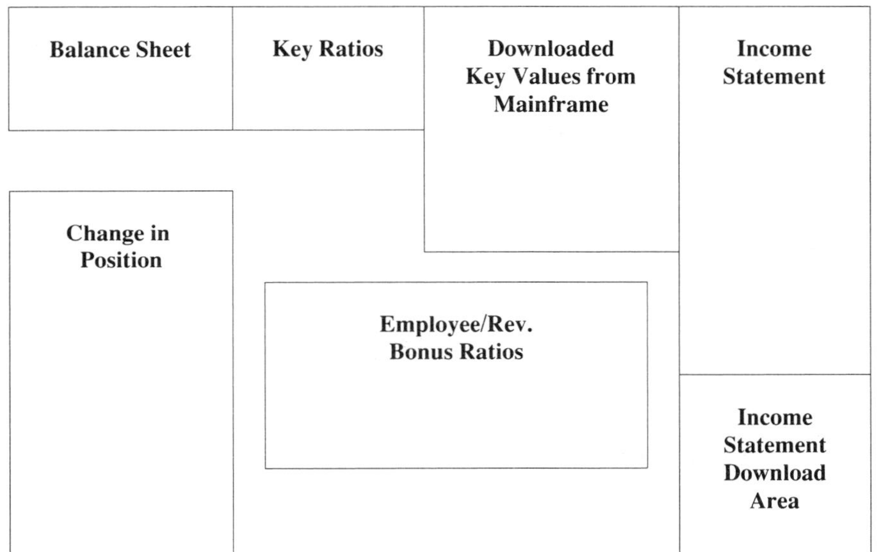

Fig. 5.11. The map of segments in a large worksheet.

The solution to a worksheet like the one in figure 5.11 is to segment it into smaller worksheets and then use external references to link the segments back together.

5.26 Tip: **Segment large worksheets and then relink them through a linkage area.**

Use the following approach to segmenting and relinking large worksheets:

1. Print a copy of the entire original worksheet and include row and column headings.

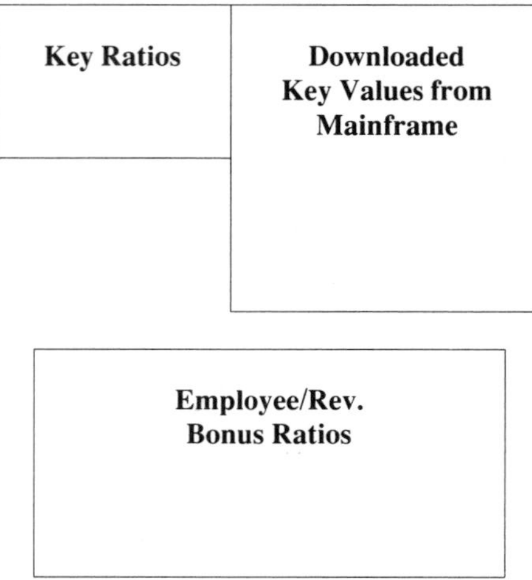

Fig. 5.12. Moving three segments to their own worksheet.

2. Segment the original worksheet into related pieces. Pieces that have a great deal of cell references among them may work better in the same worksheet. In figure 5.12, three segments are moved to a new worksheet.

   You can create segments with one of two methods. As one method, copy the segments from the large worksheet to a new worksheet. Use the **E**dit **P**aste command to paste the segments to the new worksheet in exactly the same location from which they came.

   As another method, erase unwanted segments from the original worksheet and save the worksheet using a file name appropriate to the segments that remain. Use the **E**dit Cl**e**ar command to erase the segments. Keep the wanted segments in their original locations.

   Erasing may be easier if your computer is low on memory. Once you create these isolated segments, you may see some formulas change to zero or to errors. These are some of the formulas, but not all, that require external references.

3. Close unneeded worksheets to preserve memory.

4. Save the new worksheet with an appropriate file name.

5. Open the audit macro. This macro automatically adds the A**u**dit command to the Fo**r**mula menu.

6. Activate the new worksheet if it is not active.

7. Choose the Formula Audit command. Select the **R**eport Errors option from the Worksheet Auditor box and choose OK. In the Audit Report box, select only the References to **B**lanks option and choose OK.

   In very large worksheets, the error report may take as long as 2 hours. In smaller worksheets, the report may take 5 to 10 minutes. The audit macro creates a report of all cells that contain formulas that refer to blanks. Because you have kept the segments in their original locations and erased everything that will be in other worksheets, the macro reports any formula that needs to contain an external reference. The audit report displays in a new worksheet with the cell addresses that contain formulas and the formulas that refer to blanks.

8. Print a copy of the error report for formulas that reference blank cells.

9. Create a linkage area at the top left corner of your worksheet as described earlier in this chapter.

10. Repeat Steps 1 through 9 for each worksheet you want to segment from the original. Save the worksheet with a new name and write down the file names. You do not have to reload the audit macro each time.

11. Open the first worksheet you want to link to other segments.

12. Use this worksheet's error report and the printout from the original to understand and name the needed external references. Type the external reference formulas in a linkage area. You may need to insert rows and columns to make room for this area. As you enter each external reference, check that the value it returns in the linkage area is correct. (Use range names whenever possible in your external references. You can type the range names first in the external references and later create the range names in the external worksheet. Note that range names do not return the linked value until you create the names.)

13. Leave the segmented portions of the original worksheet in their original locations so that you easily can find formulas when linking worksheets. This way you can refer to the printout of the original worksheet. Save the original worksheet with the same file name to preserve all links.

14. Repeat Steps 11 through 13 for all new worksheets that need to be linked.

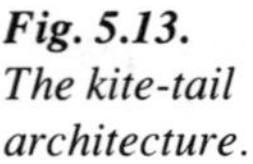

Fig. 5.13.
The kite-tail architecture.

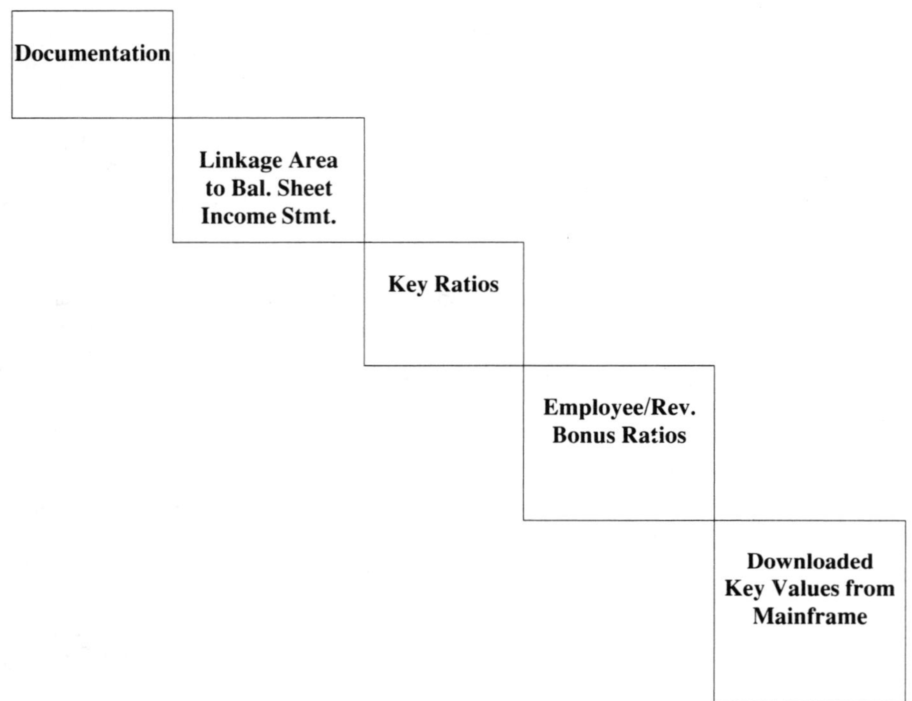

15. Once you link, debug, and verify for accuracy all worksheets, return to each worksheet and reorganize it so that the architecture is easier to maintain and enhance. Figure 5.13 shows a "kite-tail" layout that allows rows and columns to be inserted or deleted through any portion without affecting another portion.

6

Documenting and Fixing Worksheets

Any electronic worksheet can help or hurt you. The difference is whether you take the time to audit your worksheets for errors and document the worksheet so that you or others can maintain and use the worksheet. This chapter discusses tips, tricks, and traps you can use to document and audit your worksheet.

Documenting Worksheets

The layout and operation of a worksheet often seems straightforward once you complete the design, but in two or three months you may not remember why you used a specific formula or what turn of events prompted a certain assumption. You may even forget how to operate the worksheet.

If you as worksheet developer can have trouble remembering the nuances of a worksheet, imagine how difficult it can be for a new operator. These users need instructions on operation and guidelines on proper procedures.

Don't wait until you complete the worksheet to start documenting. Document as you go along. Show operating instructions in the worksheet where they are needed, show sample entries, and attach notes to appropriate cells. Once you're done, save future work by following some of the documenting tips in this section. Excel can do much of the work of documenting for you.

6.1 Tip: **Print a copy of the worksheet that shows formulas.**

Documentation for your worksheet should include a printout of the entire worksheet, showing the user's view and the formulas in each cell. Figures 6.1 and 6.2 show two printouts of a simple worksheet. Figure 6.1 shows the normal display with the **F**ile Page Se**t**up command configured for Row & **C**olumn Headings and **G**ridlines. Figure 6.2 shows the formulas behind each cell. To display these formulas, choose the **O**ptions **D**isplay command and select the Fo**r**mulas option. You may need to widen some columns to display the entire formula in a cell. Notice that the text is truncated if it exceeds the column width.

Print the worksheet showing the formulas to have a written record of how formulas interrelate. If you change column widths, don't use the same name as your original worksheet when you save the worksheet with the formulas displayed. If you do, you change your original formatting.

Fig. 6.1. *The original worksheet.*

WRKSHEET.XLS

	A	B	C	D	E	F	G
1				*Generic Quality Corporation*			
2				**Five Year Forecast**			
3							
4		1988	1989	1990	1991	1992	
5	**Sales**	$10,000	$11,000	$12,100	$13,310	$14,641	
6							
7	**Cost/Expenses**						
8	COG	3,000	3,300	3,630	3,993	4,392	
9	G&A	2,000	2,200	2,420	2,662	2,928	
10	Mktg	3,500	3,850	4,235	4,659	5,124	
13		8,500	9,350	10,285	11,314	12,445	
14	**Net Income**	$1,500	$1,650	$1,815	$1,997	$2,196	
15							

Page 1

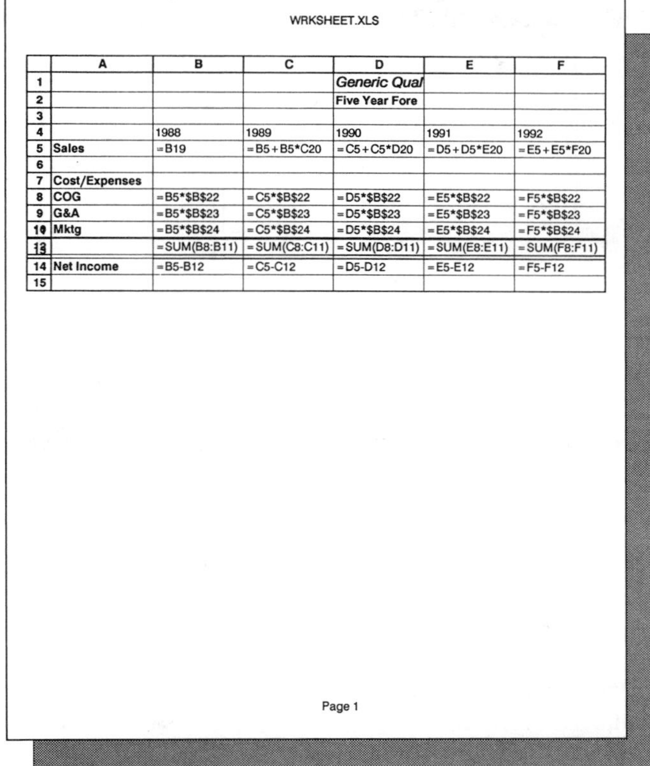

WRKSHEET.XLS

	A	B	C	D	E	F
1				*Generic Qual*		
2				**Five Year Fore**		
3						
4		1988	1989	1990	1991	1992
5	**Sales**	=B19	=B5+B5*C20	=C5+C5*D20	=D5+D5*E20	=E5+E5*F20
6						
7	**Cost/Expenses**					
8	**COG**	=B5*$B$22	=C5*$B$22	=D5*$B$22	=E5*$B$22	=F5*$B$22
9	**G&A**	=B5*$B$23	=C5*$B$23	=D5*$B$23	=E5*$B$23	=F5*$B$23
10	**Mktg**	=B5*$B$24	=C5*$B$24	=D5*$B$24	=E5*$B$24	=F5*$B$24
13		=SUM(B8:B11)	=SUM(C8:C11)	=SUM(D8:D11)	=SUM(E8:E11)	=SUM(F8:F11)
14	**Net Income**	=B5-B12	=C5-C12	=D5-D12	=E5-E12	=F5-F12
15						

Page 1

Fig 6.2. *The worksheet printed with formulas.*

6.2 Tip: **To keep track of the range names you used in the worksheet, paste a list of range names onto your worksheet.**

If you use macros with your worksheet or link worksheets, you should be using named ranges. In this case, you should create a list of all the range names used in a worksheet and the addresses associated with each name. To create such a list, move the cell pointer to an area of the worksheet where you've put other documentation or instructions; then choose Fo**r**mula Paste **N**ame. When the Paste **N**ame dialog box appears, select the Paste **L**ist option button. Figure 6.3 shows a pasted list of range names from the data-entry area of a simple worksheet. You must add the border manually.

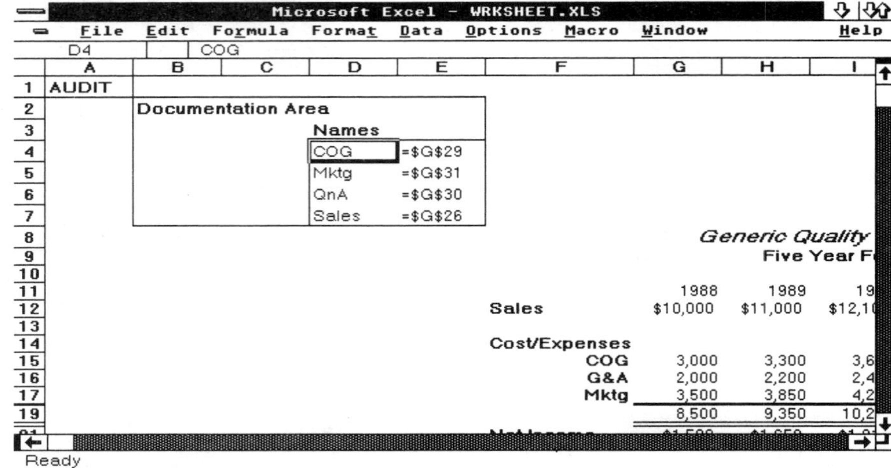

Fig. 6.3. A list of range names pasted in a worksheet.

6.3 Tip: Add a copy of the audit error report and map to your documentation.

Companies that use standardized worksheets throughout many divisions or operating entities need standardized worksheets that have been audited and include good documentation. A part of such an auditing process should be a complete error report generated by the AUDIT.XLM macro (PC) or Worksheet Auditor (Macintosh). The audit macro also can create a miniaturized map of the worksheet showing where text, constants, and formulas are located. A later section of this chapter describes how to use the audit macro. (This macro comes with Excel.)

6.4 Tip: Use the Window Show Info command to display information about a cell.

To see appropriate information about any cell in the worksheet, even the notes attached to the cell and its precedent and dependent formulas, select the cell and then choose **W**indow **S**how Info. Or press Ctrl+F2 (PC) or Command+Shift+F2 (Macintosh). Figure 6.4 shows the Info window for the selected cell—I12. By choosing the **I**nfo command, you can display additional information in the window such as precedent and dependent formulas or whether the cell is protected.

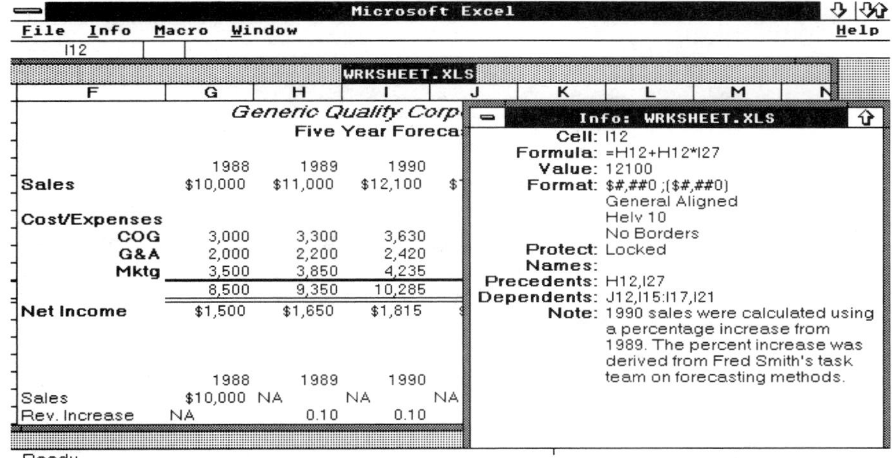

Fig. 6.4. *A window that shows cell information.*

Working with Notes

Notes are a convenient way of attaching commentary to cells—for instance, to explain why you used a certain formula or assumption. You also can use notes to document formula problems you must fix later. Notes do not show in the worksheet, but you quickly can identify cells that contain notes. You can display and print the notes along with your worksheet.

6.5 Tip: **Attach notes to cells to add explanations.**

With the Formula Note command, you can attach a text note to a cell. These notes are useful for describing how a formula works or why you chose a certain variable. You attach a note to a cell by selecting the cell, choosing the Formula Note command, and typing the note (see fig. 6.5). Don't forget that notes can contain more information than what appears in the Note box; you can scroll through the note area.

6.6 Tip: **Use notes to identify important worksheet assumptions.**

Notes may contain important worksheet assumptions such as why a specific technique was used. In firms that audit and share standardized worksheets (an excellent idea), the author's name, auditor's name, and revision dates are entered in cell A1 of the worksheet. Once audited, the worksheet should be protected with a password so that it cannot be altered.

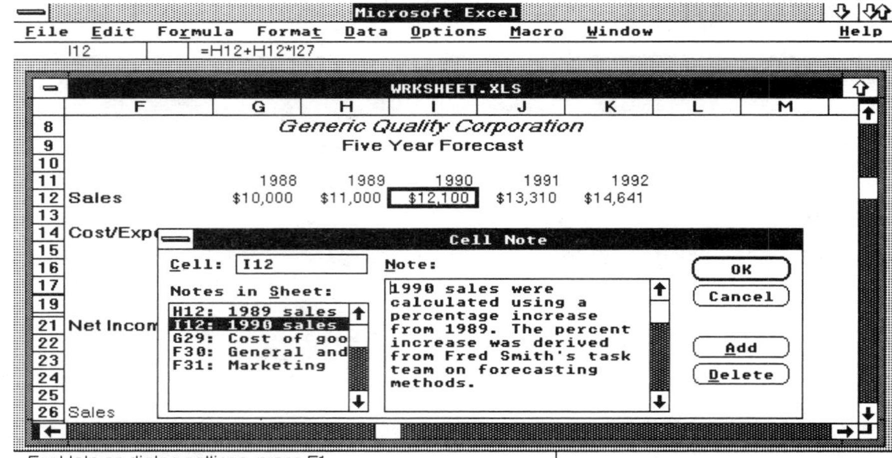

Fig. 6.5. The Cell Note dialog box with I12 selected.

When you use a password, be sure to let someone else—microcomputer manager, security administrator—know the password. If you forget the password, the worksheet becomes inoperative.

6.7 Trick: **Use Formula Find to find notes by content.**

You can use one of two ways to find a specific note. First, you can choose Formula Note and scroll through the notes in the Sheet box until you find and select the note you want. The note contents appear in the Note text box to the right.

A second method enables you to find a note that contains any key word. Choose the Formula Find command. In the Find What text box, type the key word you want to find. Select the Notes option in the Look in option box and then choose OK (see fig. 6.6). The first cell that contains a note with that key word is selected. Press F7 to find the next note that contains the key word.

6.8 Tip: **To find all cells that contain notes, use Formula Select Special.**

Find all cells that contain notes by choosing Formula Select Special, selecting the Notes option, and then choosing OK. All cells that contain notes are selected.

As a shortcut for selecting all cells that contain notes, press the Ctrl+? key (PC) or Shift+Command+O (Macintosh).

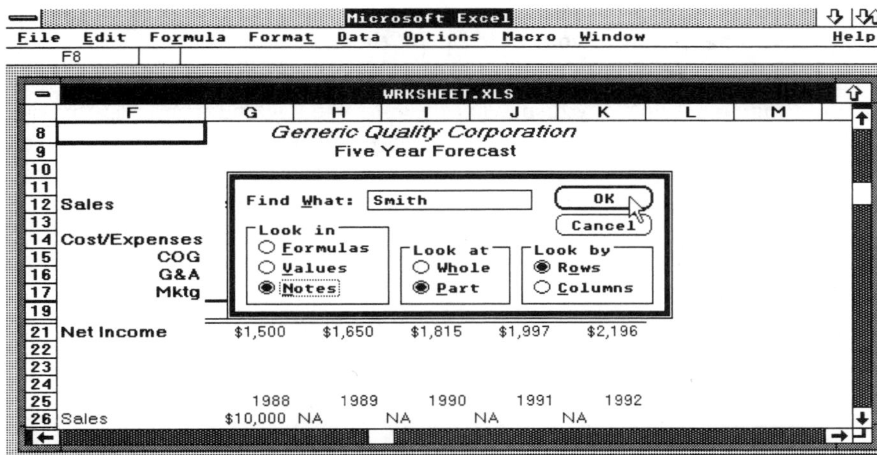

Fig. 6.6. Finding notes by content.

6.9 Tip: **To open notes quickly, double-click your mouse on the cell that contains the note.**

Open a note in a cell quickly by double-clicking on the cell. Once the note is open, you can read, edit, and save the note. From the keyboard, press Ctrl+F2 to display the Info window for the active cell. Press Ctrl+F2 again to close the window.

6.10 Trick: **To browse through notes, select all notes and then press Ctrl+F2.**

With many notes in a worksheet you may want to browse through all the notes quickly. To do so, follow these steps:

1. Press Ctrl+? (PC) or Shift+Command+O (Macintosh) to select all notes.
2. Press Shift+F2 to display the Note box.
3. Press Cancel or Esc to remove the Note box.
4. Press Tab to go to the next selected cell.
5. Repeat Steps 2–4.

6.11 Tip: **To save a hard copy of your notes, print them.**

Print individual notes by displaying the Info window and then choosing **F**ile **P**rint. Print all notes in your worksheet by displaying the worksheet and choosing the **F**ile **P**rint command. Select the **N**otes or **B**oth option and then choose OK. If you want the cell addresses to print for each note, choose the Page Se**t**up command and ensure that Row & **C**olumn Headings is selected before you print.

Finding Worksheet Problems

Two independent surveys of worksheets found that over 30 percent contained errors—even in worksheets done by "experts." The computer press has frequent stories about banks that make $100,000 errors because they aren't aware that formatting a number for 2 decimals is not the same as rounding to 2 decimals, or stories of construction companies that make $250,000 errors because a SUM function did not include the full range.

Excel contains commands and macros to help you audit worksheets and find problems. In Excel, these auditing commands and macros are an integral part of the program. You should take advantage of these built-in features to ensure that your worksheet functions accurately. In other electronic worksheets, you must buy special add-on programs to audit for errors.

6.12 Trick: **To compare results and formulas, display them both by adding a new window.**

Figure 6.7 shows both the normal display and the formulas behind the display on the same screen. This view can be helpful when checking results against the formulas that produce the results.

To display these two views, open and move the worksheet so that you have room to see a second worksheet. Then choose the **W**indow **N**ew Window command. This command opens a second window in the same worksheet. Choose the **O**ptions **D**isplay command and select the Fo**r**mulas option so that formulas display. Now you can size the windows to see them both. Each window scrolls independently. Press Ctrl+F6 to move between the two windows.

Microsoft Excel

File Edit Formula Format Data Options Macro Window Help

D17 | =PMT(B17/12,$B$11*12,C17)

MORTFRML.XLS:1

	A	B	C	D	E	F	G
15		Worst					(inclds points)
16	Periods	Rate/Yr	Balance	Pmt	IPmt	PPmt	AccumCost
17	0	0.0825	72,000.00	-540.91	-495.00	-45.91	-1,980.91
18	1	0.0825	71,954.09	-540.91	-494.68	-46.23	-2,521.82
19	2	0.0825	71,907.86	-540.91	-494.37	-46.55	-3,062.74
20	3	0.0825	71,861.32	-540.91	-494.05	-46.87	-3,603.65
21	4	0.0825	71,814.45	-540.91	-493.72	-47.19	-4,144.56
22	5	0.0825	71,767.26	-540.91	-493.40	-47.51	-4,685.47

MORTFRML.XLS:2

	C	D	E
16	Balance	Pmt	IPmt
17	=B4	=PMT(B17/12,$B$11*12,C17)	=-B17/12*C17
18	=C17+F17	=IF(B18=B17,D17,PMT(B18/12,$B$11*12,C18))	=-B18/12*C18
19	=C18+F18	=IF(B19=B18,D18,PMT(B19/12,$B$11*12,C19))	=-B19/12*C19
20	=C19+F19	=IF(B20=B19,D19,PMT(B20/12,$B$11*12,C20))	=-B20/12*C20
21	=C20+F20	=IF(B21=B20,D20,PMT(B21/12,$B$11*12,C21))	=-B21/12*C21
22	=C21+F21	=IF(B22=B21,D21,PMT(B22/12,$B$11*12,C22))	=-B22/12*C22

Ready

Fig. 6.7. *A mortgage worksheet with two windows.*

6.13 Trick: Switch between worksheet results and formulas to check your results.

You quickly can switch the display between a worksheet's results and its formulas by pressing the Ctrl+' (PC) or Command+' (Macintosh). Note that the accent mark (') key is not the apostrophe key. The accent key is located on the same key as the tilde (~) key.

Pressing Ctrl+' a second time returns you to the original display. The formula display automatically widens column widths to let you see more of each formula. If you manually widen the column to see more of a formula, the increased width also changes your original worksheet.

6.14 Tip: Check for values or formulas entered in the wrong locations.

Most worksheets do not use protection. Therefore, inexperienced operators can enter data over formulas or formulas over data accidentally. In some cases, this action produces wild results; therefore, you know an error exists. In the worst cases, the accidental entry is close enough to the original cell contents that the error isn't caught. As a consequence, the worksheet may produce slightly incorrect errors for years.

You can use Excel to find values or formulas in wrong cells. To find values entered over formulas throughout the worksheet, select a single cell. Then choose the Formula Select Special command to display the dialog box shown in figure 6.8.

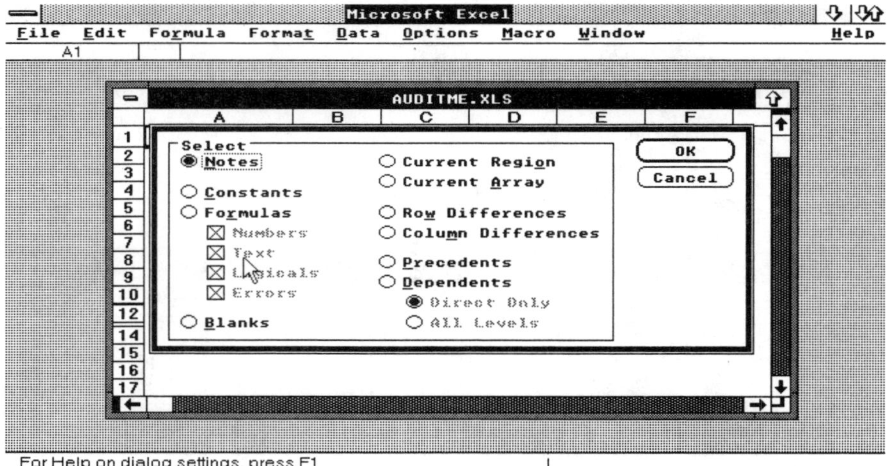

Fig. 6.8. The Select Special dialog box.

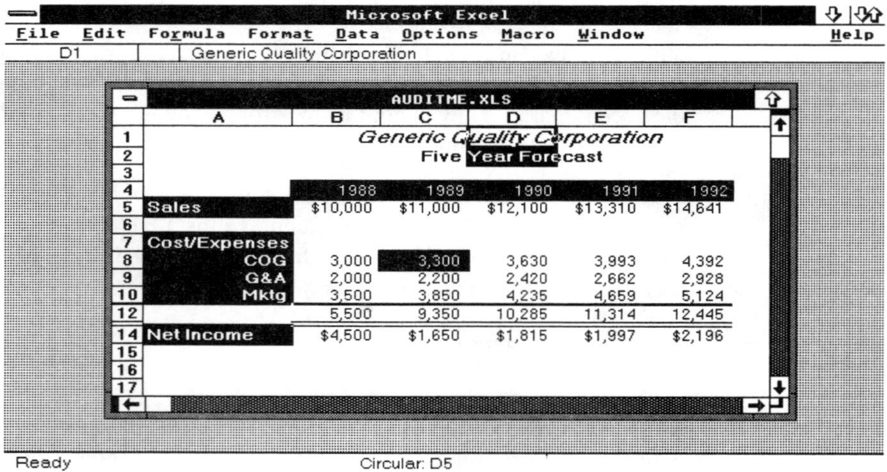

Fig. 6.9. Constants selected in the worksheet.

Select the **C**onstants option and then choose OK. Figure 6.9 shows a constant value in cell C8 selected; this value stands out in an area of formulas. If you next select a single cell and then choose Fo**r**mula **S**elect Special Fo**r**mulas N**u**mbers, Excel selects numeric formulas, and the misplaced contents of cell C8 are revealed as shown in figure 6.10. Instead of a constant, cell C8 should contain a formula like the other cells in the area. By spotting this incorrect entry, you can fix your worksheet.

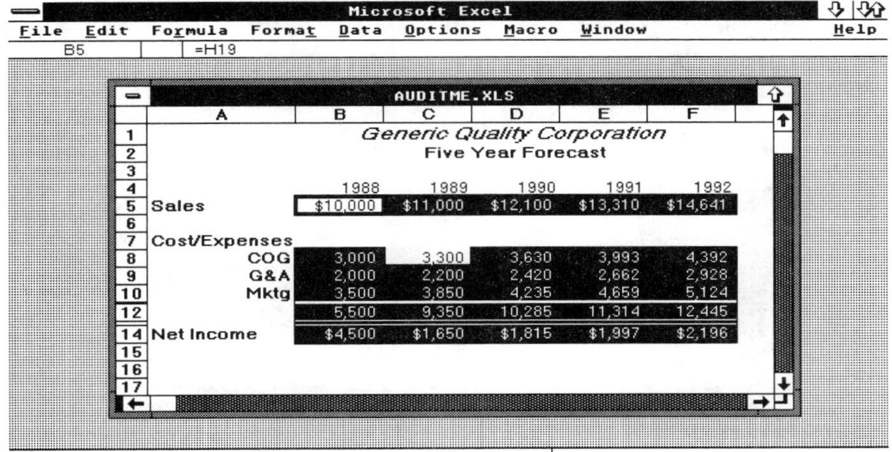

Fig. 6.10. Formulas selected in the worksheet.

6.15 Tip: **Find incorrect formulas with Formula Select Special Row/Column Differences.**

Editing or copying formulas can create accidental errors in formulas. You can find some of these incorrect formulas if all the formulas in a row or column have a similar structure. For example, in figure 6.11 all the formulas in rows 8, 9, and 10 are first entered in cells B8, B9, and B10 and then filled across. Suppose that you suspect that editing has introduced errors in some of the formulas. You can find the formulas that no longer have a "copied pattern" that is similar to their row neighbors.

Select the cells in question—cells B8:F10, in the example. Choose the Formula Select Special command, select the Row Differences option, and then choose OK. Figure 6.12 shows that cells E8 and D9 contain formulas that have a different pattern of cell references than the other formulas in the same row.

Use the Column Differences option to find formulas whose cell reference pattern differs from formulas in the same column.

6.16 Tip: **To find cells that produce #error messages, use Formula Select Special with the Errors option.**

To find cells that produce #error messages, select the Formulas Errors option from the Formula Select Special dialog box. Cells that contain #errors are selected. Press Tab to move forward to view each of these cells; press Shift+Tab to move backward.

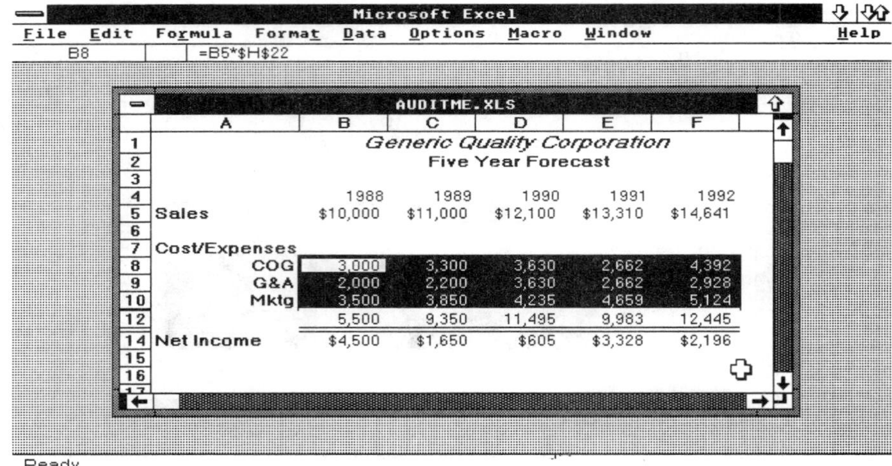

Fig. 6.11. AUDITME with rows selected.

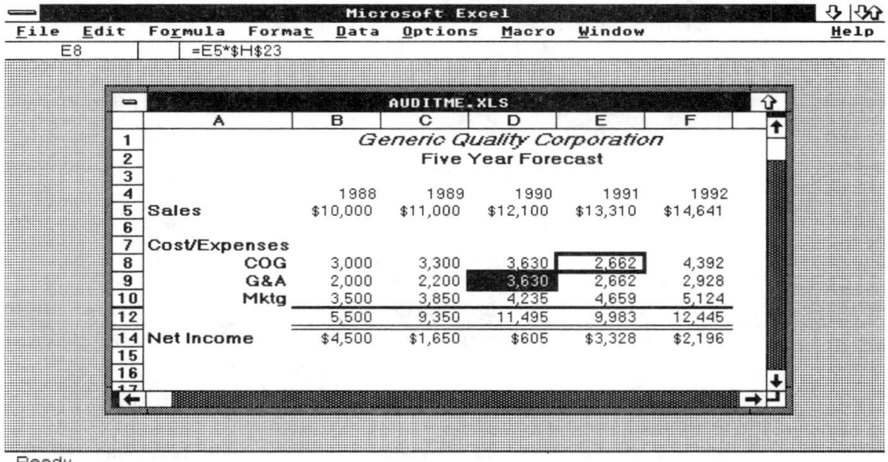

Fig. 6.12. AUDITME with aberrant cells selected.

6.17 Tip: Find formulas that precede or depend on a formula.

Find the cells that feed into a formula by choosing Fo**r**mula **S**elect Special and selecting the **P**recedents option. Select the D**i**rect Only option to select cells that feed directly into the formula. Select All Le**v**els to select all cells that eventually feed into the formula. The **D**ependents option selects all cells that depend on the selected formula.

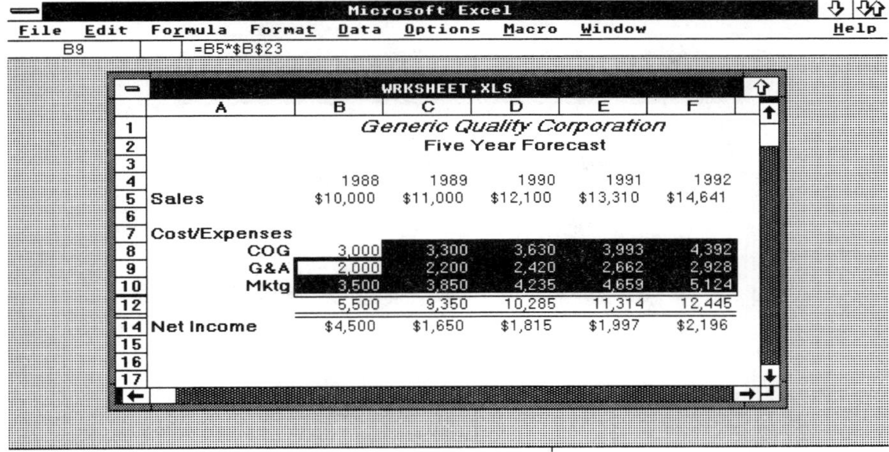

Fig. 6.13. A SUM function error showing not all cells are summed by formula in B12.

Figure 6.13 shows a SUM function error caught by using the **P**recedents option. In this example, the **P**recedents option is used to see what cells the SUM formulas in row 12 are totaling. To check, select cells B12:F12 and then use the Fo**r**mulas **S**elect Special command. Select the **P**recedents option with D**i**rect Only. The result shows that the SUM formulas in C12:F12 sum the numbers in row 8 through 11 in their respective columns. The SUM formula in B12 contains an error, however, because only cells B9 to B11 are selected. The SUM function leaves out cell B8. This type of error can be expensive. By checking the worksheet, you can find and correct this type of error.

6.18 Tip: Debug your worksheet with the audit macro.

The AUDIT.XLM macro, which comes with PC Excel, is located in the WINDOWS\LIBRARY directory on your hard disk. The Worksheet Auditor macro for Macintosh Excel is located in the Macro Library folder. Running the audit macro adds the A**u**dit command to the bottom of the Fo**r**mula menu. To find information about the audit macro beyond that described here, choose the **H**elp **I**ndex command, Macro Library, and then Worksheet Auditor. Figure 6.14 shows the Worksheet Auditor box from which you can select different types of auditing assistance.

Selecting **R**eport Errors produces another dialog box from which you can select what information you want to incorporate in the error report. The report can show all #errors, formulas that reference blank cells, all cells involved in circular errors, and names that are incorrect or not used.

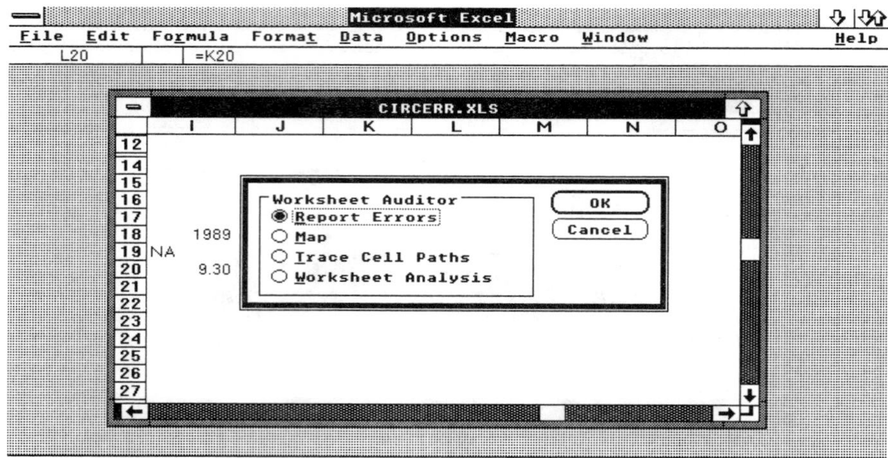

Fig. 6.14. The Worksheet Auditor.

Other features of the audit macro include a map feature that shows where formulas, text, and values are located in an overview map of the worksheet. You also can trace through the links quickly among dependent and preceding formulas. An information feature shows whether changes have been made and whether protection is turned on.

6.19 Tip: **Find all formulas involved in circular errors with the audit macro.**

A circular reference is a formula that depends on itself for input. In some cases the formula may depend on other formulas, but through a "circular" route, the other formulas eventually lead back to the first. Circular references can produce results that get bigger and bigger or smaller and smaller with each recalculation. Excel warns you with an Alert box when you create a circular reference. But a circular reference that has not been repaired may still creep into your worksheet.

A circular reference is a particularly difficult error to resolve in most electronic worksheets. In Excel, you easily can find this reference if you use the audit macro. Start the macro and then choose the Fo**r**mula A**u**dit command. (The A**u**dit command is not available unless you start the audit macro.) Select the **R**eport Errors option, choose OK, and then select the **C**ircular References report. Figure 6.15 shows the circular reference report showing all the formulas involved. You must decide which formula to change to break the circle.

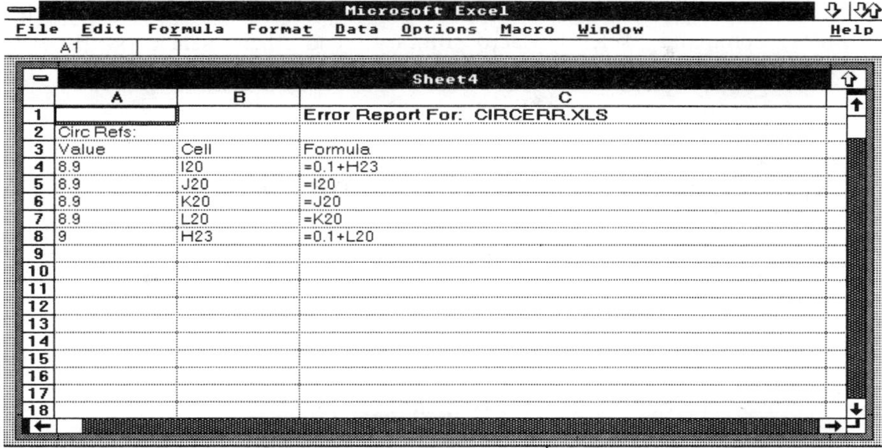

Fig. 6.15. *A circular error report.*

The circular error report in figure 6.15 shows five formulas that use each other's results in a circle of dependencies. Column A shows the value in each cell. Column B shows the cell involved in the loop, and column C shows the formula in each of the cells.

6.20 Tip: **To see how two worksheet versions have changed, compare them with the compare macro.**

If you need to compare two versions of a worksheet to see how they have changed, use the COMPARE.XLM macro that comes with PC Excel. In PC Excel, the COMPARE.XLM macro is located in the WINDOWS\LIBRARY directory on your hard disk. (With Macintosh Excel, the macro is named Worksheet Comparison and is located in the Macro Library folder.)

Running the compare macro adds the Co**m**pare command to the Fo**r**mula menu. Choosing Fo**r**mula Co**m**pare produces a dialog box that asks for the name of the worksheet you want to compare against the active worksheet. After you supply the name, the compare report is generated.

The compare macro produces a report showing the cells that differ between the two worksheets and the contents of those cells. The compare macro is best used to find minor changes between a master copy and a variant. You also can use this macro to find data-entry contents that have changed. On the other hand, some changes—such as inserting rows or columns—can produce so many differences that the report is overwhelming.

To find out more information about the compare macro, choose the **H**elp **I**ndex command, select Macro Library, and then select Worksheet Comparison.

Fixing Worksheet and Formula Problems

The following tips help you find problems that the Fo**r**mula **S**elect Special command and the Worksheet Auditor miss.

6.21 Tip: **Avoid #REF! errors by making sure that you don't delete a cell, row, or column on which other formulas depend.**

#REF! errors occur most frequently when you delete (not erase, but delete) a cell, row, or column on which other formulas depend. If you stop as soon as a #REF! error appears and choose **E**dit **U**ndo, you restore the deleted cells and prevent the error.

If you are unsure about deleting an area of the worksheet, delete it and then choose the Fo**r**mula **S**elect Special command with only the Fo**r**mulas **E**rrors option selected. This command selects any #errors that appear in the worksheet. If no errors result, you safely can delete the area. If errors do appear, check the formulas.

6.22 Tip: **Use the Format Alignment command to prevent text from filling cells.**

If you enter text into cells with the **F**ill option from the Forma**t** **A**lignment command, the text fills adjacent cells. This can be disconcerting at a later time if you are unaware of the formatting. What you enter in one cell fills other adjacent cells. To remove the problem, select all the cells that contain the filled text (except the cell you want filled) and then reformat the area with the Forma**t** **A**lignment command.

6.23 Trap: **Use ROUND( ) and the Calculation Precision as Displayed command when formulas do not produce an exact zero result.**

In a few rare cases, computers store numbers differently that appear to be the same. The difference may show up later during calculations that produce a near-zero result. Figure 6.16 illustrates this problem. In cell F7, the numbers to the left total to 0. In cell F5, the numbers to the left should total 0, but they do not. The difference from zero is a small number, –1.7E–13. Because –2555.34 in B5 is stored differently than 2555.34 in B7, the results differ.

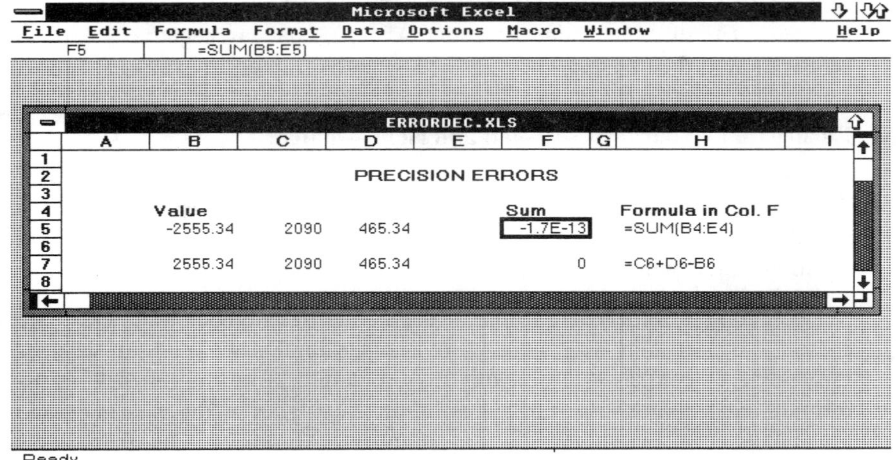

Fig. 6.16. A small number that appears as zero in General format.

To remove this problem, format the cells with a format other than General. Few financial problems work with numbers large enough to reflect an error that is 13 decimal places out.

If you want to ensure that the problem is removed, you can choose **O**ptions **C**alculation **P**recision as Displayed to round worksheet results to the same as the displayed precision. This command applies to the entire worksheet. If you want to round the precision for a single cell, enclose the resulting formula in a ROUND( ) function—for example, ROUND(SUM(B4..E4),2).

6.24 Trick: Use IF functions to check for results near zero.

Testing some formulas for zero results produces FALSE even though the results appear to be zero in the display. This action occurs because the display shows a value rounded to match the format. The actual result behind the display may be nonzero. You can see the actual nonzero result by formatting the cell with the General format.

If you want to test whether a cell is zero or approximately zero, use an IF function to check for numbers less than some small amount. For example, if you want to display the text Zero! when cell B21 is smaller than .000001, you can use an IF function such as the following:

=IF(ABS(B21).000001,"Zero!","Not Zero")

In this test, results less than .000001 are assumed to be small enough that they are zero. The absolute value function, ABS( ), changes negative values to positive; therefore, the test works for both negative and positive results.

6.25 Tip: **Ensure that all parentheses—left and right—match.**

A common problem when writing long or complex formulas is mismatched left and right parentheses, especially when the formula contains many nested functions, each with their own parentheses.

If Excel refuses to accept a formula, yet all the functions and addresses are correct, suspect that you have a missing parenthesis. To find whether mismatched parentheses are causing the problem, start at the left side of the formula and count all opening parentheses. Next, start at the right side and move left as you count all closing parentheses. If the two numbers don't match, you need to find where to add the missing parenthesis.

To find where a missing parenthesis belongs, start with the inner most pair of nested parentheses and match sets of left and right parentheses. As you work outward, you will find the missing parenthesis.

6.26 Trick: **Save incorrect formulas to be repaired later.**

If you have trouble entering a formula and Excel will not accept the entry, you can save the formula so that you don't have to retype it later. To save the formula, type a space before the equal (=) sign in front of the formula and press Enter. Adding a space changes the formula to text. At a later time, you can return to the cell and correct the error.

6.27 Trick: **Calculate terms within formulas to pinpoint errors.**

In a long formula or formula with multiple terms (segments), you may not be sure which part is causing an error. You can check the accuracy of each term in a long formula with the following steps. This procedure creates an exact duplicate of the original formula. Use this duplicate to experiment.

1. Select the cell that contains the formula.
2. Select the entire formula in the formula bar so that the equal sign to the end of the formula bar is highlighted.
3. Choose the **E**dit **C**opy command to copy the formula to the clipboard.
4. Press Esc or select the X formula box to return the formula to normal.

5. Select an unused cell.
6. Choose **E**dit **P**aste.

An exact copy of the formula is reproduced without changing relative references. You will want to examine this copy so that the original formula remains untouched. In the copy of the formula, do the following:

1. Select a segment of the formula you want to check. The formula should be highlighted.
2. Press the F9 key or choose **O**ptions Calculate **N**ow.
3. If this segment of the formula produces a correct result, return to Step 1 and choose another segment.

Once you have found the segment that produces an incorrect result, return to the original formula and correct it. Then delete the duplicate.

6.28 Tip: **Use the Formula Replace command to make multiple edits.**

If you need to replace a cell reference, range reference, range name, or a formula throughout the worksheet, use the Fo**r**mula R**e**place command. Enter the reference, name, or function to be replaced in the R**e**place box. Enter the new reference, name, or function in the **W**ith box. Using the R**e**place command ensures that you find and replace all instances of the reference, name, or formula that need to be changed.

Select the **F**ind Next button to find each individual occurrence. Then select the **R**eplace button to replace the occurrence that appears behind the Replace window. You can move the Replace window if you need to see the formula and cell that will be replaced.

Figure 6.17 shows the Replace dialog box being used to update a range used by formulas and functions throughout the worksheet. Because rows have been inserted outside the existing range, range formulas did not update automatically. You could change each function in the worksheet individually. Or you can use the Fo**r**mula **R**eplace command as a fast and accurate way to make changes.

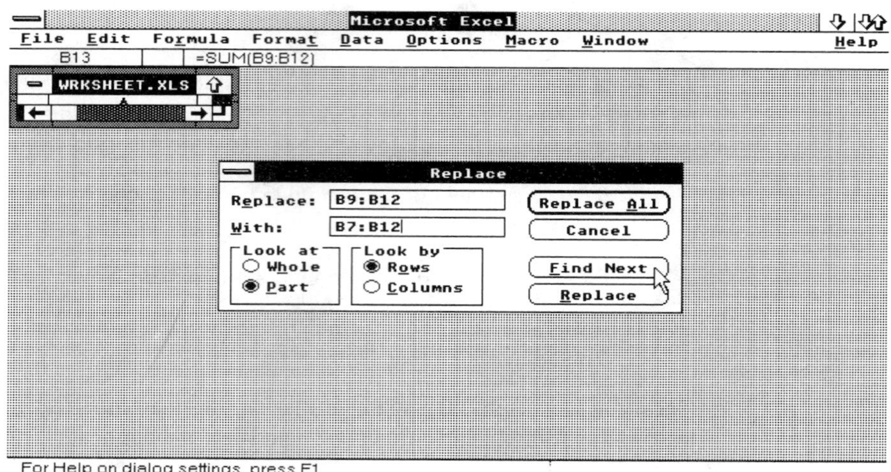

Fig. 6.17. The Replace box.

7

Opening and Saving Files

When you start Excel, you either begin creating a new worksheet or you open a current file. Opening a file brings a copy of the information stored on disk into memory. You see on-screen what resides in memory. When you work in Excel, you make changes to the file on-screen.

As you operate on the worksheet (in electronic memory) and make changes, the file on-screen no longer matches the original that resides on disk. You must save the file to the disk to store your most current work. This chapter covers tips, tricks, and traps for opening and saving your files.

Opening Files

7.1 Tip: **To work in another directory, change directories or folders.**

In PC Excel, you make permanent changes to the active directory by selecting a directory from the **D**irectories list box or by typing the disk and path name in the File **N**ame text box. Use the same path name conventions used in DOS commands when you type a new disk or path.

To move to a lower directory using the list box, select the directory name you want to open and then choose OK. (Double-click your mouse on the name as a short-cut.) To move to the parent directory of the active directory, select the [..] name in the **D**irectories box and then choose OK. (Or double-click on [..].) Change to another disk drive by double-clicking on a drive letter such as [-A-] or [-C-]. You return to the active directory last used on that disk.

To move rapidly to a listed file in one of the list boxes, drag the "thumb" at the side of the list box. Or select one name in the list box so that it is highlighted. Then type the first letter of the name you want. The pointer immediately moves to names beginning with that letter.

After selecting one file or directory from a list box, move to the beginning or end of the box by pressing the Home or End keys respectively.

In Macintosh Excel, change folders by choosing the **F**ile **O**pen command. Between the Open Document title and the list box, you see the name of the active folder. Drag down on this name to see other folders. Release the mouse on the folder you want.

7.2 Tip: **To remain in the current directory and open files in another directory, use the File Open command and type the complete file name including the directory.**

You do not need to use **F**ile **O**pen to open a DOS directory and then open files. Opening the directory in this fashion changes the current or active directory.

To open a file from another directory and remain in your current directory, choose the **F**ile **O**pen command and type in the text box the disk, path name, and file name you want to open. In figure 7.1, the active directory is C:\WINDOWS\EXCELTIP, but only part of the path is shown:

Directory is C:\...\EXCELTIP

To keep this directory active and open a file in another directory, type the complete file name, as in the following example:

C:\WINDOWS\MORTGAGE.XLS

If your file name and path name exceed the space in the text box, keep typing. The text box scrolls. Press the Home or End keys to move to the first or last character.

7.3 Tip: **To display only certain files, use DOS wild cards in PC Excel.**

In PC Excel. you can list all the files in a directory by using the DOS wild cards (*.*) in the File **N**ame box (see fig. 7.2). As the figure shows, you can see all files with any extension in the **F**iles list box.

In the **F**ile **N**ame box, use an asterisk (*) to request any group of characters at that position. Use a question mark (?) to request any single character at that exact position. For example, to display Lotus 1-2-3 files, enter ***.WK?**; this

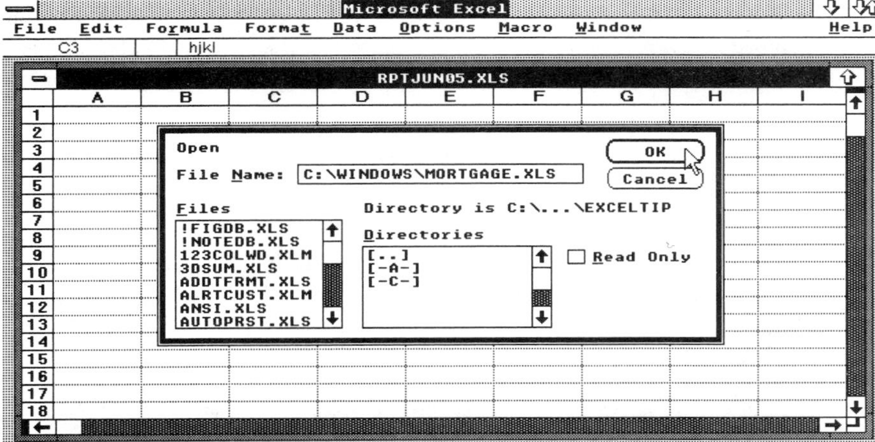

*Fig. 7.1. The **File Name** box.*

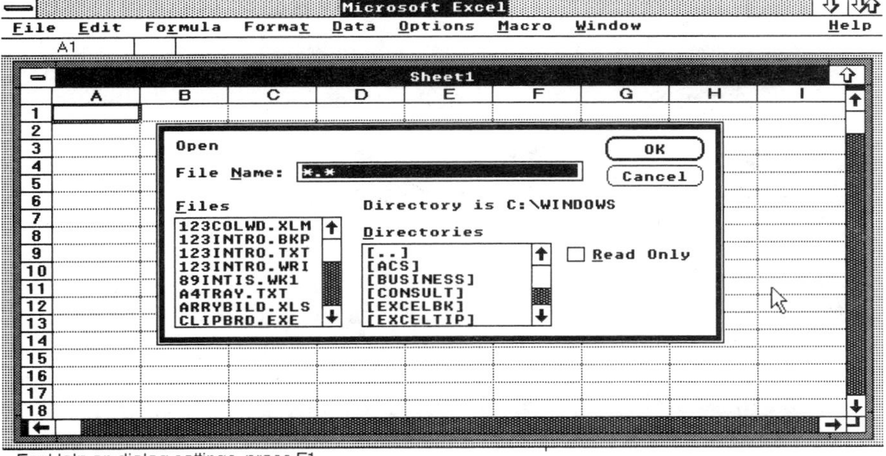

*Fig. 7.2. The **File Open** box.*

command displays files with any first name and an extension that starts with WK—in this case, all 1-2-3 files.

7.4 Tip: To open non-Excel files, display and then select the file.

Excel automatically can open and convert certain files that are not in the Excel file format. This capability makes it convenient for you to use Excel with other applications because you do not have to run a translation or conversion program.

Excel can open the following file types:

Text	ASCII text files
CSV	Comma separated values ASCII text files
SYLK	Multiplan files
WKS	Lotus 1-2-3 Release 1A
WK1	Lotus 1-2-3 Release 2.0 and 2.01
DIF	Data Interchange Format (worksheet interchange)
DBF 2	dBASE II
DBF 3	dBASE III

To open a non-Excel file, display the non-Excel files in the list box. (See the preceding tip on displaying files if you are using PC Excel.) Once you see the file name listed, select it and choose OK.

If you open and then save one of these files, Excel saves the file back to its original format. See Tip 7.16 later in this chapter for information on how to save the file in an Excel format.

7.5 Trick: **To transfer previous versions of Macintosh Excel files to newer Excel versions, save the file with the SYLK format.**

Transfer previous versions of Macintosh Excel files into newer versions of Macintosh or PC Excel by saving the file with the SYLK format. If you want to use the file with PC Excel, transfer the file to the PC using a program such as MacLink Plus. Then open the file in the newer version of Excel. When you save the file, make sure that you use **F**ile Save **A**s **O**ptions to save the file with the **N**ormal file format. This command preserves the newer Excel format.

7.6 Tip: **Save multiple related files as a workspace.**

You can prepare a group of worksheets, charts, and macros to open together by saving them as a workspace. Arrange the files and their windows as you want them to appear when you open them. Save any of the worksheets that may need a name change. Then choose **F**ile Save **W**orkspace and name the workspace. Excel adds the .XLW extension in PC Excel. In Macintosh Excel, the file name is preceded by RESUME—for example, RESUME BUDGET.

In PC Excel, open the workspace by choosing **F**ile **O**pen and selecting the appropriate file name with the .XLW extension. In Macintosh Excel, open the appropriate RESUME file.

7.7 Trap: **If you move files, resave the workspace files; otherwise, the workspace file cannot be opened.**

Workspace files keep a record of the file names in the group and the location where each file is stored. If you delete a file, move it to another directory or folder, or rename it, the workspace file cannot reopen the original files in the workspace. When opening a workspace, you receive a warning that a file cannot be found. You should open the missing file manually and resave the workspace using **F**ile Save **W**orkspace.

7.8 Trap: **Be sure to change the workspace name when you save a new workspace, or you may overwrite another workspace file.**

In PC Excel, choosing **F**ile Save **W**orkspace presents a dialog box that contains the name of the last workspace saved. Make sure that you change this name to one appropriate to the new workspace. Otherwise, you lose the previous workspace and misname the current one.

7.9 Trick: **Use Window Hide to make a file hide on opening.**

To create a worksheet, chart, or macro sheet that stays hidden when you open it, make one change to the worksheet, even if you just type and then delete text. Hide the worksheet using the **W**indow **H**ide command. Now choose **F**ile **E**xit (PC) or **F**ile **Q**uit (Macintosh). A dialog box asks whether you want to save the file. Choose OK and name the file if requested.

To test your hidden file, restart Excel and open the file you hid. This file remains hidden because that's how you saved it.

Saving, Closing, and Deleting Files

7.10 Tip: **To close all files at once, hold down the Shift key and choose the File menu.**

To close all open files, hold down the Shift key as you choose the **F**ile menu. A new command, **C**lose All, appears. Choose **C**lose All to close all worksheets. You are asked whether you want to save any worksheets that have changed since they were opened. Choose OK to save your files.

7.11 Tip: **Save your files every 15 minutes.**

Save your work to disk every 15 or 20 minutes. The worksheets on which you work reside in electronic memory, and this memory is good only as long as electrical power is on. If there is static electricity, a power surge, or power failure, you will lose your work. Saving every 15 or 20 minutes stores earlier versions of your work on disk. If needed, you can return to these versions.

7.12 Trap: **Be careful of the File Save command; this command overwrites previous versions of your file on disk.**

When you save with the **F**ile **S**ave command, your work in memory replaces the existing file of the same name stored on disk. Once you save the new version over the previous version, you cannot retrieve the information in the previous version. This can be dangerous because a localized portion of the disk may become damaged, or you may need to return to an earlier version of your work.

A much safer procedure is to use the **F**ile Save **A**s command, which allows you to change the file name. You can edit the last two characters of your file name to add version numbers. For example, you can name the file JUNRPT.XLS in PC Excel JUNRPT01.XLS, JUNRPT02.XLS, JUNRPT03.XLS, and so on. Using a two-digit version number such as 01, 02, 12, or 35 keeps the file names in alphabetical order. Once you are confident of your work, use the **F**ile **D**elete command to delete versions you do not want. In Macintosh Excel, you may want to use version names such as June Report V01, June Report V02, and so on.

Version numbers may interfere with a linked file's capability to find the file named with a new version. The linked file may look for the file with a previous version number. Prevent this from happening by keeping linked files in memory as you work. Then save all files after you save the worksheet you worked on. Chapter 5 describes how to relink multiple worksheets should they become separated because of name changes.

7.13 Tip: **Make file backups from your hard disk to a floppy disk.**

In addition to saving files on your hard disk, you should save a copy of important files on a separate disk. In PC Excel, choose **F**ile Save **A**s and type the drive letter in front of the current name (see fig. 7.3).

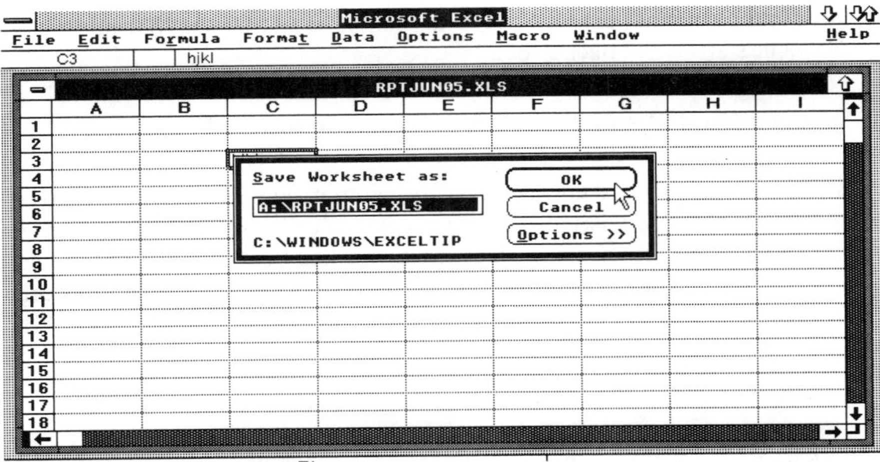

Fig. 7.3. The Save Worksheet as box.

The disk letter, A: in the figure, stays in front of the file name for additional saves. You must delete the letter manually when you want to save the file to another disk—for instance, back to the hard disk. The current directory remains the original directory used with the last **F**ile **O**pen.

On the hard disk in Macintosh Excel, save to the disk by choosing **F**ile Save **A**s, selecting the Drive button, and then saving.

7.14 Tip: **To save your file to a directory other than the current directory, type the complete file name, including the directory path.**

In addition to saving a file to a different disk, you can save a file to a different directory. You can remain in one directory and save to another. For example, in figure 7.3, you can save RPTJUN05.XLS to another hard disk directory by typing the following:

C:\BUDGET\RPTJUN05.XLS

In Macintosh Excel, you must change to the directory in which you want to save a file.

7.15 Tip: **Save backup copies of your file with the Create Backup File option.**

If you want a duplicate copy of your work in the same directory or folder as the original, choose the **F**ile Save **A**s command and select the **O**ptions button. Select the Create **B**ackup File check box. When you save the file, a second copy of the file is created in the same directory or folder. For PC Excel files, this backup copy has the DOS file extension of .BAK. On the Macintosh, the file name starts with "Backup of..."

7.16 Tip: **Save non-Excel files with the Normal file format to keep Excel features.**

Be careful when you save worksheets opened from non-Excel formats. Unless you tell Excel otherwise, the program automatically saves the information back to the same format from which it was opened. Because other formats do not support the enhanced formats or extensive functions available in Excel, any enhancements you made may be lost.

To keep your enhancements, save the file using **F**ile Save **A**s and select the **O**ptions button. Select the **N**ormal option and then choose OK.

7.17 Trap: **Although you can stop a file save that is in progress, this operation can be dangerous.**

If a file save takes an extremely long time, you may be tempted to stop the save. Press the Esc key in PC Excel to stop a file save that is in progress. In Macintosh Excel, press Command+. (period). Be careful—stopping a file while it's saving can be dangerous. Excel deletes the file from disk before saving it. By stopping the save, you are left without a file on disk and only the worksheet you see on-screen (and resides in memory). Be sure to save your on-screen work.

7.18 Tip: **In PC Excel, lead file names with ! to make them appear first on the list.**

If you want file names to appear first in the **F**ile **O**pen list box, save the file name using an ! (exclamation point) as the first character.

7.19 Trick: **Delete multiple files with the MS-DOS Executive.**

Use the MS-DOS Executive in Windows or the Desktop on the Macintosh to delete multiple files. Select the first file name or directory you want to delete. Then hold down the Shift key and click on the additional file names or icons you want to delete. Holding down the Shift key enables you to select multiple files. Choose the **F**ile **D**elete command. On the Macintosh, drag the files to the garbage can.

7.20 Trap: **Do not delete temporary files while in Windows.**

Windows creates temporary files with the extension .TMP. If you delete these files, you may have to restart Excel and Windows. If you have already deleted temporary files and cannot restart Windows or Excel, reinstall Windows and try again.

8

Printing

Excel's printing and formatting capabilities exceed those of other worksheets. Excel takes full advantage of the capabilities of the new generation of hardware—high-resolution color monitors, laser printers, font cartridges, and plotters. You can print financial proposals, budgets, and database reports that appear to have come from the typesetter, giving your reports greater impact.

As you work in an Excel worksheet or chart, the on-screen display appears close to the printed result. If you need an exact view of how the printed page will appear, you can preview pages using Excel's **P**rint **P**review option. In addition, Excel includes a print spooler so that you can print multiple documents yet continue to work in a worksheet or chart. This chapter discusses tips, tricks, and traps to help you manage the printing process.

Setting and Removing Print Areas

In this section, you learn how to define the area of your worksheet you want to print. In a new worksheet, Excel prints the entire worksheet, starting from cell A1 at the upper left and continuing down as many rows and across as many columns that contain data. You can, however, define specific areas to be printed. You can even define nonadjoining areas to print with a single print command.

8.1 Tip: **Print the entire worksheet by deleting the Print_Area range name.**

After initially creating a worksheet, choosing the **P**rint command will print the entire worksheet. If you want to print only a portion of your worksheet, select the print area you want to print and then choose the **O**ptions Set Print **A**rea command. Excel prints the range you selected when you choose the command. Choosing **O**ptions Set Print **A**rea is the same as naming a range Print_Area.

To print the entire worksheet once you have named a print area, delete the range name Print_Area. To do so, choose the Fo**r**mula **D**efine Name command and select Print_Area from the scrolling list box. Select the **D**elete button and then choose OK. Because the named range Print_Area no longer exists, Excel returns to printing the entire worksheet.

8.2 Tip: **Delete the last Print_Area name if you want to remove mandatory page breaks from the screen temporarily.**

When you first create a worksheet, the entire worksheet prints. After the first print, mandatory page breaks appear on-screen as dashed lines. These page-break markers define the edges of the print margins.

If you want to remove the dashed lines on-screen temporarily, delete the named print area. To do so, choose Fo**r**mula **D**efine Name. From the scrolling list box, select the name Print_Area, select **D**elete, and then choose OK. The mandatory page breaks reappear the next time you print or set the print area.

8.3 Trap: **Selecting the same rows and columns with Options Set Print Titles and Set Print Area causes double printing.**

The **O**ptions Set Print **T**itles command repeats selected rows at the top of a printed page and repeats columns at the left edge of a printed page. If you have selected these same rows or columns with **O**ptions Set Print **A**rea, the rows or columns print twice, once as print titles and once as the print area. Figure 8.1 shows how field names above a database print twice if selected with both Set Print **T**itles and Set Print **A**rea.

To correct this problem, reselect the range you want to print and do not include the titles range. When the print range is selected, choose **O**ptions Set Print **A**rea.

If you are unsure where the print titles are set, choose Fo**r**mula **G**oto, select the name Print_Titles from the list, and choose OK. To remove print titles completely, choose Fo**r**mula **D**efine Name, select Print_Titles, and then choose the **D**elete button.

DATABASE					
DUE DATE	DAYS DUE	FIRM	TASK	CPA	STAFF
DATABASE					
DUE DATE	DAYS DUE	FIRM	TASK	CPA	STAFF
2-Oct-88	1	R & R Consulting	Quarterly	MB	CN
10-Oct-88	9	Townsend	Quarterly	CN	CD
10-Oct-88	9	Townsley	Court Appearance	MB	CD
15-Oct-88	14	Hillside Vineyards	Fincl Plan	CN	BR
15-Oct-88	14	R & R Consulting	Business Review	CN	MB
18-Oct-88	17	Smith	Fm 1099	RP	BR
12-Nov-88	42	Smythe	Business Plan	MB	RP

Fig. 8.1. *Rows and columns printed twice.*

8.4 Tip: View all corners or resize any edge of your print area with a shortcut key.

When selecting large print areas, it's sometimes difficult to tell whether the corners of the area include all the cells you want. To see the corners of what will print, press the Goto key—F5 (PC) or Command+G (Macintosh). Select the Print_Area name and choose OK to select the area to be printed. With the area selected, press Ctrl+. (PC) or Control+. (Macintosh). Each press of the key combination moves the active cell to a different corner so that you can see each corner.

If you want to resize an existing print area, press the Goto key, select the Print_Area name, and choose OK. Press the Ctrl+. (PC) or Control+. (Macintosh) key combination until the active cell is in the corner diagonal to the corner you want moved.

Now, hold down the Shift key and press the arrow key in the direction you want to expand or contract the print area. (Holding down the Shift key preserves cells already selected.) As soon as you begin to move the corner, Excel displays the corner that is moving so that you can see the new cells you are selecting. Once you select the new area you want to print, set the print area by choosing **O**ptions Set Print **A**rea.

8.5 Trick: **Print multiple areas of the document with a single command.**

You can hold down the Ctrl key (either the Control or Command key on the Macintosh) to select nonadjoining areas with the mouse (see fig. 8.2). You can print several areas by selecting them at one time and then choosing the **O**ptions Set Print **A**rea command. All the areas are assigned the Print_Area range name.

Fig. 8.2. Selecting nonadjoining areas.

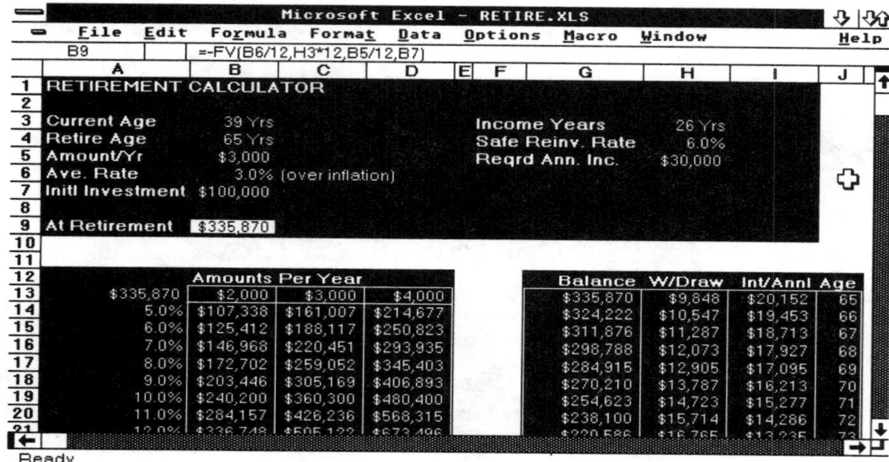

Select the areas in the order you want them to print. Excel puts page breaks between areas and prints the areas in the order you selected them. Each area prints on a separate page.

8.6 Trick: **Use named ranges to change between different print areas quickly.**

If you need to change between print areas quickly, assign each area a name using the For**m**ula **D**efine Name command. For example, you may have areas with names such as Mo_Report, Sales, Jun_Bdgt, and so on.

To select and print these reports quickly, first assign range names to the areas. Then use the Goto key to select the range name and set the print area. To do so, press the Goto key—F5 (PC) or Command+G (Macintosh). Then select a name such as Mo_Report by double-clicking on the name in the list box. Choose **O**ptions Set Print **A**rea and then choose **F**ile **P**rint. Press the Goto key again to select the next range to be printed and repeat the process.

If you always print reports in the same order, even if they are from different worksheets, save time by creating a recorded macro. Chapter 11 provides examples of macros used for printing.

8.7 Trick: **Print multiple ranges on a page by using a special print area in a linked worksheet.**

Excel prints each print area on a separate page. If a print area contains multiple nonadjoining areas, each of these areas also prints on a separate page. This placement makes it difficult to print nonadjoining areas on the same page.

To print nonadjoining areas on the same page, select a worksheet area that will contain formatted results for printing. Use simple references such as =A12 to bring text and values into the area from which you will print. Bring in results from other worksheets by using **E**dit **C**opy in the original and **E**dit Paste **S**pecial with the Forma**t**s option in the copy. Arrange the data in this print area as you want it to print.

Using a separate print area not only enables you to print physically separated information on the same page, a separate print area also gives you greater freedom in formatting. You can position this print area in a location where you can adjust column widths and row heights without affecting other areas of the worksheet.

Imagine this new worksheet as a palette used only for arranging and formatting printouts. Select all these ranges as you want them to print and use the **O**ptions Set Print **A**rea command to set the print area. Because the areas are linked to the original worksheets, the areas will contain up-to-date information.

8.8 Trick: **Print multiple ranges on a page by hiding rows or columns.**

If you need to print nonadjoining areas on the same page and the ranges are in-line vertically or horizontally, you can hide rows and columns between the printing areas to bring the printing areas together. Once the areas appear together on-screen, you can print them on the same page.

To do so, first save the worksheet with its correct row heights and column widths. Reopening this worksheet is easier than redoing many custom row heights and column widths.

In the worksheet, select the rows you want to shrink, choose Forma**t** **R**ow Height, and enter a zero height. Select the columns you need to shrink and choose Forma**t** **C**olumn Width. Enter a zero column width. Once the nonadjoining areas appear next to each other on-screen, you can select what you want to print on the same page, choose **O**ptions Set Print **A**rea, and then choose **F**ile **P**rint.

Once you have printed, close the worksheet you printed from and reopen the original worksheet. If you frequently print these areas on a single page, record a macro that will repeat the process for you.

Setting and Removing Page Breaks

Excel uses and displays three different types of page breaks on-screen. Seeing where pages will break is a convenient feature, allowing you to adjust page breaks by changing column widths, page margins, font sizes, or paper orientation. You can even insert manual page breaks to ensure that a page break occurs at exactly the location you want. Manual page breaks don't alter or destroy the worksheet as they do in some electronic worksheets.

8.9 Tip: **Use the appropriate type of page break.**

You can use one of three levels of page breaks in Excel. Each type is displayed as dashes on-screen, and each provides a different degree of control. The page break types include the following: manually inserted page breaks, automatic page breaks, and print-area boundary page breaks.

Manually inserted page breaks appear above and to the left of the active cell when you select **O**ptions Set Page **B**reak. Set manual page breaks to mark the end of printing on a page. Manual page breaks inserted above automatic page breaks cause the automatic page breaks to shift down. Manual page breaks inserted to the left of automatic page breaks cause the automatic page breaks to shift to the right.

Automatic page breaks appear within the print area at the edge of the last column and row that can print within the page margins. You cannot remove automatic page breaks with the **O**ptions Remove Page **B**reak command because they are defined by the paper size, default font, and margins. Change Font 1 (PC) or the standard font (Macintosh), the paper size, or page margins to adjust an automatic page break.

The edges of the range named Print_Area appear as *print-area boundary page breaks*. Within a print area, any nonadjoining areas that are included in the named Print_Area are separated by page breaks and print on separate pages.

8.10 Tip: **Use the Options Set Page Break command to enter page breaks.**

When you choose the **O**ptions Set Page **B**reak command, page breaks appear above and to the left of the active cell (see fig. 8.3). The page breaks display as dashed lines. You can see page breaks more easily if you choose **O**ptions **D**isplay and unselect the **G**ridlines option.

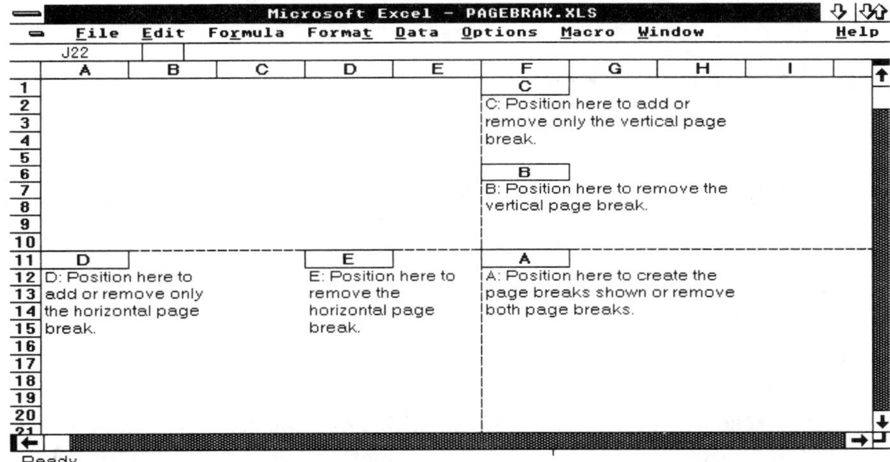

Fig. 8.3. Page breaks displayed on-screen.

If you want to insert only a horizontal page break, move the active cell into column A underneath the row where you want the page break and then choose **O**ptions Set Page **B**reak. If you want to insert only a vertical page break, move the active cell into row 1 to the right of where you want the page break; then choose **O**ptions Set Page **B**reak.

8.11 Tip: **Position the cell pointer correctly before removing page breaks.**

The **O**ptions Remove Page **B**reak command appears on the menu only when the active cell is positioned correctly next to a manual page break. If the **O**ptions Remove Page **B**reak command does not appear, the active cell is incorrectly positioned, or the page break is a mandatory page break. If the active cell is not correctly positioned to remove a page break, the command Set Page **B**reak appears on the **O**ptions menu.

To remove a manually set horizontal page break, move the active cell directly under the dashed line and choose **O**ptions Remove Page **B**reak. To remove a manually set vertical page break, move the active cell directly right of the dashed line and choose **O**ptions Remove Page **B**reak. You can remove horizontal and vertical page breaks simultaneously by positioning the active cell below the horizontal page break and to the right of the vertical page break. Figure 8.3 shows where to locate the active cell to remove page breaks.

If the active cell is positioned correctly next to a page break, but the **O**ptions Remove Page **B**reak command does not appear, the page break is an automatic page break.

Selecting and Changing Fonts

One of the features that makes Excel's printed results impressive is the capability to use your printer to its maximum capability. Within a worksheet, you can change type fonts and styles, vary type size, and add shading and borders. To use the capabilities, you must understand how to choose features that are available for your printer.

8.12 Tip: **Use shortcut keys in PC Excel to format with fonts quickly.**

In PC Excel, to format a cell's contents with a font quickly, select the cells you want to change. Then use the Ctrl key in combination with the number keys 1 through 4 to choose the fonts 1 through 4. (Do not press the function keys F1 through F4 by accident.)

To format with Font...	*Press...*
1	Ctrl+1
2	Ctrl+2
3	Ctrl+3
4	Ctrl+4

8.13 Tip: **Choose the Format Font Fonts> command and select the Printer Fonts option in PC Excel to ensure that you use fonts available on your printer.**

When choosing fonts in a worksheet or chart, you can use fonts that are not available on your printer or plotter. If you do this, the print preview shows how the worksheet or chart should appear, but when you print, the printer will make substitutions for the fonts (typefaces and sizes) that the printer does not have available.

If Excel cannot find a printer typeface that matches the typeface you used in formatting, Excel substitutes an available typeface of the same size. (Fonts of the same point size will not always print the same actual height on the page. The actual height depends on both historical and design factors in the font.) If Excel finds the font you requested, but cannot find the size you requested, it substitutes the next smaller size.

To ensure that you use only fonts available in your printer, choose the Forma**t** **F**ont command. When the dialog box appears, select the **F**onts> button (see fig. 8.4). Select the **P**rinter Fonts check box.

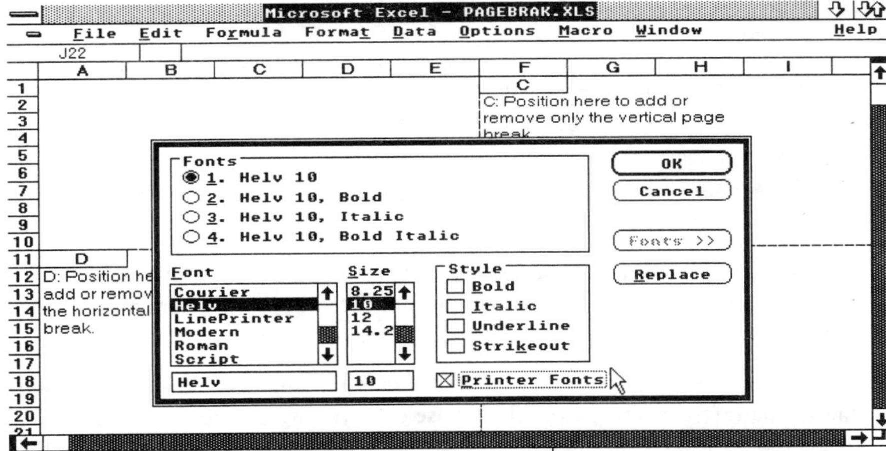

Fig. 8.4.
The Fonts box.

At this point, check to ensure that the fonts listed as fonts 1 through 4 are available in the **F**ont scrolling list. If the fonts are not available in the scrolling list, you must replace them with a font that your printer can use. Replace any of the four fonts by selecting the font (1–4) you want replaced. Next, select a font from the **F**ont list and a size from the **S**ize list. Select the **R**eplace button to replace the font with your new selection.

8.14 Trap: Available printer fonts may change depending on paper orientation.

Some printers, such as HP LaserJet printers, have different fonts available for portrait (vertical) and landscape (horizontal) paper orientation. If you have formatted a worksheet for portrait orientation and used fonts available in portrait, the worksheet may not print correctly when you change the orientation to landscape. The printer may not have the same fonts available in landscape and may substitute a landscape font for the font it does not have.

To avoid font changes caused by orientation changes, choose the Forma**t** **F**ont F**o**nts> command and select the **P**rinter Fonts check box when you do your original formatting. When you change paper orientation, return to the Forma**t** **F**onts F**o**nts> dialog box and see whether the fonts you originally chose are still available. If the fonts are not available, you must substitute new fonts.

8.15 Tip: **Use Font 1 in PC Excel as the main worksheet font to make reformatting easier.**

Font 1 is the default font used throughout the worksheet. This font is used in row and column headings and as the default font when you enter data. The width of a standard Font 1 character defines the column width.

Use Font 1 for the body of your worksheets. For Font 1, choose a font that enables you to print the body of your worksheet on the page. If you need to adjust the size of the worksheet later, you need to replace only Font 1.

8.16 Tip: **Select the default font for Macintosh Excel with the Options Standard Font command.**

In Macintosh Excel, you select the default font by choosing **O**ptions **S**tandard Font. Choosing a new standard font changes all entries throughout the worksheet that were made using the default standard font.

If you want entries that use the standard font to remain in that font (even when the standard font is changed), select those cells you want to remain unchanged. Then choose the Forma**t** **F**ont command. In the **F**ont dialog box, unselect the **S**tandard Font check box to prevent the selected cells from changing when you choose a new standard font.

8.17 Trick: **Use fonts as style sheets to make quick formatting changes to worksheets.**

In Excel for Windows, you can use four fonts numbered 1 through 4 in a worksheet. You can view these four fonts as aids in setting worksheet styles. Use each of the four fonts for a specific purpose.

Use Font...	*To format...*
1	Body copy, headers, and footers
2	Worksheet labels or database field names
3	Second level titles
4	Main titles

If you use this convention, you can easily adjust any of your worksheets because you will know how each of the fonts is used. Normally, you will use Font 1 for the largest amount of text in the worksheet.

8.18 Tip: **Use Font 1 in PC Excel to select fonts for the header or footer.**

The body copy, header, and footer are normally Font 1. If you want headers or footers that differ from the body's font, choose Font 1 to fit your header or footer. Then choose Font 2 for the body copy. Set Font 2 as the default body font by selecting the entire worksheet (click in the blank space directly left of the column headers). Now choose Forma**t** **F**ont **2**. Replace Font 2 with the font you want in the body. This process leaves Font 1 for headers and footers and Font 2 for body copy.

8.19 Tip: **Use screen fonts in PC Excel to print the maximum number of characters per page when small fonts are not available.**

Even if your laser printer does not have a small font available, you may still be able to print with small fonts when you need to fit the maximum amount of characters on a page. Try changing Font 1 to Modern with a 6- or 8-point size. Modern, a font designed for use on-screen, prints even if the font is not available in the printer. The characters are not shaped as well as cartridge or soft fonts, but this method works.

8.20 Trap: **Printing with screen fonts from PC Excel can be helpful, but unpredictable at different resolutions.**

Screen fonts such as Modern, Roman, and Script are designed for use on-screen and not on the printer. Therefore, screen fonts may not print as well as a font designed for the printer. When printing with screen fonts, choose the **F**ile P**r**inter Setup command, select the **S**etup button, and select a graphics resolution of 300 dots per inch (dpi). Using screen fonts with a printing resolution of 75 or 150 dots per inch produces unusually formed characters.

8.21 Tip: **Display worksheets and fonts judiciously to save memory while printing.**

Each worksheet can have its own fonts, independent of the fonts used in other worksheets. However, each additional font uses memory. Using the same fonts across different worksheets and charts saves memory.

Fitting Text to a Page and Setting Page Layout

You can use a number of commands in Excel to position printing on the page. You also can define how much text fits on the page. The capability to fit large financial reports on a page can be useful. This section includes tips to help you fit more information on the page.

8.22 Trick: **Use one of several techniques to fit the maximum amount of characters on a page.**

When you need to fit the most information possible on a page, use one or more of the following techniques until your copy fits.

Use smaller fonts: Change Font 1 (PC) or the standard font (Macintosh) to a smaller point size. The numbers that describe a font size are the height of a font in points. There are 72 points per vertical inch. Proportionally spaced fonts cannot be measured by their widths because each character has its own special width. This "proportional" width enables text to pack more closely, giving the same appearance as typesetting. (A small point size corresponds to a large number of characters per inch.) The smallest default font for HP LaserJets without cartridges or soft fonts is LinePrinter. If you do not have a small point size available for your printer, you may be able to use the Modern screen font in a 6- or 8-point size to print small characters. Many PostScript printers print fonts as small as 4 points. If a small font or odd size is not listed for your PostScript printer, try typing the size you need in the text box underneath the **S**ize scrolling list.

Set smaller margins: Margins determine how much white space surrounds the body of text on a page. Smaller margins mean more copy on the page. Set margins using the **F**ile Page Se**t**up command. Margins on many laser printers cannot be smaller than .25 inches; this is a physical limitation of the printer.

Change to landscape paper orientation: Printing sideways on the page enables you to print longer lines of text. This print method is useful in large forecasts and budgets. Choose the paper orientation in PC Excel by choosing the **F**ile Printer Se**t**up command. Then select the **S**etup button and select landscape orientation. Be aware that available printer fonts may be different in portrait and landscape orientations. In Macintosh Excel, change paper orientation by choosing **F**ile Page Se**t**up and selecting the paper orientation icon of your choice.

Hide unneeded rows or columns: Fit pertinent information on the page by hiding nonpertinent rows or columns before printing. Reduce row heights to zero and column widths to zero to hide unwanted rows and columns. Chapter 3 on formatting describes how to reduce and enlarge row heights and column widths.

Reduce column widths: Column widths that are wider than necessary can waste horizontal space. Make column widths as wide as needed to separate contents—but no wider—if you want the most text possible. Change multiple columns simultaneously by holding down the Shift key as you select the columns. Drag the right column-heading divider to change the widths of all selected columns.

Reduce row heights: You can reduce the row heights by a small amount to fit a few more lines of text per page. Excel automatically sets the row heights according to the height of the tallest text in a row. Excel adds a small amount of space above each character for visual room between lines. You can reduce the row height by a small amount and still leave room for characters. If a line has a tall font that forces an entire row to print too tall, you may be able to reduce the row height of the print area significantly.

Reduce multiple rows by holding down the Shift key as you select adjacent row headings. Drag the bottom divider between row headings to change the height of all selected columns. Return to original row heights by choosing the Forma**t** **R**ow Height command and selecting the **S**tandard Height option.

Change paper size: Select a larger paper size to print more on the page. If you do not have the correct paper tray, you may need to feed the paper manually.

Use reduction mode: With Macintosh Excel, you can reduce (or enlarge) PostScript print size by choosing **F**ile Page Se**t**up and entering a number less than 100 (or greater than 100) in the Reduce/Enlarge box.

8.23 Trick: Print with double- or triple-spacing by changing row height.

To print double- or triple-spaced reports, select the rows you want double- or triple-spaced. Select rows that have the same original spacing. Choose the Forma**t** **R**ow Height command. If all rows were the same original height, you see a row height number in the **R**ow Height text box. Enter a number twice this amount for double-spacing or triple the amount for triple-spacing. Change rows that have different standard heights separately. Once you change all rows, print the area.

Return to normal row height by choosing the Forma**t** **R**ow Height command and selecting the **S**tandard Height option.

8.24 Tip: **Position printing on the page by changing margins.**

Move printed results anywhere on the page by adjusting the top and left margins. Printed copy always prints from the top margin down and from the left margin across. If the print area does not fill the page, you can position the print area on the page by moving the top and left margins to move the top and left edges of the printout. Before printing, use the **F**ile **P**rint command with the **P**review option to see the position of printing on the page.

8.25 Tip: **If text exceeding the rightmost printed column is cut off when printed, adjust the worksheet.**

Text that exceeds the right mandatory page break is truncated so that only the text to the left of the page break prints. The page boundaries act as you would expect them to act, cutting off text that goes outside the page margins and printing text inside the margins.

To adjust the worksheet so that "too wide text" will print, you must do one of the following. Reselect and set a wider print area; decrease the left and right print margins; use a smaller font; decrease column widths to the left of the wide text; or increase the column width of the column containing the truncated text.

In some cases, increasing the column width of the column containing the text causes the right page break to move so that the truncated text prints on a following page. Once the text is completely to the left of the rightmost page break, the text will print.

Adding Headers, Footers, and Page Numbering

To enhance your printout further, you can use two other Excel features: headers and footers. Headers print at the top of each page, footers at the bottom. You can automate headers or footers to include page numbers, dates, and times. You can even start page numbers at a page number you specify.

Another useful feature, **O**ptions Set Print **T**itles, can duplicate top or left side headings on pages so that you can always see labels or headings on printouts that cover multiple pages.

8.26 Trick: Customize your headers and footers with special codes.

Headers and footers appear at the top and bottom of every page. Type your desired header or footer by choosing the **F**ile Page Se**t**up command and entering the text in the **H**eader or **F**ooter boxes. Default headers and footers print one-half inch from the top or bottom of the page and three fourths of an inch from the side of the page regardless of page margin settings. Headers and footers print in Font 1 in PC Excel.

You can enhance, format, and add features to headers and footers with the special codes in table 8.1. You can, for example, use the header/footer options to include the date and name of your worksheet to make it easier to keep track of different revisions.

Table 8.1
Header and Footer Codes

Code	*Effect*
Position Codes	
&L	Align against the left margin
&C	Center between margins
&R	Align against the right margin
Style Codes	
&B	Print in bold
&I	Print in italics
&S	Print in strikeout (Macintosh)
&U	Print in underline (Macintosh)
&O	Print in outline (Macintosh)
&H	Print in shadow (Macintosh)
&&	Print an ampersand
Font Codes	
&"font name"	Print in specified font. Enclose the font name in quotation marks (Macintosh).
&"size"	Print in specified size (Macintosh)

Code	*Effect*
Automatic Codes	
&D	Print the computer's date
&T	Print the computer's time
&F	Print the name of the worksheet or chart
Page Codes	
&P	Print the page number
&P+# or &P–#	Print the page number plus or minus a starting number

Combine codes with text to create custom headers and footers. For example, if the computer's date is 12/4/89 and this is the first page of the print area, the following header or footer code

&L&D&C&BAccounting Report&RPage &P+1

prints as

12/4/89	**Accounting Report**	Page 2

The code &P+1 added one to the actual page number.

8.27 Trick: **Print page numbers starting at a specific number.**

Automatic page numbering begins with page one as the first page in the print area. The print area is defined when you choose **O**ptions Set Print **A**rea. If you want page numbers to start on a greater or lesser page number than the automatic page numbering, use the &P code and add or subtract page numbers.

For example, if you have selected a large print area that contains 20 pages and in the **F**ile **P**rint dialog box you have requested printing from page 15 to 20, pages will be numbered from 15 to 20 by the code &P. However, if you want page numbering for this range to be from page 1 through 6, use a code of &P-14. Similarly, if a page normally prints with a page number of 1 and you want a page number of 12, use the code &P+11.

8.28 Trick: **Stop headers and footers from overlapping printed worksheets by adjusting margins.**

Headers and footers print one-half inch from the top and bottom of the page. If printed worksheets or charts overlap the header or footer, change the top and bottom margins of the print area using the File Page Setup command.

If you are printing a worksheet and need headers that are located differently from the default headers, use Trick 8.30 to create custom headers using print titles.

8.29 Trap: **Use Options Set Print Titles to repeat headings on each printed page.**

Wide worksheets and long databases cross multiple pages when printed. This can produce a difficult-to-read printout that shows data, but does not show labels from the left column of the worksheet or field names from the top of the database. If you want a column of row labels or a row of field names to print on every page, you need to use print titles.

To print repeating titles, follow these steps:

1. Select the entire row(s) or column(s) you want repeated on every page. These rows and columns do not have to be adjacent to the actual print area, but they must be aligned with the print area. Figure 8.5 shows headings selected above a long mortgage table. These headings repeat at the top of each page.

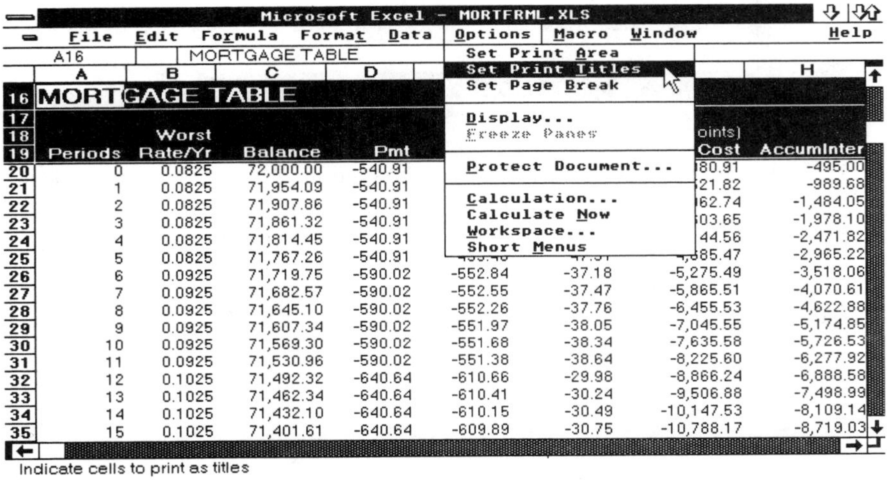

Microsoft Excel - MORTFRML.XLS

File Edit Formula Format Data Options Macro Window Help

A16 MORTGAGE TABLE

Options menu: Set Print Area / Set Print Titles / Set Page Break / Display... / Freeze Panes / Protect Document... / Calculation... / Calculate Now / Workspace... / Short Menus

	A	B	C	D	E	F	G	H
16	MORTGAGE TABLE							
17								
18		Worst					oints)	
19	Periods	Rate/Yr	Balance	Pmt			Cost	AccumInter
20	0	0.0825	72,000.00	-540.91			80.91	-495.00
21	1	0.0825	71,954.09	-540.91			21.82	-989.68
22	2	0.0825	71,907.86	-540.91			62.74	-1,484.05
23	3	0.0825	71,861.32	-540.91			03.65	-1,978.10
24	4	0.0825	71,814.45	-540.91			44.56	-2,471.82
25	5	0.0825	71,767.26	-540.91	[illegible]	[illegible]	[illegible]85.47	-2,965.22
26	6	0.0925	71,719.75	-590.02	-552.84	-37.18	-5,275.49	-3,518.06
27	7	0.0925	71,682.57	-590.02	-552.55	-37.47	-5,865.51	-4,070.61
28	8	0.0925	71,645.10	-590.02	-552.26	-37.76	-6,455.53	-4,622.88
29	9	0.0925	71,607.34	-590.02	-551.97	-38.05	-7,045.55	-5,174.85
30	10	0.0925	71,569.30	-590.02	-551.68	-38.34	-7,635.58	-5,726.53
31	11	0.0925	71,530.96	-590.02	-551.38	-38.64	-8,225.60	-6,277.92
32	12	0.1025	71,492.32	-640.64	-610.66	-29.98	-8,866.24	-6,888.58
33	13	0.1025	71,462.34	-640.64	-610.41	-30.24	-9,506.88	-7,498.99
34	14	0.1025	71,432.10	-640.64	-610.15	-30.49	-10,147.53	-8,109.14
35	15	0.1025	71,401.61	-640.64	-609.89	-30.75	-10,788.17	-8,719.03

Indicate cells to print as titles

Fig. 8.5. Setting the print titles.

2. Choose the **O**ptions Set Print **T**itles command. The row(s) or column(s) you selected are assigned the range name Print_Titles.

Figures 8.6 and 8.7 show the first and second printed pages from the mortgage table. Notice that the headings selected in figure 8.5 are repeated.

Fig. 8.6. *Page 1 of the mortgage table.*

MORTGAGE TABLE

	Worst					(inclds points)	
Periods	**Rate/Yr**	**Balance**	**Pmt**	**IPmt**	**PPmt**	**AccumCost**	**AccumInter**
0	0.0825	72,000.00	-540.91	-495.00	-45.91	-1,980.91	-495.00
1	0.0825	71,954.09	-540.91	-494.68	-46.23	-2,521.82	-989.68
2	0.0825	71,907.86	-540.91	-494.37	-46.55	-3,062.74	-1,484.05
3	0.0825	71,861.32	-540.91	-494.05	-46.87	-3,603.65	-1,978.10
4	0.0825	71,814.45	-540.91	-493.72	-47.19	-4,144.56	-2,471.82
5	0.0825	71,767.26	-540.91	-493.40	-47.51	-4,685.47	-2,965.22
6	0.0925	71,719.75	-590.02	-552.84	-37.18	-5,275.49	-3,518.06
7	0.0925	71,682.57	-590.02	-552.55	-37.47	-5,865.51	-4,070.61
8	0.0925	71,645.10	-590.02	-552.26	-37.76	-6,455.53	-4,622.88
9	0.0925	71,607.34	-590.02	-551.97	-38.05	-7,045.55	-5,174.85
10	0.0925	71,569.30	-590.02	-551.68	-38.34	-7,635.58	-5,726.53
11	0.0925	71,530.96	-590.02	-551.38	-38.64	-8,225.60	-6,277.92
12	0.1025	71,492.32	-640.64	-610.66	-29.98	-8,866.24	-6,888.58
13	0.1025	71,462.34	-640.64	-610.41	-30.24	-9,506.88	-7,498.99
14	0.1025	71,432.10	-640.64	-610.15	-30.49	-10,147.53	-8,109.14
15	0.1025	71,401.61	-640.64	-609.89	-30.75	-10,788.17	-8,719.03
16	0.1025	71,370.85	-640.64	-609.63	-31.02	-11,428.81	-9,328.65
17	0.1025	71,339.84	-640.64	-609.36	-31.28	-12,069.46	-9,938.01
18	0.1125	71,308.55	-692.59	-668.52	-24.07	-12,762.05	-10,606.53
19	0.1125	71,284.48	-692.59	-668.29	-24.30	-13,454.64	-11,274.82
20	0.1125	71,260.18	-692.59	-668.06	-24.53	-14,147.24	-11,942.89
21	0.1125	71,235.65	-692.59	-667.83	-24.76	-14,839.83	-12,610.72
22	0.1125	71,210.89	-692.59	-667.60	-24.99	-15,532.42	-13,278.32
23	0.1125	71,185.90	-692.59	-667.37	-25.22	-16,225.01	-13,945.69
24	0.1225	71,160.68	-745.69	-726.43	-19.26	-16,970.70	-14,672.12
25	0.1225	71,141.42	-745.69	-726.24	-19.45	-17,716.39	-15,398.36
26	0.1225	71,121.97	-745.69	-726.04	-19.65	-18,462.08	-16,124.39
27	0.1225	71,102.31	-745.69	-725.84	-19.85	-19,207.77	-16,850.23
28	0.1225	71,082.46	-745.69	-725.63	-20.06	-19,953.46	-17,575.86
29	0.1225	71,062.40	-745.69	-725.43	-20.26	-20,699.15	-18,301.29
30	0.1325	71,042.14	-799.77	-784.42	-15.35	-21,498.93	-19,085.72
31	0.1325	71,026.79	-799.77	-784.25	-15.52	-22,298.70	-19,869.97
32	0.1325	71,011.27	-799.77	-784.08	-15.69	-23,098.47	-20,654.05
33	0.1325	70,995.58	-799.77	-783.91	-15.86	-23,898.25	-21,437.96
34	0.1325	70,979.71	-799.77	-783.73	-16.04	-24,698.02	-22,221.70
35	0.1325	70,963.68	-799.77	-783.56	-16.22	-25,497.80	-23,005.25
36	0.135	70,947.46	-812.64	-798.16	-14.48	-26,310.44	-23,803.41
37	0.135	70,932.98	-812.64	-798.00	-14.64	-27,123.08	-24,601.41
38	0.135	70,918.33	-812.64	-797.83	-14.81	-27,935.72	-25,399.24
39	0.135	70,903.52	-812.64	-797.66	-14.98	-28,748.36	-26,196.91
40	0.135	70,888.55	-812.64	-797.50	-15.14	-29,561.00	-26,994.40
41	0.135	70,873.40	-812.64	-797.33	-15.32	-30,373.64	-27,791.73

If you select complete rows and choose the **O**ptions Set Print **T**itles command, the only cells from these rows that print are cells in the same columns as the print area. These cells print above the print area on the page.

If you select columns and choose the **O**ptions Set Print **T**itles command, the only cells from these columns that print are the cells in the same rows as the print area. These cells print to the left of the print area on the page.

MORTGAGE TABLE

Periods	Worst Rate/Yr	Balance	Pmt	IPmt	PPmt	(inclds points) AccumCost	AccumInter
42	0.135	70,858.09	-812.64	-797.15	-15.49	-31,186.28	-28,588.88
43	0.135	70,842.60	-812.64	-796.98	-15.66	-31,998.92	-29,385.86
44	0.135	70,826.94	-812.64	-796.80	-15.84	-32,811.56	-30,182.66
45	0.135	70,811.10	-812.64	-796.62	-16.02	-33,624.20	-30,979.29
46	0.135	70,795.08	-812.64	-796.44	-16.20	-34,436.84	-31,775.73
47	0.135	70,778.89	-812.64	-796.26	-16.38	-35,249.49	-32,572.00
48	0.135	70,762.51	-812.64	-796.08	-16.56	-36,062.13	-33,368.07
49	0.135	70,745.95	-812.64	-795.89	-16.75	-36,874.77	-34,163.97
50	0.135	70,729.20	-812.64	-795.70	-16.94	-37,687.41	-34,959.67
51	0.135	70,712.26	-812.64	-795.51	-17.13	-38,500.05	-35,755.18
52	0.135	70,695.13	-812.64	-795.32	-17.32	-39,312.69	-36,550.50
53	0.135	70,677.81	-812.64	-795.13	-17.52	-40,125.33	-37,345.63
54	0.135	70,660.30	-812.64	-794.93	-17.71	-40,937.97	-38,140.56
55	0.135	70,642.58	-812.64	-794.73	-17.91	-41,750.61	-38,935.28
56	0.135	70,624.67	-812.64	-794.53	-18.11	-42,563.25	-39,729.81
57	0.135	70,606.56	-812.64	-794.32	-18.32	-43,375.89	-40,524.14
58	0.135	70,588.24	-812.64	-794.12	-18.52	-44,188.53	-41,318.25
59	0.135	70,569.72	-812.64	-793.91	-18.73	-45,001.18	-42,112.16
60	0.135	70,550.99	-812.64	-793.70	-18.94	-45,813.82	-42,905.86
61	0.135	70,532.05	-812.64	-793.49	-19.16	-46,626.46	-43,699.35
62	0.135	70,512.89	-812.64	-793.27	-19.37	-47,439.10	-44,492.62
63	0.135	70,493.52	-812.64	-793.05	-19.59	-48,251.74	-45,285.67
64	0.135	70,473.93	-812.64	-792.83	-19.81	-49,064.38	-46,078.50
65	0.135	70,454.12	-812.64	-792.61	-20.03	-49,877.02	-46,871.11
66	0.135	70,434.09	-812.64	-792.38	-20.26	-50,689.66	-47,663.49
67	0.135	70,413.83	-812.64	-792.16	-20.49	-51,502.30	-48,455.65
68	0.135	70,393.35	-812.64	-791.93	-20.72	-52,314.94	-49,247.57
69	0.135	70,372.63	-812.64	-791.69	-20.95	-53,127.58	-50,039.27
70	0.135	70,351.68	-812.64	-791.46	-21.18	-53,940.22	-50,830.72
71	0.135	70,330.50	-812.64	-791.22	-21.42	-54,752.87	-51,621.94
72	0.135	70,309.08	-812.64	-790.98	-21.66	-55,565.51	-52,412.92
73	0.135	70,287.41	-812.64	-790.73	-21.91	-56,378.15	-53,203.65
74	0.135	70,265.50	-812.64	-790.49	-22.15	-57,190.79	-53,994.14
75	0.135	70,243.35	-812.64	-790.24	-22.40	-58,003.43	-54,784.38
76	0.135	70,220.95	-812.64	-789.99	-22.66	-58,816.07	-55,574.36
77	0.135	70,198.29	-812.64	-789.73	-22.91	-59,628.71	-56,364.09
78	0.135	70,175.38	-812.64	-789.47	-23.17	-60,441.35	-57,153.57
79	0.135	70,152.21	-812.64	-789.21	-23.43	-61,253.99	-57,942.78
80	0.135	70,128.79	-812.64	-788.95	-23.69	-62,066.63	-58,731.73
81	0.135	70,105.09	-812.64	-788.68	-23.96	-62,879.27	-59,520.41
82	0.135	70,081.14	-812.64	-788.41	-24.23	-63,691.91	-60,308.82
83	0.135	70,056.91	-812.64	-788.14	-24.50	-64,504.56	-61,096.96

Fig. 8.7. Page 2 of the mortgage table.

8.30 Trick: Create custom or additional header lines with the Options Set Print Titles command.

Add custom header lines in addition to those from **F**ile Page Set**u**p by typing your header in one or more rows in the same columns as the print area. Select the rows containing your custom header and choose **O**ptions Set Print **T**itles. Do not reselect these rows when you choose **O**ptions Set Print **A**rea. Doing so causes the print titles to print twice.

One advantage to headers created using print titles is that you can create headers using all formatting features. These headers can have different size fonts, use underlining and shading, and stay within the margins as defined by the **F**ile Page Set**u**p command. Add dates and times to these headers by entering the NOW( ) function in a cell and formatting the cell with any date or time format. Note that you will not be able to add page numbers that change automatically with each printed page when you use this method.

If your print area includes different areas that are not aligned on the same columns, you must print each area separately with its own header. If you print this area frequently, record a macro to reselect each area and each custom header.

8.31 Tip: **Use File Page Setup to turn on or off gridlines and headings on printed pages.**

Gridlines and headings for printing are controlled separately from the gridlines and headings displayed on-screen. To add or remove gridlines and headings from printing, choose the File Page Setup command and select or unselect the Row & Column Headings box or the Gridlines box.

8.32 Tip: **Print notes to document your worksheet.**

You can put hidden notes behind cells using the Formula Note command. These notes enable you to document changes, include comments or ideas during worksheet construction, and enhance the worksheet with business information. When you print a worksheet, you will probably want to print the notes in the same area.

To print notes, choose the File Print command. From the print dialog box, select Notes to print only the notes in the print area, or select Both to print the worksheet area and the notes.

When you print with Notes selected, the cell address where the note is located appears above the note. When you print with Both, the note addresses appear only when you have selected Row & Column Headings in the File Page Setup command. This makes sense because the only time you will be able to refer from a note's address to the worksheet is when the worksheet contains row and column headings.

Installing Printers and Fonts

You may have one of many different printers, each with its own unique capabilities. To get the most from your printer and the available fonts, you must install the printer and the fonts correctly.

8.33 Tip: **Use the Control Panel to add or delete printers or fonts in PC Excel.**

Add or delete printers and soft fonts through the Control **P**anel in Windows or PC Excel. If you have already installed Excel, you can add additional printers or fonts by selecting the Application Control menu icon with the mouse or by pressing Alt+space bar. Then choose the R**u**n command. Select the Control **P**anel option and then choose OK.

Choose the **I**nstallation Add **N**ew Printer command or Add Ne**w** Font command. Insert the disk that contains the new printer driver or new fonts into drive A and choose OK. Follow the instructions on-screen to select and add a print driver or font to Excel.

Once you have added a print driver, choose the **S**etup **C**onnections command and select the new printer and the printer port to which the printer is connected. Two printers cannot simultaneously occupy the same printer port. Install extra printers to the None port until you want to reconnect the printers.

Select the default printer, the printer you normally use, by choosing **S**etup **P**rinter and then selecting the default printer. Normally you will not change Printer Timeout settings.

If your printer is a serial printer, choose the **S**etup **C**ommunications **P**ort command and set the communication settings appropriate for the printer you have attached to COM1 or COM2. These settings are listed in the printer manual or are available from your dealer.

Close the Control **P**anel by selecting the Application Control menu icon with the mouse or by pressing Alt+space bar. Then choose **C**lose.

8.34 Trap: **Use the Control Panel to delete unwanted soft fonts from PC Excel or Windows.**

Do not delete soft fonts from the hard disk with DOS commands or with the MS-DOS Executive. Use the Control **P**anel as described in the preceding tip. Choose the **I**nstallation De**l**ete Font command and select the fonts you want deleted.

Deleting fonts from the hard disk using DOS commands or the MS-DOS Executive does not delete internal settings and font lists kept within Windows. Windows and Excel will consider those fonts still available.

If you have already deleted soft fonts without using the Control **P**anel, you may experience difficulty using your fonts, or nonavailable fonts may appear in the Forma**t** **F**ont list. To repair this problem, reinstall Windows if you are using the full version of Windows, or run the program WINSU.EXE to reinstall the Excel-only (run-time) version of Windows.

8.35 Trick: **Check the README files in the WINDOWS directory for information on your printer.**

To get the most out of your individual printer, check the WINDOWS or EXCEL directory for README files that describe your printer. These files contain information about using your printer to its best capabilities. Some example file names include READMEE9.TXT for nine-pin Epson printers, READMEHP.TXT for HP LaserJets, and READMEPS.TXT for PostScript printers.

These files are ASCII or text files that most word processors can read. Windows Write or Windows Notepad, simple word processors that come with Windows, can read and print these files also.

8.36 Tip: **Install the Generic/Text Only printer if your printer driver is not available on the Installation disk.**

If you do not find your printer on the printer disk for Windows or for Excel, check your printer's manual to see whether your printer emulates one available in Windows. If so, change any settings required for the printer to run in emulation and select the printer driver that the printer emulates during installation. Many printers emulate either the Epson FX family or the IBM ProPrinter family.

If you cannot find a printer resembling yours and your printer does not emulate another, select the Generic/Text Only printer. This printer enables you to print worksheets with the default character set for the printer. You will not be able to select different fonts or character styles such as bold or italic from within Excel, and you will not be able to print charts. Contact your dealer, the printer manufacturer, or the Microsoft support hotline for a print driver. New print drivers are being developed all the time. Tip 8.33 describes how to install new print drivers.

8.37 Trick: **Select two print cartridges on HP LaserJets by holding down the Shift or Ctrl keys.**

If you use two cartridges with your HP LaserJet, select them both from the **F**ile Pri**n**ter Setup command by selecting the **S**etup button. From the **C**artridges list box, select your first cartridge. Use a mouse to scroll to the second cartridge and hold down the Shift key as you click on the second cartridge name.

Using the keyboard, select the first cartridge by scrolling to it. Select the second cartridge by holding down the Ctrl key, scrolling to the cartridge, and pressing Ctrl+space bar.

Printing

You have chosen fonts correctly, selected the print range, added page breaks, and defined the page layout. The only thing left to do is to print. These tips show you how to print to a file and help you control the print spooler in Windows so that you can work while multiple documents print.

8.38 Trap: **Calculate the document before printing.**

If your worksheet or chart is set for manual recalculation, you need to calculate before printing, or you may print incorrect results. If the word Calculate appears in the status bar at the bottom of the screen, a recalculation may be necessary. If you set the worksheet for automatic recalculation except tables, the calculation warning may not appear at the bottom of the screen.

To recalculate all worksheets, press F9 or choose the **O**ptions Calculate **N**ow command. To recalculate only the active worksheet, press Shift+F9.

8.39 Trick: **With PC Excel, print to a file for later printing from any computer.**

You can print a text file to disk by setting up a dummy printer port that is a file on disk. This file receives the characters and printer control codes that would have gone to the printer.

Print to a file, for example, when you need to print on a PostScript printer or LaserJet printer, but do not have one readily available. You can print to file and then later move the file to a computer with a laser printer. From this computer, you can use a DOS command to copy the file to the printer. The printout will print just as though it came directly from Excel. Printing a file to disk also enables you to create an ASCII text file that other programs can read.

To create a disk file, use a word processor to add the following line to the WIN.INI file under the [ports] section:

```
OUTPUT.PRN=
```

Substitute any file name for "output" if you want. Save WIN.INI back to the EXCEL or WINDOWS directory as an ASCII text file. (Do not use Excel's text file features to modify WIN.INI.) Restart Windows or run-time Excel to make the new WIN.INI active.

Connect your printer to the OUTPUT.PRN= file just as though the file was a printer port. To do this from Excel, follow these steps:

1. Press Alt+space bar and choose R**u**n.
2. Select the Control **P**anel and choose OK.
3. Choose **S**etup **C**onnections.
4. Select the printer you want from the printer list.
5. Select the OUTPUT.PRN or another .PRN file from the **C**onnection list and choose OK.
6. Close the Control **P**anel by pressing Alt+space bar and then selecting **C**lose.

Now when you print, information will be sent to the .PRN file in the active EXCEL directory instead of to the printer port.

If you want to create a standard ASCII text file for use with a word processor or database, install the Generic/Text Only printer and print the file to a .PRN file.

To print the .PRN file to the printer, return to DOS or use the MS-DOS Executive to copy the file to the parallel port to which your printer is attached. From the MS-DOS Executive, select the OUTPUT.PRN file or the .PRN file you want to print and then choose the **F**ile **C**opy command. Enter the To location as LPT1 or LPT2 and choose OK.

From DOS, use the COPY command. If you are in the directory containing the file, use a syntax such as the following:

```
COPY OUTPUT.PRN LPT1
```

8.40 Tip: **Contact the typesetter before formatting your document for a typesetting machine.**

With Excel, you can format worksheets and charts that can be printed by true typesetting machines such as Linotronic or Compugraphic models. You can take the Excel files directly to a typesetter if the typesetter has a copy of Excel. The typesetter then can print directly to the typesetting machine from Excel.

If your typesetter does not have a copy of Excel, but can work with PostScript files, create a Linotronic, Compugraphic, or Apple LaserWriter "print ready" file on disk. (Some typesetting machines will read PostScript file created for Apple LaserWriter.) Your typesetting company should then be able to copy this file to the typesetting machine. If you create such a file, ensure that you have thoroughly previewed the file before "printing" it to disk. Also be sure that the last time you printed or previewed the file you asked Excel for a single copy—the PostScript file will record the number of copies you last requested. If you printed more than one copy to disk, you may end up with charges for multiple typesetting jobs.

Before formatting worksheets or charts for the typesetter, call them to find out the type of machine they use (Linotronic, Compugraphic, or Apple LaserWriter compatible), the model number, the model's recommended resolution (dots per inch), and the available fonts. Use these settings in the **F**ile P**r**inter Setup command to select the correct Postscript printer and graphics resolution.

Use the recommended fonts when you format a worksheet or chart. In the same way that you can add fonts to laser printers, typesetting machines come with a base set of fonts. The individual typesetters add other fonts. If you use fonts that the typesetter does not have available, you will be charged for converting the worksheet or chart to available fonts. Also, the fonts the typesetters use may not be fonts that give the appearance and impact you want.

If a local typesetter cannot assist you, check with a major copying company, such as AlphaGraphics. They can send your file via modem (telephone line) to a national typesetter, and you can have your finished results by express mail the next day.

8.41 Trick: With PC Excel, manage the print spooler for better printer control.

In Windows, the Spooler program stores and controls jobs sent to the printer, enabling Windows applications to continue working independent of the printer. If you have sent multiple print jobs to the spooler, you can control those jobs and the spooler operation.

If you are in Excel and have sent jobs to the printer, press Alt+Tab until you see the name Spooler appear in its own window or as text at the lower left of the screen.

With spooler active and print jobs in the print queue waiting to print, you see a Spooler window similar to figure 8.8. In this figure, you can see which files have been sent to the HP LaserJet and which have been sent to the Apple

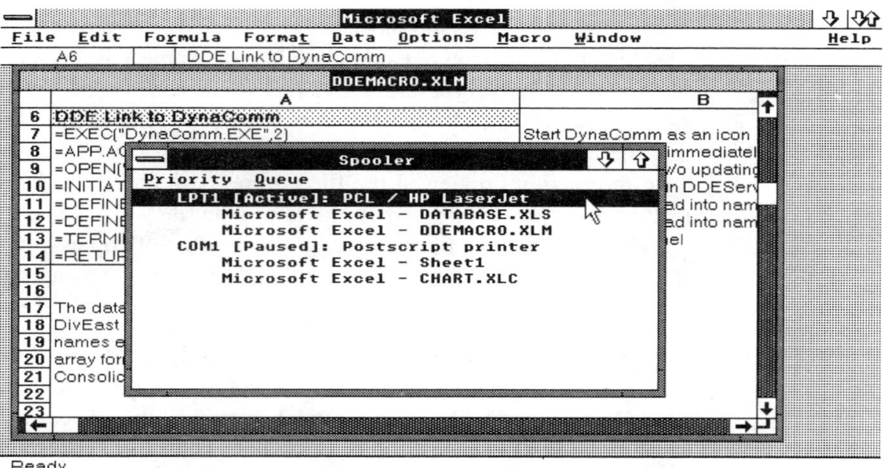

Fig. 8.8. *A Spooler window.*

LaserWriter (PostScript). Notice that you can pause a printer so that the spooler holds its print jobs until told to continue printing.

Use the following commands to control printing from the spooler.

Action	*Option*
To make Excel faster	Choose **P**riority **L**ow
To make the printer faster	Choose **P**riority **H**igh
To pause a printer temporarily	Select the printer and then choose **Q**ueue **P**ause
To restart a printer	Select the printer and then choose **Q**ueue **R**esume
To terminate a job	Select the job, choose **Q**ueue **T**erminate, and then choose OK

If you want to close the spooler, you can wait until all print jobs are finished; then the spooler will close by itself. If you want to close the spooler and stop jobs waiting to be printed, press Alt+space bar and choose **C**lose. You are asked whether you want to terminate jobs currently waiting to print. Choose OK.

8.42 Trick: **With PC Excel, load the print spooler and then print while the printer is available.**

If you have Windows, you can save time if you load the spooler with print jobs and then print them all when you are not working on the computer or printer. If you have Windows and are in Excel, press Alt+space bar until the MS-DOS Executive appears. Change to the WINDOWS or EXCEL directory and double-click on SPOOLER.EXE, or select SPOOLER.EXE and then press Enter. This action starts the spooler even though it has nothing to print.

Once you start the spooler, pause the printers that you will be printing to by selecting the printers and then choosing the **Q**ueue **P**ause command. Now return to Excel by pressing Alt+Tab. Print files from Excel to the printer you paused. When you are ready to print all the files stored by the spooler, press Alt+Tab to return to the spooler, select the paused printer, and then choose **Q**ueue **R**esume. You now can do something else, and the spooler will manage the printing.

8.43 Tip: **With PC Excel, leave disk space and memory available to print with the print spooler.**

The print spooler uses the hard disk to store files waiting to be printed. If there is not enough room on the hard disk, you get an error when you try to print. To fix this problem, delete files from disk or print without the spooler.

The spooler also requires memory to print. If there isn't enough memory for the print spooler to work correctly, you receive an out of memory error. Use one of these solutions to fix this problem:

1. Close unneeded applications or worksheets to make more memory available.
2. Restart Windows without TSR (terminate-and-stay-resident) applications you may be using.
3. Use a word processor to change the WIN.INI file to Spooler=NO. Save the WIN.INI file as a text file and then restart run-time Excel or Windows. This action turns off the spooler. You won't be able to print and work simultaneously, but you can work under low memory or low disk space conditions.

Use any or all the techniques described in Chapter 13 to gain additional memory.

8.44 Trap: **Printing with copier labels in a laser printer can gum up the works.**

Gum-backed copier labels and gum-backed laser printer labels are different. Using copier labels in a laser printer may cause the labels to roll up into sticky wads that jam up your printer. Special laser printer labels are available. If they are not immediately available, ask your office supplier to order them.

8.45 Tip: **To print selected pages, watch the page number in print preview.**

When previewing what is about to print, check the title bar. Excel displays the page number of what you are previewing. By noting page numbers in the title bar, you can determine which pages you want to print. Return to the **F**ile **P**rint dialog box and enter the selected pages in the **F**rom and **T**o text boxes.

9

Creating and Using Databases

An Excel database makes it easy for you to store, sort, find, extract, and analyze data. Excel's database capabilities range from quick and easy to custom and complex. You can use the data form that Excel automatically creates for you and have a database up and running in 15 minutes or less. Or you can create a custom database using macros and dialog boxes for data entry and then generate complete statistics about the database contents.

In Excel databases, you can use a number of shortcuts to speed your work. If you are finding or extracting information, you'll want to know how to create criteria that can answer any question you want to ask of the database. Excel also can help you pull meaningful management information from a database. You can produce accounting totals by job cost code or produce a statistical analysis of sales results. All these different capabilities are discussed in this chapter.

Sorting Data

Even if you don't want to learn how to use Excel's database capabilities, you'll want to learn how to sort data. Sorting is useful to reorder any type of list or report. You can sort on as many rows or columns as you need—there is no limit.

9.1 Tip: **Use the mouse or arrow keys to enter the sorting column.**

When you choose the **D**ata **S**ort command, the dialog box shown in figure 9.1 appears. To enter the column you want to sort, first select the text box of the key you want to sort on. Next click your mouse in the column or press the arrow keys to move the active cell to the column you want to sort. Finally, choose the OK button.

The active cell in figure 9.1 is cell E13. The address you select does not have to be within the database. If the dialog box hides cells you need to see, move the box. (Drag the title bar to move the Sort window.)

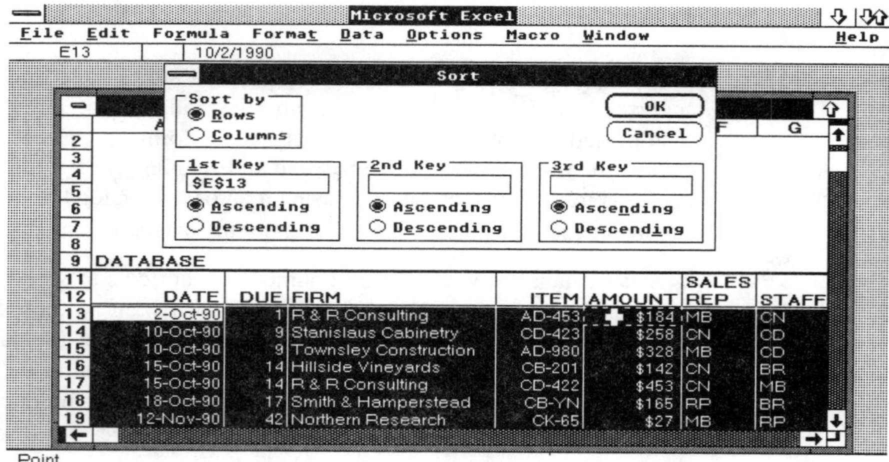

Fig. 9.1. The Sort window.

If you are entering more than one key, be sure that you reposition the cursor to the next key text box before selecting the address of the next column you want to sort.

9.2 Tip: **Use range names to enter the column on which you want to sort.**

You can make sorting easier by entering a range name in the **1**st Key, **2**nd Key, or **3**rd Key text box. To name the columns so that you can use range names, select the entire database. If you have already used **D**ata Set Data**b**ase to set the database name, an easy way to select the database is to press the Goto key, F5 (PC) or Command+G (Macintosh), and then double-click on the name Database. This action selects the data and field names. Choose the

Formula Create Names command, select Top, and choose OK. This command sequence assigns the field names to each column in the database.

Reselect the range you want to sort, but do not include the field names. After choosing the Data Sort command, you can enter the key (column) you want to sort on by typing the field name of that column.

9.3 Trap: **Sort the full width of your database.**

Before choosing the Data Sort command, make sure that you have selected the full width of the database. In some cases, it may appear that you have selected all the database, but there is more data off-screen. Make sure that you scroll far enough to the right to verify that you have included the full width of the database.

If you sort without including the full width of the database, the left side of the database will be in a different order than the right side. If you immediately recognize the problem, you can select Edit Undo Sort, or you can close and reopen the worksheet. However, if you continue working, you cannot undo the change. And if you save the missorted database over the original, you destroy your original database by replacing it with scrambled data.

You do not have to select all rows within a database to sort. However, you must select the full width of the rows that you do select.

9.4 Tip: **Name a sort range within your database.**

Naming a sort range can save you time. Name the sort range by selecting all data below the field names. Do not include the field names. Choose the Formula Define Name command, enter a name for the sort range, such as Sort_Sales, and then choose OK.

Once you name the sort range, you can select the range by pressing the Goto key, F5 (PC) or Command+G (Macintosh), and double-clicking on the sort name. Then choose Data Sort.

9.5 Trick: **Return a sorted database to its original entry order with an index field.**

You can return a database to its original order by including an additional column that contains index numbers or dates. Figure 9.2 shows a database where column G, with the field name INDEX, contains a list of sequential index numbers. After sorting the data, you can return the database to the original order by sorting on the column that contains the index numbers.

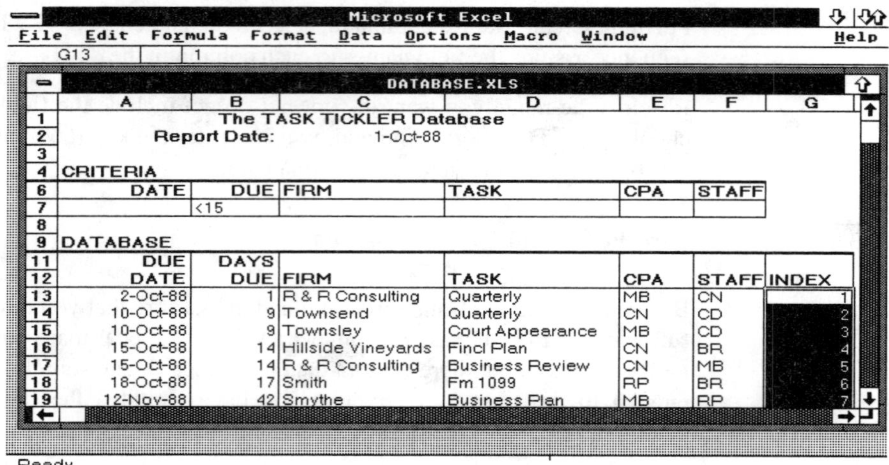

Fig. 9.2. *A database with an index field.*

To enter your own column of index numbers, insert or add a column to the database. Reset the database range to include the column by using the **D**ata Set Data**b**ase command. Enter a sequential series of numbers down the column by typing **1** in the first cell at the top of the column. Now select the cell that contains the 1 and all cells down that column that you want to contain a sequential series. (Do not select the entire column.)

Choose the **D**ata Se**r**ies command. Select the options **C**olumns and **L**inear, and set the **S**tep Value equal to 1. You do not need a St**o**p Value because the series will stop at the last selected cell. Choose OK. A series of numbers starting at 1 and increasing by 1 fills the column. You can sort on this column whenever you want to return the database to the original order. As you add more records (rows), you will have to enter an index number for each record.

Another form of indexing uses the date and time when a record was entered. In PC Excel, press Ctrl+; (semicolon) to enter the date and Ctrl+: (colon) to enter the time. You can enter the date and time together in a cell by pressing Ctrl+;. Then press Ctrl+: and then Enter. In Macintosh Excel, press control+; (semicolon) to enter the date and Command+; (semicolon) to enter the time. Sorting on a column containing the entry date and time will return the database to the order in which data was entered.

9.6 Trick: Sort multiple times to sort with an unlimited number of keys.

Although Excel shows three sort keys in the Sort dialog box, you can sort on an unlimited number of fields. To sort on more than three fields, you sort multiple times beginning with the lowest key first, then moving to higher keys, and finally ending with the first, second, and third keys.

For example, if you want to sort columns A through F so that A is the first key, B the second, and so on, you need a sort like the following:

Key	1	2	3	4	5	6
Column	A	B	C	D	E	F

Using Excel's three sort keys, start with and sort the lowest three levels first:

Key	1	2	3
Column	D	E	F

To get the final results, sort again with these keys:

Key	1	2	3
Column	A	B	C

9.7 Trick: **Count related records by sorting and selecting them.**

To count a number of records manually, you can use a counter that few Excel users even notice. As you select a range, Excel displays to the left of the formula bar the number of rows and columns in your selection. If you select cells in the database, the display will show how many rows are selected.

To count the records, first group the records of interest together by sorting the database or listing the field(s) in which you are interested. Next, select a cell in the first record you want to count and then continue the selection down the column so that the selection includes all the records you want to count. As you select records, watch to the left of the formula bar. A display such as the following means that there are 25 rows (records) and 2 columns selected:

```
25RX2C
```

When you release the mouse button, the display disappears. To bring the display back, hold down the Shift key and click on the bottom cell in the selection.

Using the Automatic Data Form

Excel contains a powerful feature—the data form—that enables you to begin using a database immediately. With this form, you can add new records to a database, delete existing records, and edit data. The data form is also a quick way to perform simple searches. Figure 9.3 shows Excel's automatic data form over the database with which the form is used.

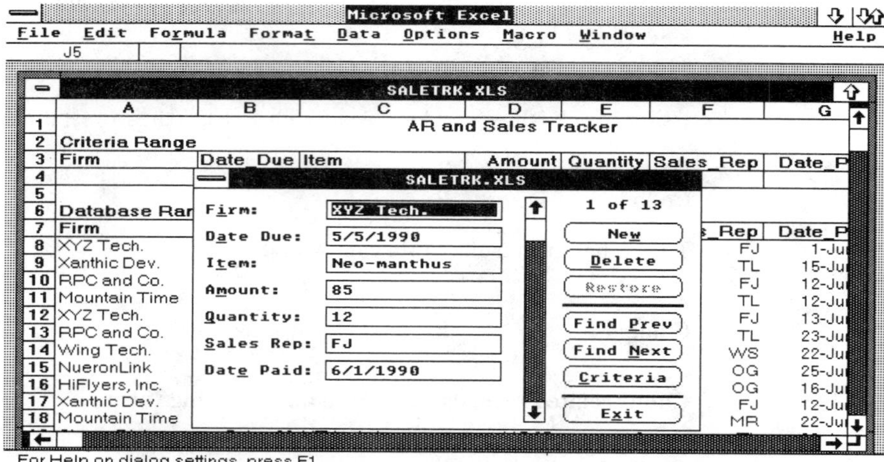

Fig. 9.3. *An automatic data form.*

9.8 Tip: **Follow four steps to set up an automatic data form.**

You can create a data form to enter, edit, and find data by following these steps:

1. Enter unique text field names in a row above each column that will contain data. Do not begin field names with numbers or symbols.

2. Enter one row of data below the field names. Format the data in the row as you want it to appear in the database.

3. Define the location of the database by selecting the field names and the single row of data. Choose the **D**ata Set Data**b**ase command. This command applies the range name Database to the range you selected.

4. Choose the **D**ata Fo**r**m command to display the automatic data form. Select the appropriate buttons to enter new data or to enter criteria for a question.

9.9 Tip: **Leave space after the last row of a database if you want to add records with the database form.**

The data form will not insert new rows or push down existing data when you add new records. Instead, when you use the form, Excel adds new records in the blank cells at the bottom of the database. If there is no blank space, you are warned that you cannot enter additional records.

If your database runs out of blank area below the database, you can make additional room for more records in two ways. The first method pushes down existing cells directly below the database to make more room. To do this, select a range below the database as wide as the database, with as many rows as you will need to add. Choose the **E**dit **I**nsert command and then select the Shift Cells **D**own option. This command sequence pushes down only the cells directly below the database.

The second method inserts additional rows below the database. These rows cross the entire worksheet and "push down" all rows below the database. To do this, select the first row below the database and continue to select down as many rows as you need for blanks. Choose the **E**dit **I**nsert command, and the rows are inserted immediately. Be careful when using this method. Inserting rows can disturb distant parts of the worksheet. You may be inserting a row through a data-entry area, a lookup table, or a list.

9.10 Trap: **Formula results do not appear in the data form until the data is entered.**

When you first enter data in the data form, calculated results will not appear in their fields. These results calculate after you add the new record by pressing Enter or moving to another record. When you return to the record you just added, the calculated results will be displayed. If calculation is set to manual, results will not appear. You must return to the worksheet and recalculate to see calculated fields in this case.

9.11 Trap: **Limit field names to use the automatic form.**

The automatically generated data form has a limit of approximately 15 fields on the PC and 10 on the Macintosh. Automatic forms display fields vertically in the form. If you need to display more fields with a data form or arrange the fields as you like, create a custom data form as described in the next tip.

9.12 Tip: Create a custom data form.

You can create custom data forms that include titles, instructions, examples, allowable choices, and custom layouts without using macros. You can control the layout and appearance of Excel's automatic data form by entering layout information in the worksheet and then naming the area containing the information Data_Form.

Rather than manually calculating the X and Y (horizontal and vertical) position for each item in the form, you can use the dialog editor that comes with Excel to "draw" data forms. You then can use the **C**opy command to copy the form from the dialog editor and then paste the numeric results onto your database worksheet. The dialog editor is described in Chapter 12.

Figure 9.4 shows a custom data form that contains a title, field labels, and rearranged fields. Figure 9.5 shows the information necessary to create that form.

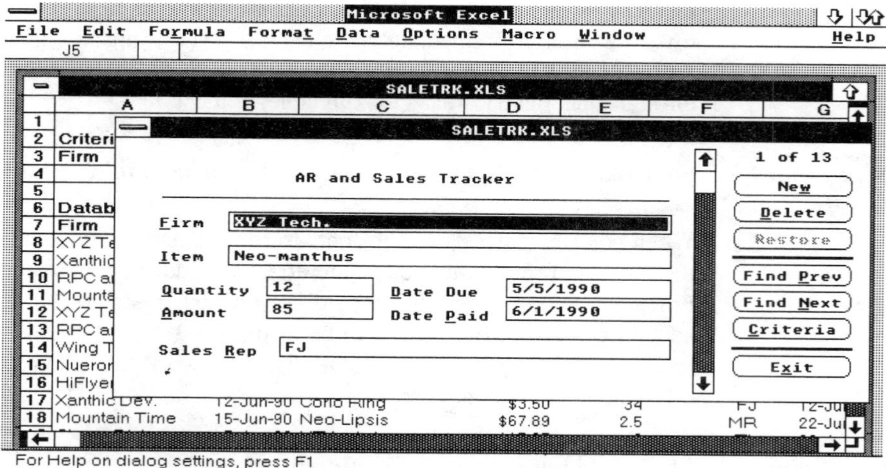

Fig. 9.4. A custom data form.

Note that custom data forms cannot contain check boxes, option buttons, or scrolling list boxes.

In figure 9.5, the labels in row 4 are for description; these labels are not part of the data form. The range J5:P21 contains the data form information and has been named Data_Form with the Fo**r**mula **D**efine Name command. The first row of numbers inside the range defines the outline of the data form.

Microsoft Excel - SALETRK.XLS

File Edit Formula Format Data Options Macro Window Help

O7

	I	J	K	L	M	N	O	P
3				Custom Data Form				
4		Type	X	Y	DX	DY	Text	Init_Result
5	Outline=>		69	11	420	232		
6		5	130	27			AR and Sales Tracker	
7		5	26	42	800			
8		5	33	69			&Firm	
9		6	82	66	322			Firm
10		5	33	99			&Item	
11		6	82	97	322			Item
12		5	35	129			&Quantity	
13		6	110	124	78			Quantity
14		5	201	130			&Date Due	
15		6	284	124	120			Date_Due
16		5	34	151			&Amount	
17		6	110	145	78			Amount
18		5	200	152			Date &Paid	
19		6	284	145	120			Date_Paid
20		5	32	183			Sales &Rep	
21		6	120	178	285			Sales_Rep
22								

Ready

Fig. 9.5. The information used to create the data form in fig. 9.4.

The numbers in the Type column describe what information is in each row and are either 5 (a label) or 6 (a field name). Other type numbers are not used.

The X and Y columns contain the X (horizontal) and Y (vertical) positions of the upper left corner for each piece of text or entry text box in the form. These numbers are the dot-position from the top left corner of the screen and are calculated automatically if you use the dialog editor. The DX and DY columns contain the width and height of each label box and entry text box. In cell O7 an underline used under the form's title extends outside the form area.

The Text column contains the text used as labels in the form. If you want to be able to select a label by pressing a key, indicate the letter to be underlined and selected by preceding it with an ampersand (&).

The last column, Init_Result, contains the exact field headings of the database. Information will be sent to these fields from the data form. These field names must be in a row with a type of 6.

Once you have created a form, either with the dialog editor or manually, assign the range enclosing the information the name Data_Form. Finally, choose the **D**ata **Form** command to check the appearance of your form.

Creating custom data forms by manually entering the numbers is difficult work. Learn to use the dialog editor described in Chapter 12 to be more productive.

9.13 Tip: **Cross-check a custom data form if it doesn't work.**

If your custom data form doesn't work, check these common problems:

1. Be sure that the range containing the form information is named Data_Form.
2. Check for blank rows. The top row of the data form information range can be blank, but it normally contains data describing the size of the form. No other rows can be blank in the Data_Form range.
3. Names in the Init_Result column define the database field where entered information will be put. Make sure that these names match the database field names exactly.
4. Make sure that the database is set as a normal database with unique text field names and defined with the **D**ata Set Data**b**ase command.
5. You can use two number types, 5 (a label in the form) and 6 (a field name). You cannot use other types of numbers.

Designing Databases

Your database will be easier to use and will cause fewer problems as your worksheet grows if you abide by some of the design considerations described in this section. In addition, Excel has features that make databases easier to view and use.

9.14 Tip: **Check for common accidents if you have problems with your database.**

You can resolve most database problems by checking these frequent problem causes:

Database or criteria range incorrectly set: Check that the database and criteria range names are correct by pressing the Goto key, F5 (PC) or Command+G (Macintosh), selecting Database or Criteria, and choosing OK. This selects the database or criteria range. Ensure that the ranges include the field names in the top row. Ensure that the criteria range includes one row below the field names.

Space character in the criteria range: Pressing the space bar to clear a cell in the criteria range appears to clear the cell, but actually enters a space character in that cell. This space causes the next **D**ata **F**ind to look for a space character below that field name. Because there probably isn't one, the search that should work, does not. Find cells that contain a blank by selecting the criteria range. Choose the Formula Find command and type a space in the Find What text box. Choose OK. If there is a space character in a cell, that cell will be selected. Remove the space character by using Edit Clear to clear the cell.

Calculated criteria below a field name: You must enter criteria that involve functions or formulas below a blank or nonexistent field name in the criteria range. Do not enter a calculated criteria below a field name that exists in the database.

Incorrectly selected extract range: You must select the extract field names before you choose the Data Extract command. No command is used to set the extract range as is done with the database or criteria range. Extract field names are a third set of field names, separate from the database and criteria field names.

9.15 Tip: **Make sure that field names in the database, criteria, and extract ranges match.**

Field names in the database, criteria, and extract ranges must be spelled exactly the same. The easiest way to ensure that field names match is to enter the field names at the top of the database; then use Edit Copy and Edit Paste to duplicate the field names into the criteria and extract ranges.

9.16 Trick: **Add text notes to your database to provide further explanation; find notes by content with the Formula Find command.**

In some databases, you'll want to add lengthy descriptions or textual notes. These notes can add valuable detail to databases containing such things as project information, accounting data, or survey results. Excel has the capability to find notes in your database according to their content.

Use the Formula Note command to add notes to any active cell in the database. Figure 9.6 shows a note that has been attached to a firm's name in an expense register database. You may even want to create a specific field in each record that will contain notes.

To find notes that contain specific information, select the database range and then choose Formula Find. In the Find What text box, type a word that is in the note for which you are looking. Select the Notes and Part options. If the database is large, do not select the whole database. Instead, select the column containing notes and select the Columns option. Choose OK. All cells containing the desired word in a note are selected. Move to the next appropriate note by pressing F7. Move to the previous note by pressing

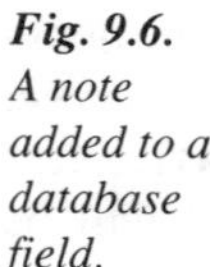

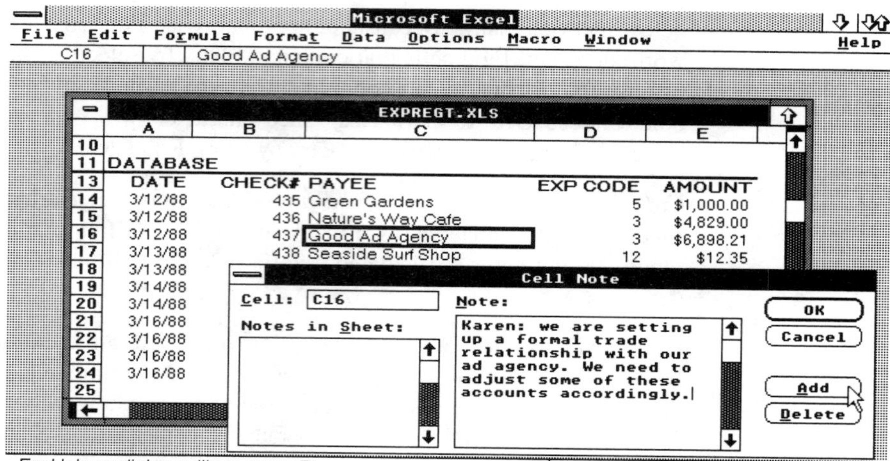

Fig. 9.6. A note added to a database field.

Shift+F7. Read the current note through the information window by pressing Ctrl+F2 (PC) or Command+Shift+F2 (Macintosh). Read and edit the current note through the Cell Note dialog box by pressing Shift+F2.

9.17 Tip: **Change between databases quickly using the Goto key.**

Excel can have only one active database at a time, but with a few keystrokes, you can switch between databases. To do so, use the Fo**r**mula **D**efine Name command to name each database and criteria range with a unique name.

To select a new database, press the Goto key, F5 (PC) or Command+G (Macintosh), and select the name of the database you want. Then choose the **D**ata Set Data**b**ase command. Repeat the process for the matching criteria range. You can assign this entire process to a single keystroke if you create the range names and then record the switching process with the macro recorder.

9.18 Tip: **Use Q+E with Excel for large disk-based databases.**

Excel databases reside in the worksheet and therefore can contain only as much information as will reside in memory. If you want to create a large database that can stay on disk, but from which Excel can extract information as needed, consider using Q+E. Q+E enables you to use Excel to create dBASE files on disk, edit records, add records, delete records, and extract data. The dBASE database stays on disk; Excel brings into the worksheet only the data that matches criteria you specify. Q+E also can create Dynamic Data Exchange (DDE) links to dBASE databases on disk. DDE links enable

Windows or Presentation Manager applications to exchange information when the information changes. In this case, if the dBASE file changes, the linked area in the Excel worksheet also changes. Q+E is sold by Microsoft and by Pioneer Software.

Entering Data in a Worksheet Database

You can use one of a number of shortcut keys for speeding your work with Excel databases. In addition to the information described in this section, review how to use the automatic data form (described previously in this chapter) as an "instant" method of entering data.

9.19 Tip: **Always insert new database rows through the middle of the database.**

Insert new database rows or columns through the middle of the database to preserve the database range. If you insert a row at the bottom or insert a column at either edge of the database, the row or column will not be included in the Database range name. (The data form automatically extends the Database range name to include records that it adds.)

If you do not like the order after inserting records in the middle, use the **D**ata **S**ort command to rearrange the records. If you prefer to add records at the end of a database or add columns on the edges, make sure that you redefine the database location with the **D**ata Set Data**b**ase command.

9.20 Trick: **Use shortcut keys to enter or delete rows quickly.**

Enter or delete rows quickly in a database by selecting the rows you want to insert or delete and then pressing Ctrl++ (plus) to insert or Ctrl+– (minus) to delete. Ctrl++ is the same as **E**dit **I**nsert, and Ctrl+– is the same as **E**dit **D**elete. On the Macintosh, use control++ or control+–.

9.21 Tip: **Increase the speed of data entry by turning off automatic recalculation.**

When you enter new data, Excel recalculates. In large or complicated worksheets, the time required to recalculate may slow your data entry. You can do two things to reduce this recalculation time.

Excel will stop its nontable recalculations if you continue to work. Excel detects that you are entering data or choosing a command and puts the recalculation on hold. If you don't do anything for a few seconds, the recalculation continues until it is finished.

To turn off recalculation completely, choose the **O**ptions **C**alculation command and then select **M**anual. To recalculate the active worksheet, you must press Shift+F9. To recalculate all worksheets in memory, press F9, press Ctrl+= (PC) or control+= (Macintosh), or choose **O**ptions Calculate **N**ow.

9.22 Tip: **See and change the corners of the database range quickly.**

To see the corners of the database range, press the Goto key, F5 (PC) or Command+G (Macintosh), and select Database. Press Ctrl+. to move the active cell between corners of the database. You can press Shift+arrow key to expand or contract the selection at the corner diagonally opposite the active cell.

9.23 Trick: **If necessary, make formula references in the database absolute references.**

Any formula reference in a database record that refers to a single cell outside the database must be an absolute reference. For example, in figure 9.7 the formulas below the DUE field name calculate the number of days due by subtracting the date in the DATE field from the Report Date in cell C2.

Cell C2 is outside the database. This location can cause problems if you sort the database or add data. If you aren't careful, references to cells outside the database will adjust when the database moves. To keep the reference C2 from

Microsoft Excel

File Edit Formula Format Data Options Macro Window Help

B13 =A13-$C$2

DATABASE.XLS

	A	B	C	D	E	F
1		The TASK TICKLER Database				
2	Report Date:		1-Oct-88			
3						
4	CRITERIA					
6	DATE	DUE	FIRM	TASK	CPA	STAFF
7		<15				
8						
9	DATABASE					
11	DUE	DAYS				
12	DATE	DUE	FIRM	TASK	CPA	STAFF
13	2-Oct-88	1	R & R Consulting	Quarterly	MB	CN
14	10-Oct-88	9	Townsend	Quarterly	CN	CD
15	10-Oct-88	9	Townsley	Court Appearance	MB	CD
16	15-Oct-88	14	Hillside Vineyards	Fincl Plan	CN	BR
17	15-Oct-88	14	R & R Consulting	Business Review	CN	MB
18	18-Oct-88	17	Smith	Fm 1099	RP	BR
19	12-Nov-88	42	Smythe	Business Plan	MB	RP

Ready

Fig. 9.7. An absolute reference in a database formula.

adjusting, make it an absolute reference—edit the reference to include a $ sign before the C and before the 2. To change a reference to absolute quickly, click on the C2 in the formula bar and press F4 (PC) or Command+T (Macintosh).

9.24 Tip: **Use shortcut keys for entering data in the database.**

Use the following shortcut keys in the data form and in a worksheet database to speed data entry.

Action	*PC Key*	*Macintosh Key*
Enter the computer's time	Ctrl+;	Command+;
Enter the computer's date	Ctrl+:	control+;
Copy the formula above without adjusting cell references	Ctrl+'	control+'
Copy the value from the cell above	Ctrl+"	control+"

Finding Data

The purpose of a database is to give you ready access to information. In addition to Excel's automatic data form, you can ask complex questions to find specific information. This section describes how to ask questions to find almost any type of information.

9.25 Tip: **Read Chapter 4 to learn how to use functions to analyze your database.**

Chapter 4 describes how to use worksheet functions. This chapter also describes the use of range names, array math, and data tables. You can apply all these capabilities to analyze the contents of your database.

9.26 Trick: **Use the Formula Find command to find data quickly without using a criteria range.**

To find information quickly without using the criteria range, choose the Formula **F**ind command, enter what you are looking for in the Find **W**hat text box, and select whether the information is in a formula, value, or note. Choose OK. Press F7 to find the next occurrence or press Shift+F7 to find the previous record.

9.27 Trick: **Use the Formula Replace command for easy editing.**

If you have a consistent change to be made throughout the database, use the Formula Replace command. Select the database and then choose Formula Replace. Type the text or value you want replaced, such as **Generic Quality Corp.**, into the Replace text box and type the replacement, such as **Generic Quality Co.**, into the **W**ith text box. Use the **F**ind Next and **R**eplace buttons to check changes before you make them, or use the Replace **A**ll button to replace all occurrences in the database. Figure 9.8 shows the Replace window with the text being searched for and text being replaced.

Fig. 9.8. Searching and replacing text in your database.

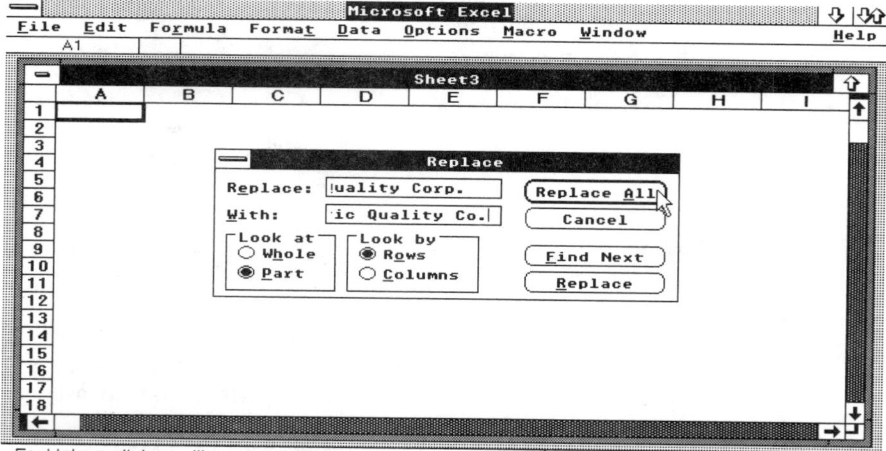

9.28 Tip: **Move the active cell so that it is outside the database range before choosing Data Find or pressing F7.**

When Excel searches a database using **D**ata **F**ind and the active cell is in the database, Excel begins at the row of the active cell and searches downward. This method saves time when you are finding multiple records. Just keep the active cell on the last record found and press F7 or choose **D**ata **F**ind again. If you are not aware of how Excel searches, you may miss data.

To ensure that Excel begins its search with the first record, move the active cell so that it is outside the database range before choosing **D**ata **F**ind or pressing F7.

9.29 Trick: **Use the asterisk (*) wild card anywhere in a text query.**

The asterisk (*) wild card used in a text criteria finds any group of characters at the same location in the text for which you are searching. Unlike the restricted use of the asterisk (*) wild card in DOS, you can use the asterisk (*) wild card anywhere within Excel criteria. For example, if you want to find a large dollhouse of any color in your toy inventory, you can enter the following criteria below the Description field name:

Large * Dollhouse

This criteria finds the following records:

Large Red Dollhouse
Large Blue Dollhouse
Large Yellow Dollhouse

9.30 Tip: **Use a formula to find exact text matches.**

When you type text into a criteria range, Excel assumes that you want to find data that begins with those characters, as though your text criteria were followed by an asterisk (*) wild card. For example, typing **Smith** below the Last_Name field will find these records:

Smith
Smithington
Smithers

If you want to find exactly the word Smith, enter the criteria as a text formula:

=C13="Smith"

Because this is a calculated criteria, you must enter the criteria below a dummy or blank field name. Calculated criteria will not work when entered below a criteria field name that exists in the database. This subject is described in more detail elsewhere in this section.

9.31 Trick: **Search for text entries within a range of characters.**

You can search for a range of characters just as you search for a range of numbers. This capability can be convenient if you want to select a partial list of names.

In figure 9.9 the criteria >L searches below the CPA field for all initials that begin with M or following. As the next tip describes, you can also search for inclusive ranges of text—text that starts with a letter between two letters.

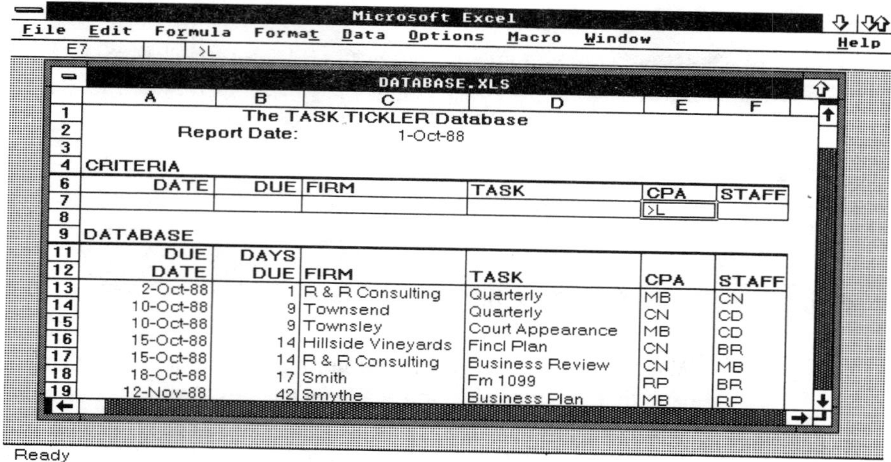

Fig. 9.9. Searching for a range of characters.

9.32 Tip: **Insert multiple field names in the criteria to ask AND questions.**

If you want to find information that involves an AND question, add a second field name that is the same as the first. For example, in figure 9.10, the criteria range contains two DUE field names. To find all records where the number of days until due is between 10 and 20, enter two criteria that create the question:

Find records where
DUE >10
AND
DUE <20

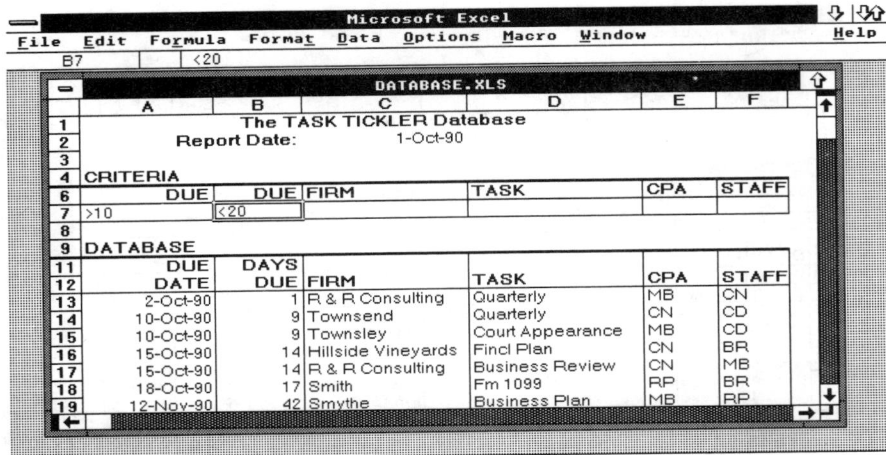

Fig. 9.10. Asking AND questions.

9.33 Tip: **Insert additional criteria rows to ask OR questions.**

If you want to find information that involves an OR question, add an extra row to the criteria range and enter the second half of the OR question in the second row of the criteria range. In figure 9.11, the criteria creates the question:

Find records where
CPA is MB
OR
CPA is CN

9.34 Tip: **Enter calculated criteria below a dummy field name.**

If your criteria involves worksheet functions or any calculation that produces a TRUE or FALSE result, you are using a calculated criteria. You must enter calculated criteria in the criteria range below a heading that *does not exist in the database*. This means that you will have to add either a blank name (no name) or a dummy field name above calculated criteria. Calculated criteria entered below a real field name will not work correctly. Be sure that you expand the criteria range to include any dummy field names you add.

A calculated criteria is used to compare a value inside the database with a value outside the database—for example, the following, where B35 is the top cell in the AMOUNTS column:

=B35$C$12

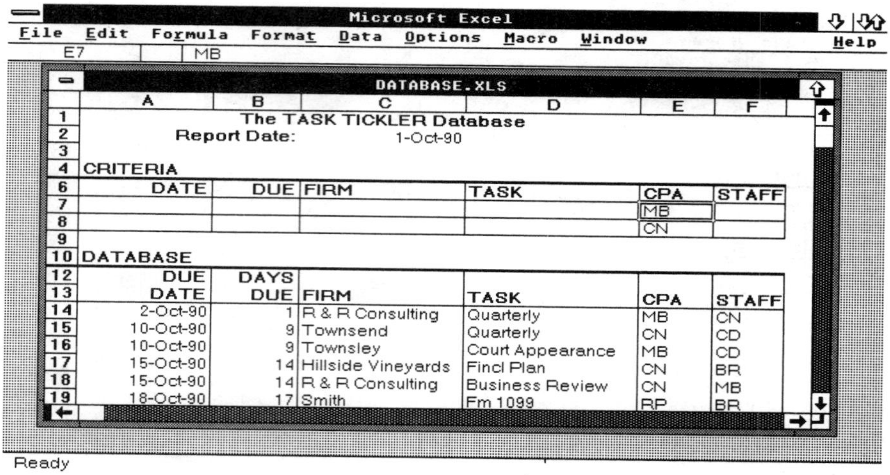

Fig. 9.11. *Asking OR questions.*

Microsoft Excel

File Edit Formula Format Data Options Macro Window Help

E7 MB

DATABASE.XLS

	A	B	C	D	E	F
1		The TASK TICKLER Database				
2	Report Date:		1-Oct-90			
3						
4	CRITERIA					
6	DATE	DUE	FIRM	TASK	CPA	STAFF
7					MB	
8					CN	
9						
10	DATABASE					
12	DUE	DAYS				
13	DATE	DUE	FIRM	TASK	CPA	STAFF
14	2-Oct-90	1	R & R Consulting	Quarterly	MB	CN
15	10-Oct-90	9	Townsend	Quarterly	CN	CD
16	10-Oct-90	9	Townsley	Court Appearance	MB	CD
17	15-Oct-90	14	Hillside Vineyards	Fincl Plan	CN	BR
18	15-Oct-90	14	R & R Consulting	Business Review	CN	MB
19	18-Oct-90	17	Smith	Fm 1099	RP	BR

Ready

C12 is outside the database and contains the maximum amount for any item spent. This criteria will find records where the amount in the database exceeds the maximum amount entered in C12. An absolute reference, $C$12, is used for C12 because it is outside the database.

You could enter the calculated criteria, in this case =B35$C$12, in the criteria range below any field name that does not exist in the database. Additional examples of calculated criteria are provided in the following tips.

9.35 Tip: Use AND criteria for numeric ranges and OR criteria for text.

The English language defines the terms AND and OR differently than they are defined in computer queries. Because of this difference, users often type incorrect queries when they need to find records within a range of numbers or when they need to find multiple persons or text items.

In computer queries, the AND operator means that the first condition AND the second condition must be true at the same time. The OR operator means that either one condition OR the other condition can be true for a record to be found.

If you want to find a numeric or date range, use an AND criteria. For example, in figure 9.12 the AND condition is used because you want due dates that are *both* greater than 9 AND less than 20. Because this is a calculated criterion, it is entered below a blank field heading.

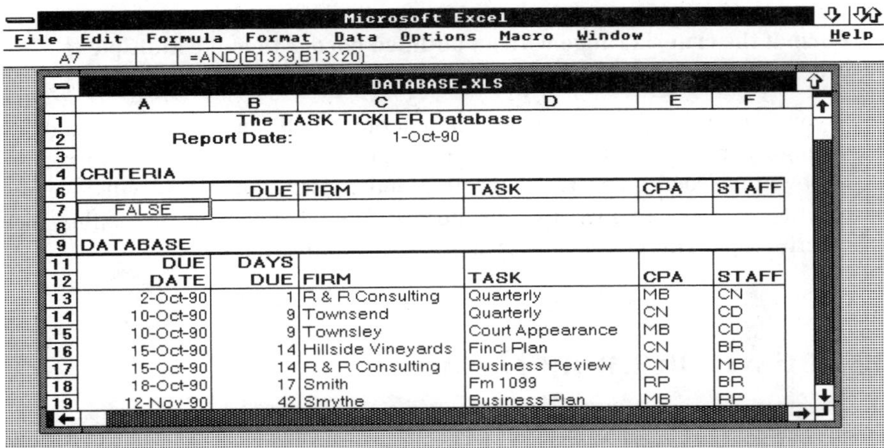

Microsoft Excel

File Edit Formula Format Data Options Macro Window Help

A7 =AND(B13>9,B13<20)

DATABASE.XLS

	A	B	C	D	E	F
1		The TASK TICKLER Database				
2		Report Date:	1-Oct-90			
3						
4	CRITERIA					
6		DUE	FIRM	TASK	CPA	STAFF
7	FALSE					
8						
9	DATABASE					
11	DUE	DAYS				
12	DATE	DUE	FIRM	TASK	CPA	STAFF
13	2-Oct-90	1	R & R Consulting	Quarterly	MB	CN
14	10-Oct-90	9	Townsend	Quarterly	CN	CD
15	10-Oct-90	9	Townsley	Court Appearance	MB	CD
16	15-Oct-90	14	Hillside Vineyards	Fincl Plan	CN	BR
17	15-Oct-90	14	R & R Consulting	Business Review	CN	MB
18	18-Oct-90	17	Smith	Fm 1099	RP	BR
19	12-Nov-90	42	Smythe	Business Plan	MB	RP

Ready

Fig. 9.12. Using the AND condition.

Microsoft Excel

File Edit Formula Format Data Options Macro Window Help

A7 =OR(E13="MB",E13="RP")

DATABASE.XLS

	A	B	C	D	E	F
1		The TASK TICKLER Database				
2		Report Date:	1-Oct-90			
3						
4	CRITERIA					
6		DUE	FIRM	TASK	CPA	STAFF
7	TRUE					
8						
9	DATABASE					
11	DUE	DAYS				
12	DATE	DUE	FIRM	TASK	CPA	STAFF
13	2-Oct-90	1	R & R Consulting	Quarterly	MB	CN
14	10-Oct-90	9	Townsend	Quarterly	CN	CD
15	10-Oct-90	9	Townsley	Court Appearance	MB	CD
16	15-Oct-90	14	Hillside Vineyards	Fincl Plan	CN	BR
17	15-Oct-90	14	R & R Consulting	Business Review	CN	MB
18	18-Oct-90	17	Smith	Fm 1099	RP	BR
19	12-Nov-90	42	Smythe	Business Plan	MB	RP

Ready

Fig. 9.13. Using the OR condition.

If you want to find multiple text items, use OR criteria. For example, in figure 9.13 the OR condition is used to find CPAs with the initials MB OR RP. If you used an AND criteria, Excel would look for a CPA that had the initials MB AND RP at the same time. Because this is impossible, no records would be found.

9.36 Tip: **Format the criteria range with an outlined border to make multiple criteria rows visible.**

If you add rows to the criteria range in order to ask OR questions, you could be setting yourself up for trouble. If you clear the criteria rows but forget to remove unneeded blank rows, the find and extract commands will find all records. To prevent this, use the Format Border command to outline the criteria range. This outline makes unused criteria rows obvious.

Extracting and Maintaining Data

Excel's extract feature enables you to make a copy of selected data for use in reports or analysis. But these reports won't be of value if you don't maintain your database and keep it current. Use the tips in this section to help you extract data and keep your database current.

9.37 Tip: **To extract data, create a third set of field names.**

You must create a third set of field names in addition to the database and criteria field names. Select this third set of names before choosing Data Extract. You do not have to include all field names in the extract range. The field names can be in any order. This enables you to create a report using the field names that you want in the order you want.

9.38 Trap: **Don't put anything below an unlimited extract range.**

If you select only the field names and choose the Data Extract command, Excel assumes that you want to get rid of any previous data below the field names and clears all cells below the field names. This action can be disastrous if part of your worksheet is below the extract range. To prevent this deletion, put the extract range at the bottom of the worksheet or limit the worksheet extract range.

To limit an extract range, select the field names as the top row and then select as many rows below as you want to be filled with data. Excel will display an alert box to let you know if there is more data in the extract than will fit in the range you have selected.

9.39 Trap: **Extracted data are values; therefore, if calculated information within the database changes, the data in the extract range will not change.**

When you use the **D**ata **E**xtract command, calculated fields within the database are pasted into the extract area as values. This means that if calculated information within the database changes, the data in the extract range will not change. You must redo the **D**ata **E**xtract for an update.

9.40 Trick: **Extract to another worksheet for reports or analysis.**

One of the safest ways to extract data and a convenient way to create a report that can use any formats or column widths is to extract information from one worksheet to a different worksheet.

To extract data from a database in worksheet A and put the extract in worksheet B, complete these steps:

1. Create a criteria range in worksheet B.
2. Create a set of extract field names in worksheet B.
3. Choose the Fo**r**mula **D**efine Name command and enter the name **Database** in the **N**ame text box and enter **=A.XLS!Database** in the **R**efers to: text box.
4. Enter your criteria for the extract in the criteria range in worksheet B.
5. Select the extract field names in worksheet B.
6. Choose the **D**ata **E**xtract command.

When Excel receives the **E**xtract command, it looks for the range name Database. The range Database is defined as being in another worksheet; therefore, Excel extracts information from the external database.

9.41 Trick: **Use a unique extract to spell-check database entries.**

Spell-check your database contents by selecting a single field name such as ITEM as the extract range. Choose the **D**ata **E**xtract command with the **U**nique Records Only option selected. Excel will produce a list of each unique word in that field. Sort the list. You will find slightly misspelled words adjacent to each other in the list. Use the Fo**r**mula **F**ind command on the database to find which records contain the misspelled words.

9.42 Tip: **Delete multiple data records by sorting first.**

If you need to select and delete several records, insert a column through the middle of your database. Mark records you want to delete by typing **1** in the inserted column in the row to be deleted. Next, sort all the records using the inserted column as the first key. This action brings all the records with a 1 in the column to the top of the database. Because the records are all together, you can easily select and delete the records with a few shortcut keys or commands.

10

Creating Charts

Creating Excel charts in a worksheet is far easier than it has ever been before. But even with this ease and with the excellent charting capability of Excel, you will find that creating even simple charts can be done faster and easier with a few tips.

10.1 Tip: **Put series data in the long direction of the data range to use automatic charting.**

When you select data and then open a new chart, Excel automatically creates a chart. Excel uses a simple rule to determine how to plot the chart. That rule defines how the data will be grouped together—which data is in series 1, series 2, series 3, and so on.

When creating charts automatically from a selected range of data, Excel always makes the data series run the long direction in the range. For example, in figure 10.1 the long direction in the range, B5:E7, is horizontal. This means that the data series run horizontally. Series 1 is from B5 to E5, for example.

The category labels, Point 1, Point 2, and so on, always appear along the top or left of the long side of the data series. In figure 10.1, the category axis labels appear along the top, running the same direction as the long side.

Figure 10.2 shows the same data, but arranged so that the long side is vertical. Notice that the chart appears the same as that in figure 10.1. The direction the data runs doesn't affect how the chart is plotted. What matters is which direction is the longest. Again, the long direction is used to determine the direction in which a data series runs.

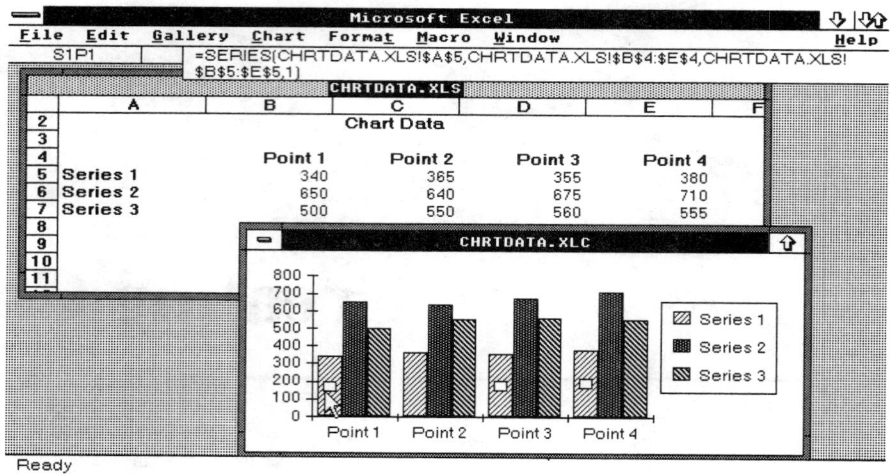

Fig. 10.1. An automatic chart created from a horizontal data series.

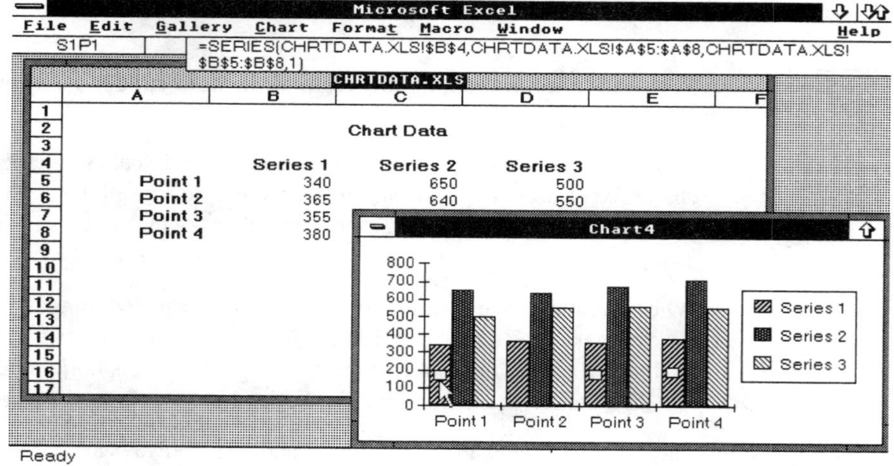

Fig. 10.2. An automatic chart created from a vertical data series.

Therefore, remember that if there are more data points than data series, you must create the chart manually. The next tip shows you how to do just that.

10.2 Tip: Use Paste Special to create charts that you can't create with automatic charting.

In cases where you have more data series than data points, like the worksheet in figure 10.3, Excel's automatic charting won't work. The automatic chart in figure 10.4, for example, plots the data incorrectly. Excel's automatic charting considers the long side of the data range to be the direction of the data series. Instead, you want a chart like the one shown in figure 10.5

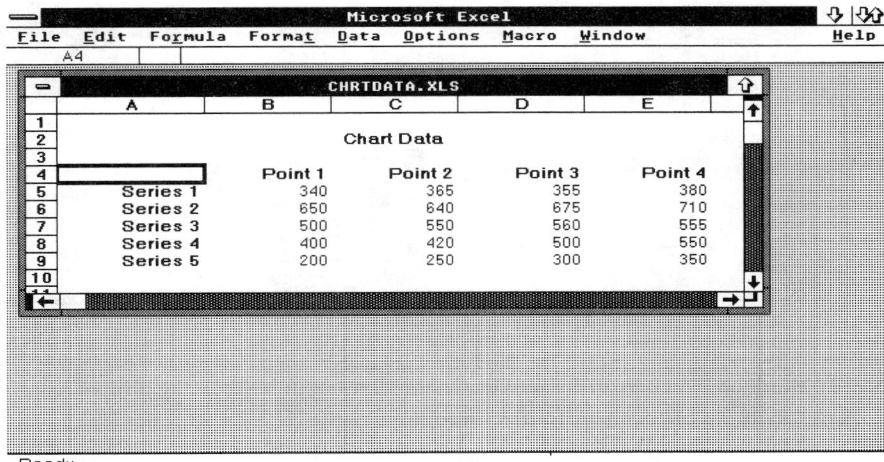

Fig. 10.3. Chart data with more data series than data points.

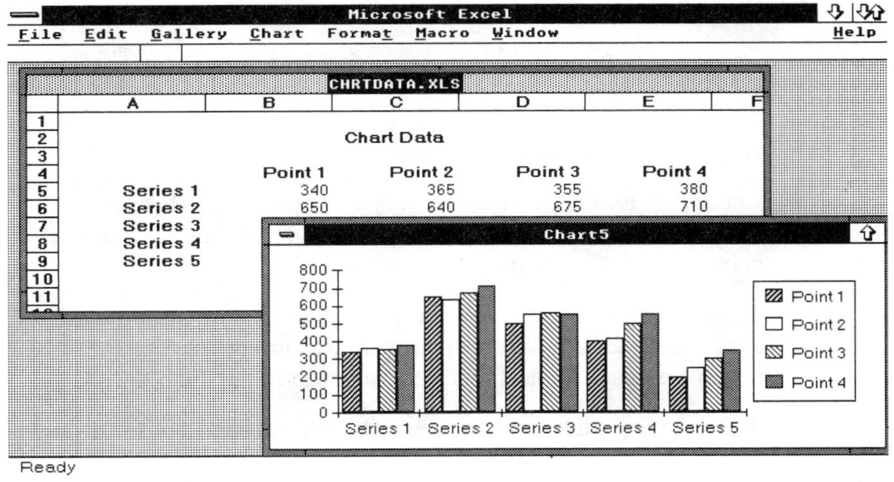

Fig. 10.4. An incorrect automatic chart.

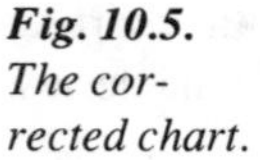

Fig. 10.5. *The corrected chart.*

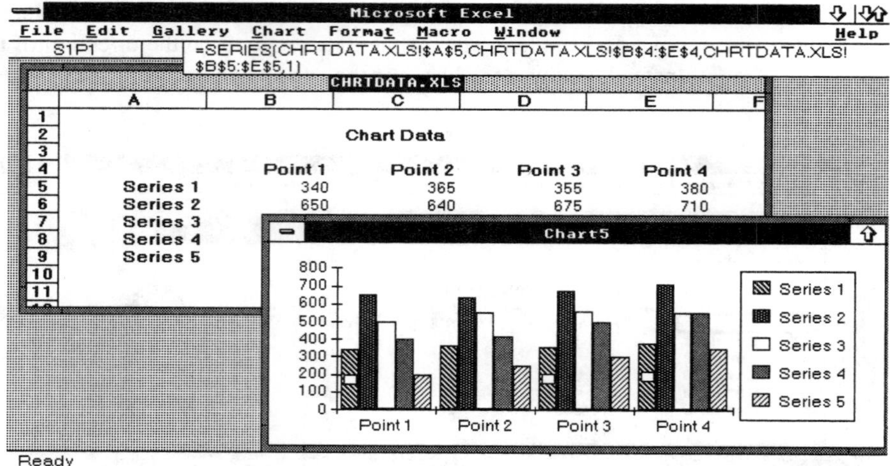

To produce the chart in figure 10.5 manually, begin by creating a blank chart. To produce a blank chart, follow these steps:

1. Select an empty worksheet cell and then choose the **F**ile **N**ew **C**hart command.

2. Reactivate the worksheet and select the range to be plotted, including the labels.

3. Choose the **E**dit **C**opy command.

4. Activate the blank chart by clicking on its window or choosing the chart with the **W**indow command.

5. Choose the **E**dit Paste **S**pecial command to paste the data from the worksheet onto the blank chart. Notice that this is the Paste **S**pecial command, not the normal paste command.

   The Paste Special dialog box appears with the Values in **C**olumns option selected. Choose the opposite of the current selection; remember that this selection for the automatic chart did not work.

6. Select the opposite option, Values in **R**ows, and then choose OK.

10.3 Tip: **Create automatic charts even faster by using shortcut keys.**

Creating automatically generated charts is already quick to do in Excel. You just select the worksheet area containing the chart data and labels and then open a new chart sheet. But you can make this process even faster with shortcut keys.

If you want to chart a worksheet range, such as range A4:E7 in figure 10.1, follow these steps for a quick chart:

1. Select any cell within the rectangular area of the data.
2. Press the Ctrl+* (asterisk) key to select the area of data surrounded by blank cells. This is shortcut key for the Formula Select Special command with the Current Region option.
3. Press the F11 key to open a new chart sheet. On the Macintosh, press F1 on the Enhanced Keyboard or choose File Open Chart.

10.4 Tip: **Select an arrow before deleting it.**

The command to delete an arrow appears on the Chart menu only when you have selected the arrow you want to delete. Therefore, first select the arrow you want to delete and then choose Chart Delete Arrow.

10.5 Tip: **Unselect all text objects before entering unattached text.**

Excel does not have a menu command to add unattached or floating text. Just select a nontext object before typing unattached text. If attached or unattached text is selected when you type, your typing will replace it.

10.6 Tip: **Make rapid changes to charts by double-clicking on chart elements.**

Double-clicking on chart elements such as a column in a chart displays the Pattern dialog box for that chart element. Within that dialog box, you can double-click on a color, pattern, or border width. Double-clicking makes the selection you want and chooses the OK button. Double-clicking on an element in the chart that contains text displays the Pattern dialog box with a Font button; this button enables you to format the text for that element.

10.7 Tip: **Edit a chart's series formula if you want to alter, repair, or enhance charts.**

Data series in a chart link to a worksheet or database through a formula containing an absolute reference. For example, in figure 10.6, the chart's first series of columns is selected as shown by the white "handles" in some of the columns.

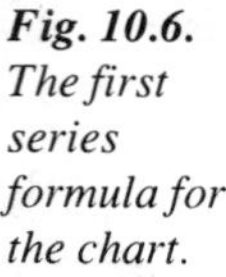

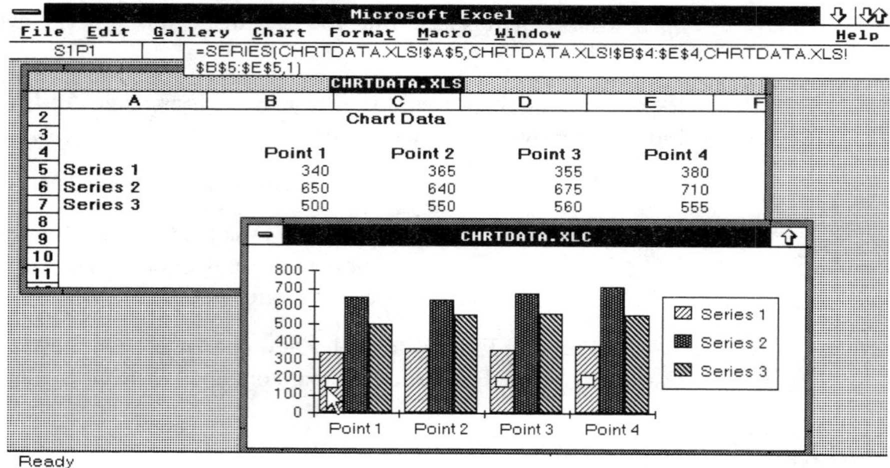

Fig. 10.6. *The first series formula for the chart.*

The formula for the series is

=SERIES(CHRTDATA.XLS!$A$5,CHRTDATA.XLS!$B$4:$E$4, CHRTDATA.XLS!$B$5:$E$5,1)

This series formula describes everything related to this data series. You can understand it by looking at the following series formula template and descriptions:

=SERIES(*series_name,category_reference,values_reference,marker_order*)

series_name is either text enclosed in quotation marks or an external reference to the cell that contains the label for the data series. This label is used as the title if there is only one series and is used in the legend for multiple series. In figure 10.6, the *series_name* is $A$5.

category_reference is an absolute external reference or external name that references the labels for the category axis. In figure 10.6, the row of point numbers, $B4:$E$4, is the *category_reference.*

values_reference is an absolute external reference or external name that references the values for the series. In figure 10.6, the *values_reference* is $B$5:$E$5.

marker_order is an integer number that positions this data series among the other data series. In figure 10.6 the first of the data series is shown.

Once you create a chart, you can reorganize data series, remove data series, change data series, and write custom legends by editing the series formula.

10.8 Tip: **Enter custom legend titles in the series formula.**

The legend for a data series does not have to be the legend at the left or top of the data series. After you create your chart, you can change the series formula to use either the text in a worksheet cell or actual text you type into the series formula. Notice that the *category_reference* is the second argument in the series formula. This argument can be either an absolute external reference to any worksheet or text enclosed in quotation marks.

In figure 10.6 the series formula uses the text in cell $A$5 of worksheet CHRTDATA.XLS as the legend for series 1:

```
=SERIES(CHRTDATA.XLS!$A$5,CHRTDATA.XLS!$B$4:$E$4,
CHRTDATA.XLS!$B$5:$E$5,1)
```

If you want a different cell's content as the legend, replace that external reference. For example, to use the text in M12 as the legend, edit the series formula:

```
=SERIES(CHRTDATA.XLS!$M$12,CHRTDATA.XLS!$B$4:$E$4,
CHRTDATA.XLS!$B$5:$E$5,1)
```

If you want an unchanging piece of text instead of a cell reference as the legend, type the text enclosed in quotation marks:

```
=SERIES("Text Legend for Series1",CHRTDATA.XLS!$B$4:$E$4,
CHRTDATA.XLS!$B$5:$E$5,1)
```

10.9 Tip: **Use range names in the series formula if the data range in the worksheet could move.**

If the cells that your chart references move, the chart's series formula does not change automatically to reflect the moved cells. In other words, the chart loses track of the location of the data, causing bars, columns, or lines to shift. If the data moves completely out of the formula's referenced range, the chart may lose all bars, columns, or lines.

To make sure that your charts stay accurate, even when worksheet data moves, replace the ranges in the series formula with named ranges. To do so, you must activate the supporting worksheet and use the Formula Define Name command to name the same range as that in the series formula. Return to the chart and edit each series formula so that the name is used. Save the worksheet and chart to preserve the new names and series formulas.

After adding names, the series formula that was the following

=SERIES(CHRTDATA.XLS!$A$5,CHRTDATA.XLS!$B$4:$E$4, CHRTDATA.XLS!$B$5:$E$5,1)

might appear as this

=SERIES(CHRTDATA.XLS!Lgnd_One,CHRTDATA.XLS!Cat_Labels, CHRTDATA.XLS!SeriesOneData,1)

10.10 Tip: **Delete series from a chart by deleting the series formula.**

To remove a data series from a chart, select the marker (bar, column, or line) for the series. When the series formula for that marker appears in the formula bar, use normal editing techniques to delete it. Use the Backspace key, for example. Once the formula bar is empty, press Enter.

10.11 Tip: **If the category labels disappear when you delete a series formula, enter a new absolute external reference to the range with the category axis labels.**

Excel takes its category labels from the second argument of the series formula for the first series formula. If you delete the first series formula and the second series does not have a second argument, the category labels on the x-axis will disappear. If you reorder the markers (bars, columns, line markers) within a chart and the new first series does not have a second argument, again the category axis labels will disappear.

To repair this problem, enter a new absolute external reference that refers to the range containing the category axis labels.

10.12 Tip: **Reorder columns, bars, or line markers by changing the *marker_order* number in the series formula.**

You can reorder the markers (bars, columns, or lines) that appear in your charts by simply editing the series formula. Select the marker you want to move and then replace the current *marker_order* number with the order number you want for this data series.

For example, in figure 10.7 the second data series has been selected. Notice that its *marker_order* number is 2. Replace this number with a 3, and the marker moves into third place. The other markers slide forward to fill the gap (see fig. 10.8).

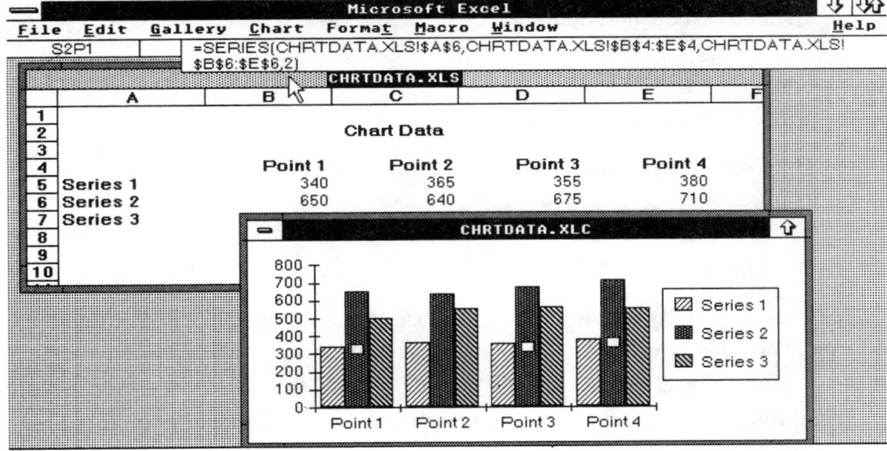

Fig. 10.7. Moving the second data series.

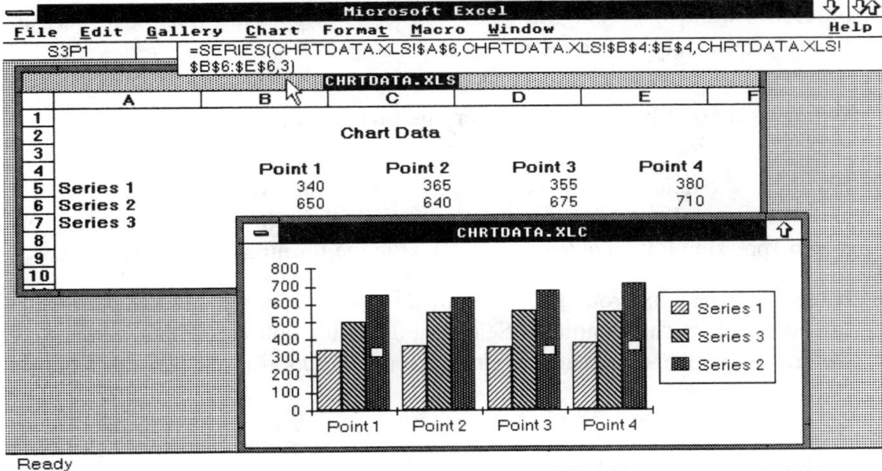

Fig. 10.8. The re-arranged data series.

10.13 Tip: Use blank charts to draw on or to chart entered data series manually.

Blank charts are excellent to use for drawing with unattached text, lines, and arrows. To create a blank chart, follow these steps:

1. Select a blank cell in the worksheet.
2. Choose the **F**ile **N**ew command.

3. Select the Chart option.

Or

1. Open an existing chart.
2. Choose the Chart Select Chart command.
3. Select the Edit Clear command.
4. Choose Select All.

Then add text by typing in the formula bar and pressing Enter. Move this text around and add new text, arrows, and lines, as needed.

10.14 Tip: **Select data ranges in the order in which you want the markers to appear.**

Excel decides the order in which it plots data series by the order in which you select the range of cells containing the data. If you want to select data in a specific order but the data is not arranged in that order, select the data in the order you want by holding down the Ctrl (PC) or control (Macintosh) key as you select the ranges with the mouse.

10.15 Tip: **Delete chart text by deleting it from the formula bar.**

It's so easy to delete attached or unattached text that it may not be obvious. To delete it, select the text item on the chart. Select the formula bar by clicking on it or by pressing F2; then delete all the text in the formula bar and press Enter.

If the text has a box around it, delete the box by selecting it and then choosing the Format Patterns command. Select the Invisible option for both border and pattern and make sure that the Shadow border option is unselected. Choose OK.

10.16 Tip: **Add data to charts by copying and pasting.**

Add data to an existing chart by selecting the data and label in the worksheet and choosing the Edit Copy command. The number of points plus the label must equal the same number as you selected when creating the original chart.

Activate the chart. Choose the Edit Paste command. The data and label are pasted into the chart. Tip 10.12 in this chapter describes how to change the position of the data series you pasted so that the markers (bars, columns, or lines) are in the order you need.

Formatting Charts

You can customize any item in an Excel chart that you can select. Select the item by clicking on it; then choose the Forma**t** command to change its appearance. For example, you can change the x- and y-axis by changing the placement of the tick marks, the style of the axis, and the thickness of the axis. Even novice Excel users can create polished charts. With some of the tips you learn in the following sections, you'll be able to format faster to create presentation-quality charts.

10.17 Tip: **Return to default chart formats with the Automatic option.**

If you've been experimenting with all the colors and patterns you can put in a chart and you've built something that others might call aesthetically offensive, you might want to return to the original color and pattern settings chosen by Excel. To do this, select the chart item and choose the Forma**t** **P**atterns command. Move to the pattern or border you want to change, select the Automatic option, and then choose OK.

10.18 Tip: **Draw with lines, dashed lines, and boxes.**

On a blank or completed chart, you can add enhancements with lines and boxes. On a blank chart, you can even create flow charts and organizational diagrams.

Create lines by adding an arrow to the chart with the **C**hart Add A**r**row command. With the arrow still selected, choose the Forma**t** **P**atterns command and select an Arrow Shaft **S**tyle for the arrow shaft. From the **W**eight group, select the line thickness. At the bottom right in the Arrow **H**ead **S**tyle group, you can select a headless arrow to use as a line.

To create stretchable, movable boxes, use an unattached text box with or without text. Create unattached text boxes by first ensuring that no text item is selected. Then type text or even a single blank space and press Enter. Use the Forma**t** **P**atterns box to change the border and pattern of the box. Use the Forma**t** **F**ont box to change the pattern behind the text or blank space inside the box. Stretch the box by dragging its corners or edges with the mouse or use the Forma**t** Si**z**e command and arrow keys. Move the box by dragging from the inside or use the Forma**t** **M**ove command and arrow keys.

Remove text boxes by selecting the box, deleting the text in the formula bar, and pressing Enter. Then choose the Format Patterns command and make the borders and pattern invisible. Unselect the shadow border.

10.19 Tip: **Move and align text boxes, lines, and arrows precisely with arrow keys.**

You can align text boxes, lines, and arrows precisely by positioning them with the arrow keys. Select the chart item and choose the Format Move command. Press the arrow keys to move in large jumps in the direction of the arrow. Press Ctrl+arrow key to move in single dot increments.

10.20 Trick: **Use movable lines as guides to align unattached text or other lines and arrows.**

A horizontal line and a vertical line kept at the bottom and side of a chart act as convenient straight-edges or alignment tools when drawing boxes and lines on a blank chart. When you need to check alignment, drag the "straight-edge" into position by dragging from its middle. Figure 10.9 shows two such lines being used to align text boxes when producing a flow chart.

To create these lines, add two arrows. Then select one arrow, select a straight line for the Arrow Head Style, and position the line vertically. Do the same for the second arrow, but position this line horizontally.

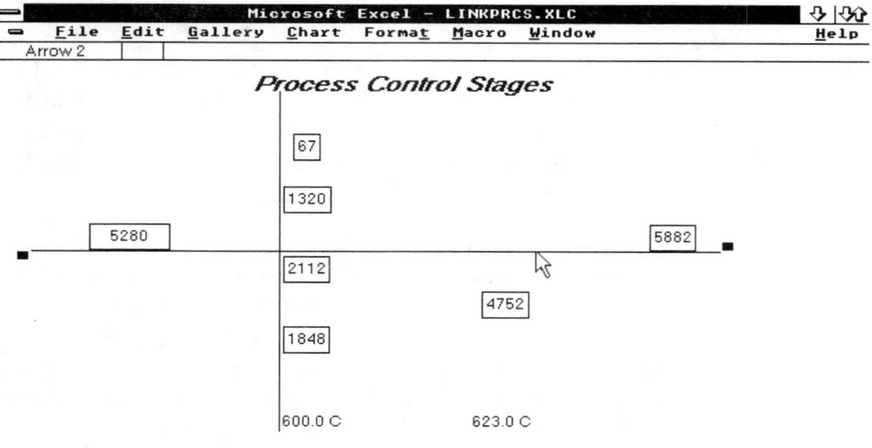

Fig. 10.9. Aligning text boxes.

10.21 Tip: **Format the value axis by formatting the first data point in the first data series.**

The format numbers on the data axis depend on the format used by the first point in the first data series in the worksheet. This formatting method gives you a great deal of power. You can use custom numeric formats on the first data series, and they will appear in the linked chart. Note that formatting does not carry over to charts you create manually. Chapter 3 describes in detail how to create custom formats that can include international characters and text.

10.22 Tip: **Reposition and reorient chart axes to either side, top, or bottom.**

Figure 10.10 shows how you can reposition the axes of charts. Select the axis you want moved by clicking on the other axis. For instance, if you want to move the y-axis, select the x-axis. Then choose the Format Scale command. Select the option Category Axis Crosses at **M**aximum Value to move the axis to the chart's opposite side. Select the Values in **R**everse Order option to reorient the direction of the scale.

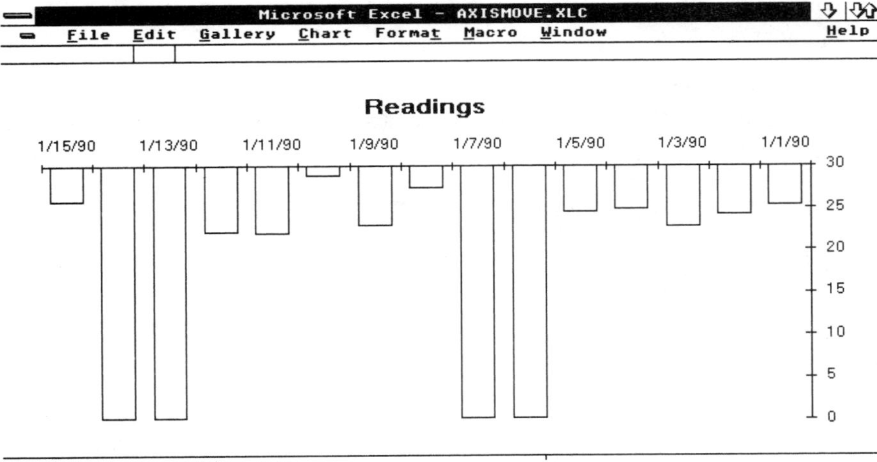

Fig. 10.10. Repositioning the chart axes.

Customizing Charts

Excel is not a drawing applications, but its charting features equal those of many stand-alone chart applications. In fact, some of its features, such as linking floating text and data directly to worksheet cells, aren't possible in many chart applications. Use the tips in this section to customize your charts.

10.23 Trick: **Draw your own custom legends.**

Use empty text boxes to draw legends that you can position at any location on-screen. Draw each box within the custom legend as a separate item and then choose a color or pattern for the box with the Forma**t** **P**atterns command. Make each piece of text a separate item and position it by dragging it into location.

10.24 Trick: **Move the chart on-screen to gain more room at the top, bottom, or left side.**

With this trick, you can push a chart down, up, or left in the screen and printing area as shown in figure 10.11. In the space you gain, you can put explanations, figures linked back to the worksheet, or a custom legend drawn with text boxes.

You can push the chart in three directions by adding attached text, blank text, or blank lines to the title, category axis (x-axis), or value axis (y-axis). In most

Fig. 10.11. Repositioning the chart.

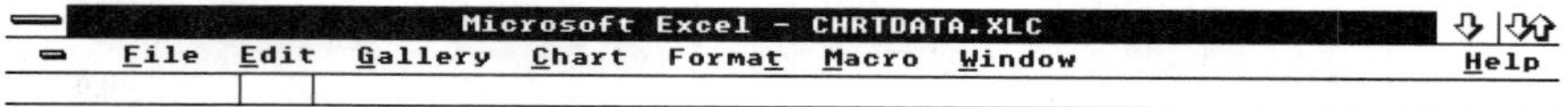

Reposition Charts When You
Need White Space or Room for Text

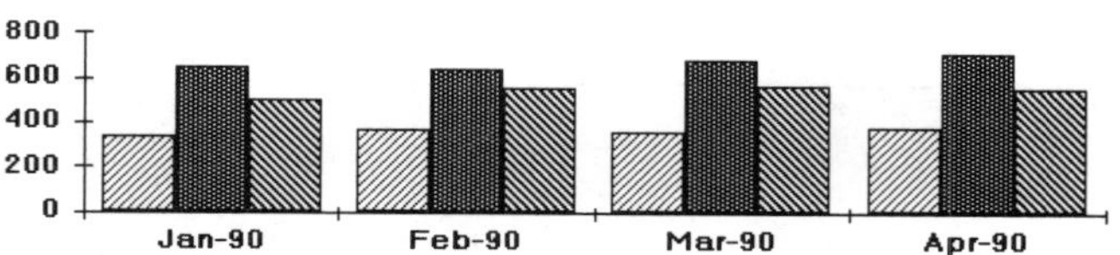

Ready

cases, it's best to add blank lines or spaces to the attached text. This action enables you to add unattached text where you want.

To push the chart to the right, follow these steps:

1. Choose the **C**hart Attach **T**ext command.
2. Select the **V**alue Axis and then choose OK.
3. Delete the Y in the formula bar and replace it with as many spaces as needed to move the chart right.
4. Press Enter to enter the text and move the chart. The chart will move up to one quarter of a screen to the right.

To move the chart up or down, follow these steps:

1. Choose the **C**hart Attach **T**ext command.
2. Select the **T**itle option to move the chart down or select the **C**ategory Axis option to move the chart up.
3. Delete the title or X in the formula bar and type any text you need. Position the chart by adding blank lines after the text. Add lines by pressing Ctrl+Enter.
4. Press Enter to enter the text and move the chart.

10.25 Tip: **Link worksheet comments or numeric tables to comments in Excel charts.**

Excel has the extremely powerful feature of linking comments or numbers in your worksheet to text in your chart. Figure 10.12 demonstrates how the text in cell A1 of the worksheet appears in the unattached text box in the chart. (The extra white space in the chart was created by repositioning the chart using the preceding trick.)

With this feature, you can have special numbers, ratios, dates, or text comments appear in the charts. Because they are linked to the worksheet, they are up-to-date and save you the time of manually editing the chart.

To create this link, use the preceding trick to shift the chart to the right to provide room for extensive text comments. Then unselect all text items on the chart and type an equal sign (=). An equal sign appears in the chart's formula bar. Activate the worksheet by clicking on it and then select cell A1. The absolute external reference formula is entered in the formula bar:

```
=CHRTCMNT.XLS!$A$1
```

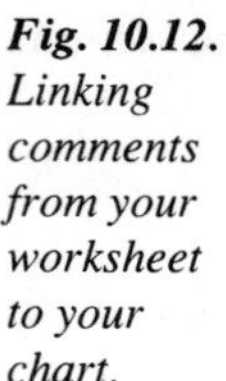

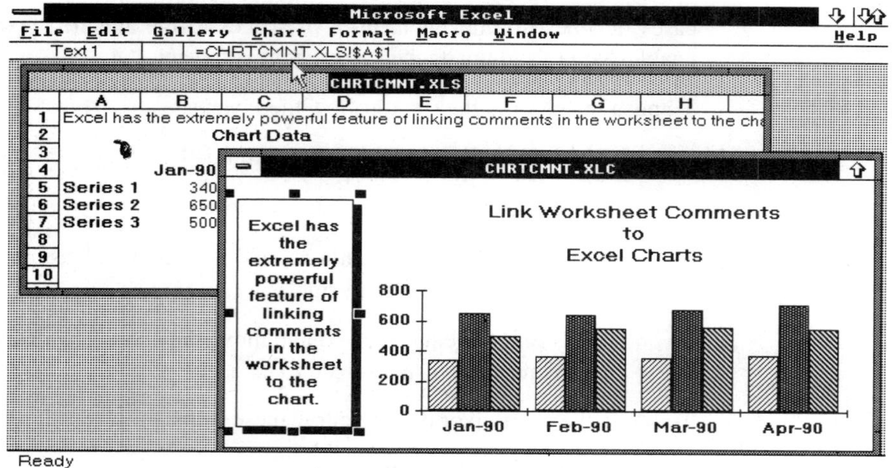

Fig. 10.12. Linking comments from your worksheet to your chart.

Press Enter to complete the link. Editing the text in cell A1 of the worksheet produces the same change in the charts text box.

10.26 Trick: Make text and numbers change in charts depending on calculated results.

Figure 10.13 shows a simple process flow chart that links to the worksheet in figure 10.14. The text boxes that make up the measurement points in the flow chart link to cells in the worksheet. As the worksheet changes, the results displayed in the flow chart change. The links are created by entering within an unattached text box an absolute external reference that references a cell in the worksheet. The same technique is used in the preceding tip.

What is unique about this trick is that you can create invisible flags that appear in charts when specific conditions are met. These might be financial flags, inventory reorder points, or process control limits. In figure 10.13, a warning appears above Stage 2 and overlapping the temperature indicator. The Over Limit warning appears when the temperature limit formula in cell G7 of the worksheet is exceeded.

The warning signal in the chart is an external absolute reference to cell G7 in the worksheet. This cell contains the IF( ) formula displayed in the worksheet's formula bar. When the limit is exceeded, the text warning appears in the worksheet cell. Because the cell is linked to the chart, the warning also appears in the chart. The font for the warning in the chart is formatted red so that it will stand out better.

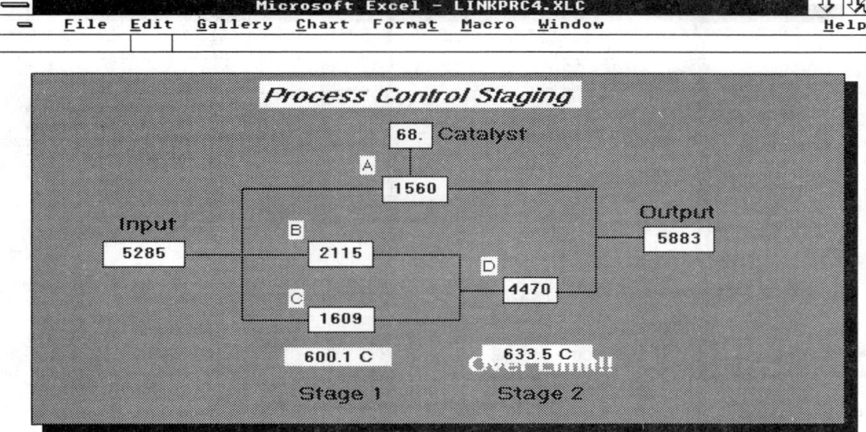

Fig. 10.13. A process flowchart.

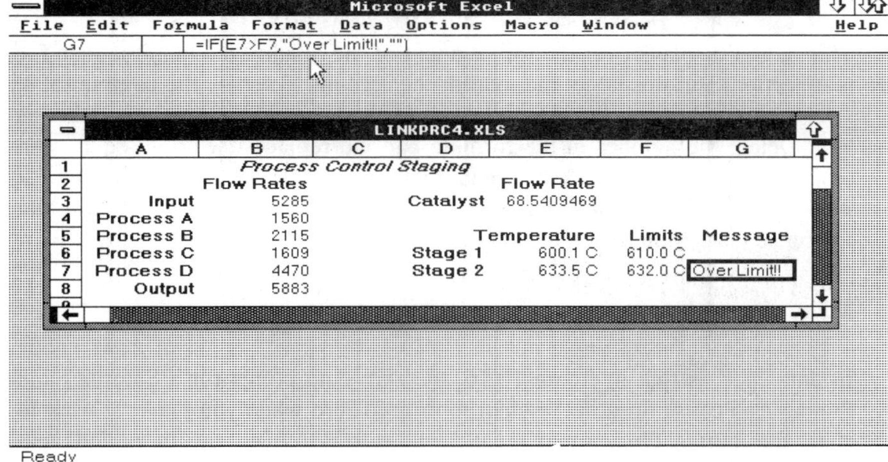

Fig. 10.14. The process worksheet.

10.27 Trick: Make totals appear above columns.

Figure 10.15 demonstrates that you can make a total appear at the top of a stacked column. The displayed total moves with the top of the column and changes to reflect the new total.

You can create figure 10.15 by first creating a stacked column chart. The stacked column chart is selection 3 in the column gallery. Once you create a

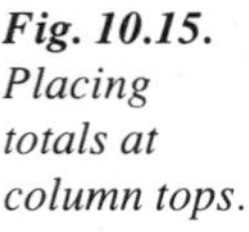

Fig. 10.15. Placing totals at column tops.

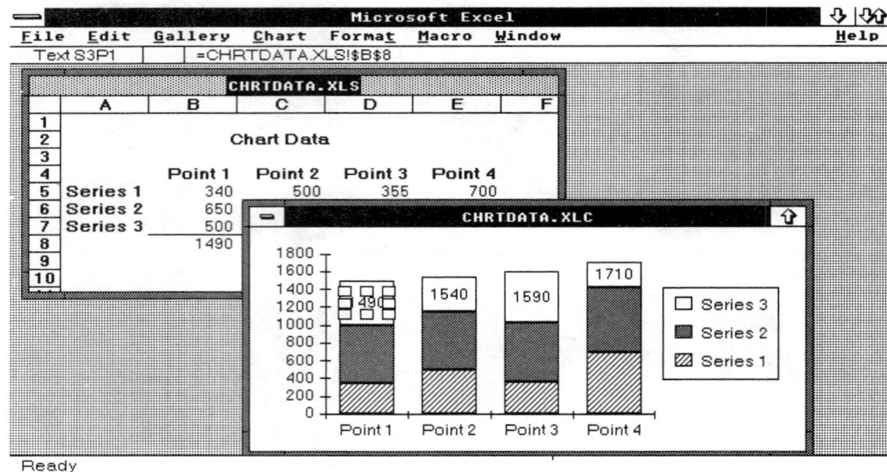

stacked column, select the top of each column by clicking on it. Now choose the **C**hart Attach **T**ext command. Choose OK.

This action displays over the top segment of the column the numeric data for that portion. But this is not the total of the column. To show the column total, select the number by clicking on it. The formula bar will show the number as text. Delete the number in the formula bar and replace it with an equal sign (=). Now activate the worksheet and click on the cell containing the total for that column. The formula bar in figure 10.15 shows the external absolute reference that produces the total at the top of the Point 1 column.

10.28 Trick: Make charts skip over zero points in data.

In data such as that in figure 10.16, the zero data points for a Saturday and Sunday can cause lines in the chart to drop to zero when you may not want to chart zero points. Or you may want the lines to skip over specific periods, but you don't want to go to the trouble of extrapolating data points over the skipped area just to get a smooth line on the chart. There is an easy solution to both of these problems.

The solution is to enter NA for the zero points or to use a formula that produces #NA whenever you want data skipped. In the chart of figure 10.17, the readings for Saturday and Sunday are skipped. This is accomplished by calculating the day of the week in cell B2 from the following formula:

```
=WEEKDAY(A2)
```

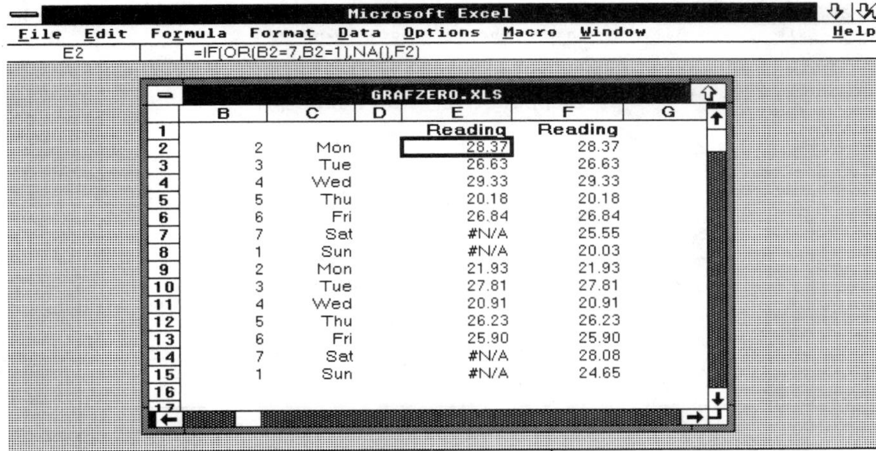

	B	C	D	E	F	G
1				Reading	Reading	
2	2	Mon		28.37	28.37	
3	3	Tue		26.63	26.63	
4	4	Wed		29.33	29.33	
5	5	Thu		20.18	20.18	
6	6	Fri		26.84	26.84	
7	7	Sat		#N/A	25.55	
8	1	Sun		#N/A	20.03	
9	2	Mon		21.93	21.93	
10	3	Tue		27.81	27.81	
11	4	Wed		20.91	20.91	
12	5	Thu		26.23	26.23	
13	6	Fri		25.90	25.90	
14	7	Sat		#N/A	28.08	
15	1	Sun		#N/A	24.65	
16						

Fig. 10.16. Data that includes zero points.

Column C shows the day of the week. This date is produced in cell C2 by referencing cell A2. Cell C2 is then formatted with the custom format ddd.

The data that is charted in column E is produced by the formula shown in the formula bar. This formula determines whether column B is a Saturday or Sunday. If it is, the formula results in #N/A. If it is a weekday, the formula results in the data.

The chart in figure 10.17 is from the data in column E. Notice that the lines that cross Saturdays and Sundays appear as straight-lines from Friday to Monday. The data point at the last Friday does not continue to the right because there is no Monday data to which to plot a line.

10.29 Tip: **Enhance Excel charts with advanced graphing and drawing applications.**

One of the advantages to the Windows environment is the sharing of data, even charts. With graphics and advanced drawing packages, you can create your charts in Excel and then copy them through the clipboard to applications such as CorelDRAW and Designer where you can polish them to the quality of that produced by professional graphics artists.

Fig. 10.17. Skipping data points.

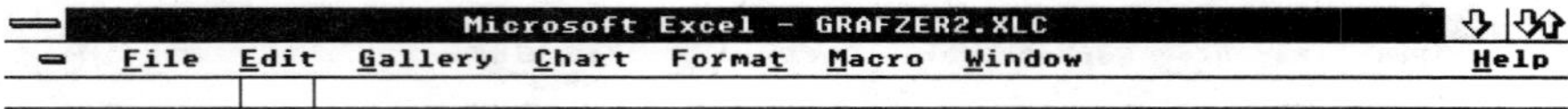

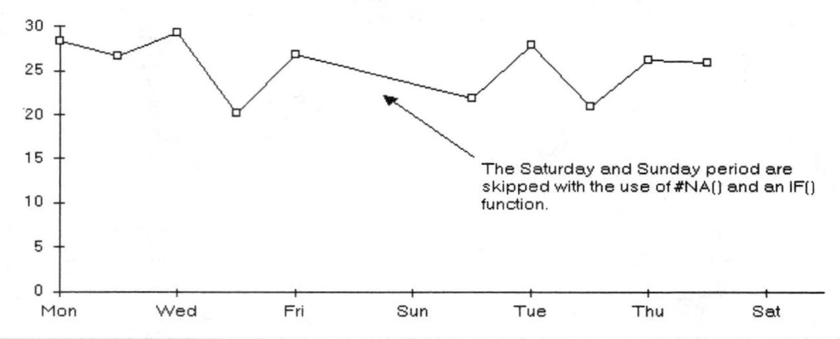

11

Creating and Editing Macros

Excel contains an excellent macro recorder that records your commands and keystrokes and translates them into a command macro. You can use the macro recorder to name and create complete macros, or you can use the recorder to add to macros that already exist. Once you are comfortable recording macros, look at the section on "Modifying Recorded Macros." Modified macros look like custom programming, yet they are quick and productive.

11.1 Tip: **Group macros of a similar type in the same macro sheet.**

Put similar macros together in the same macro sheet so that they are more convenient to recall and to use with other worksheets or charts. For example, grouping a collection of formatting macros together in one sheet enables you to open that macro sheet for use with any worksheet you need to format.

11.2 Tip: **Set the location where a recorded macro is stored.**

If you are documenting and recording your macros correctly, you will want to specify where the macro is stored. To specify in which macro sheet a macro is placed and which cell is used for the beginning of the macro, follow these steps:

1. Activate the macro sheet in which you want to place the macro.
2. Select the cell where you want to start the macro.
3. Choose the **M**acro Se**t** Recorder command.

4. Activate the worksheet or chart in which you will record the macro.

5. Choose **M**acro Re**c**ord to name and start the macro.

   or

   Choose **M**acro **S**tart Recorder to record macro functions without naming the macro.

11.3 Tip: **Look in the Macro Run list box to find a macro's shortcut key.**

If you have created a macro and given it a shortcut key but have not entered that key in the documentation, you may forget the key. If you do, you can find the shortcut key by choosing the **M**acro **R**un command and looking in the left column of the **R**un scrolling list box (see fig. 11.1).

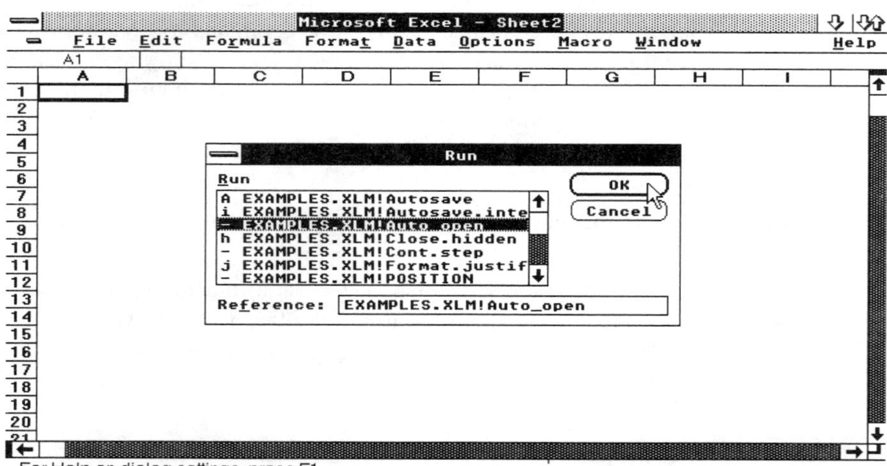

*Fig. 11.1. The **Run** list box.*

To run a macro by using a shortcut key in PC Excel, hold down the Ctrl key as you press the shortcut key. To run a macro on the Macintosh with a shortcut key, hold down Option+Command and press the shortcut key. On both PC and Macintosh, there is a difference between upper- and lowercase shortcut keys. Use the Shift key if the letter is uppercase.

Modifying Recorded Macros

With Excel, even the novice can create macros that are highly professional and polished. By first recording a macro and then making a few special modifications, you can create macros that display input dialog boxes, prompt the user for information, and cross-check data.

As an intermediate or advanced Excel user, you can modify recorded macros for use as building blocks and as a basic structure for your custom applications. Modifying a recorded macro is an excellent way to build test applications quickly or to build subroutines for more intricate macros.

11.4 Tip: **Edit macros as you edit in the worksheet.**

You can edit macro functions using the same keystrokes and commands as you use on formulas in a worksheet. When modifying recorded macros, you can use shortcuts keys to insert or delete cells, rows, or columns. These keys are useful when inserting a blank cell for an additional macro function or when deleting a macro function from a macro.

To insert or delete, select the cells, rows, or columns and then press Ctrl++ (plus) to insert or Ctrl+– (minus) to delete on the PC or control++ and control+– on the Macintosh. If you have selected cells, a dialog box appears asking the direction in which you want cells moved. If you have selected rows or columns, Excel immediately performs the insert or delete operation.

11.5 Tip: **Even though inserting a row through a macro will not stop the macro, try to avoid this practice.**

Inserting a blank row through one macro may insert a blank row through another macro at a different location in the same row. A blank cell will not stop a macro from running, but it may affect the macro's well-kept appearance when you document the macro.

11.6 Trick: **Test rows or columns for formulas and constants before deleting them.**

Be careful when deleting a row. You may inadvertently delete a row that contains a formula or value used by a macro. Deleting a formula or value in the macro will probably cause it to run incorrectly.

Before you delete a row or column, test it for formulas or constants. To do so, select the row or column and then choose Formula Select Special. Select the

Constants option. Then choose the command again but with the Formulas option to make sure that the row or column is empty.

11.7 Tip: **Select Relative or Absolute Record before you start recording your macro.**

If you want to record a macro that you can use in any location, choose Macro Set Recorder. Then choose the Macro Relative Record command before you begin recording your macro or as the first step after starting a macro. If you want the macro to duplicate the exact cell locations used during macro recording, choose the Macro Absolute Record command.

These two commands are toggles. The command that is displayed in the Macro menu is the command that is not active. For example, if Relative Record is already enabled, Absolute Record is displayed.

11.8 Tip: **Insert a ? before dialog box macro functions to display the dialog box.**

One of the first and easiest ways you can customize recorded macros is to insert a ? (question mark) in command macro functions so that the macro displays a dialog box. The ? mark in certain command macro functions pauses the macro so that the user can confirm the selection or enter a new selection.

As initially recorded, command macros run using the dialog box options you select during the macro recording. As the macro runs, you don't see the dialog box appear, nor do you have a chance to change the dialog box selections. In figure 11.2 for example, the macro was recorded with Relative Record on. When a worksheet is active and this macro runs, the FORMULA( ) function in cell A2 in the macro sheet enters the number 49 in the active worksheet cell. The FORMAT.NUMBER( ) function then formats the number as currency, and the BORDER( ) function turns off all borders. Finally, the SELECT( ) function moves the active cell to the next cell down.

With two simple edits, you can make the format and borders dialog boxes pause for input. To do so, type a question mark in front of the leading parenthesis of the FORMAT.NUMBER( ) and BORDER( ) functions. These functions should appear as FORMAT.NUMBER?( ) and BORDER?( ). Notice that both functions duplicate a menu command that produces a dialog box. The macro should appear as shown in figure 11.3.

Now activate the worksheet and run the macro. FORMULA( ) again enters the number 49 in the active cell, but the Format Number dialog box pauses on-screen for you to make changes. Notice that the selections you made during the macro recording are now used as default settings for the dialog box (see

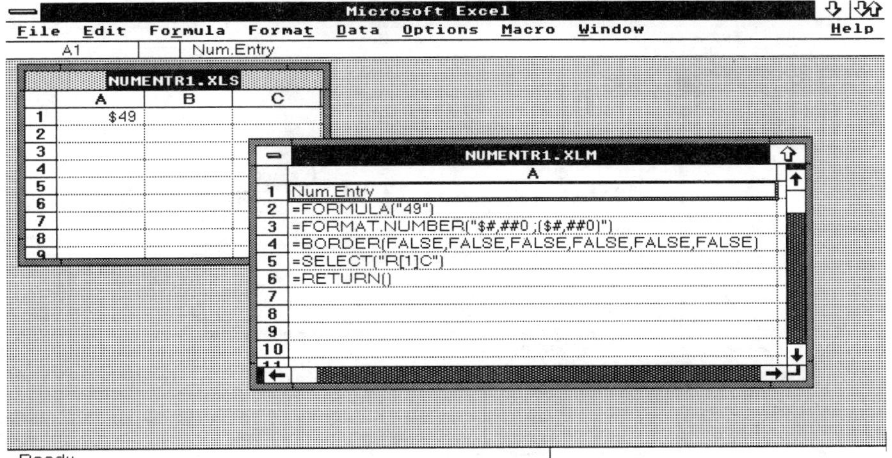

Fig. 11.2. Recording a macro without ?.

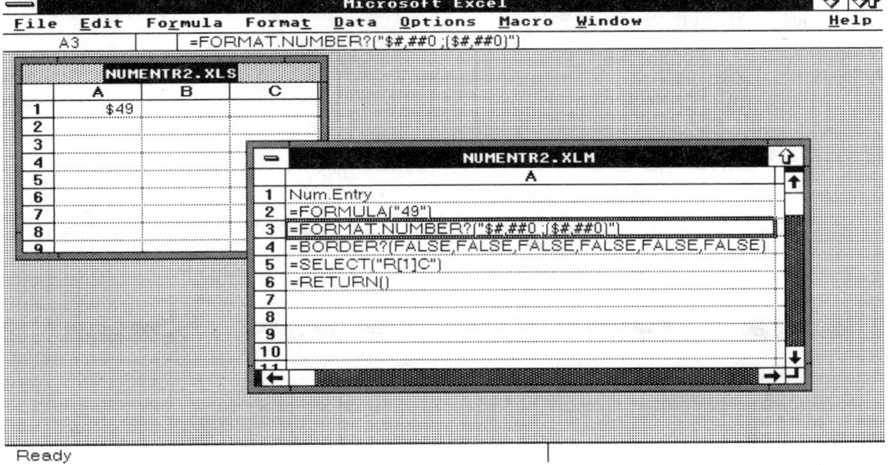

Fig. 11.3. Recording a macro with ?.

fig. 11.4). You can accept this setting or enter a new one. When you choose OK, the macro continues. In this case, the Format **B**order dialog box also appears and pauses. Because you made no selections in this box during the macro recording, it will be blank. Make your selections and choose OK.

As you record macros, remember that you can make dialog boxes appear during macro operation by typing ?. This capability allows you to create macros that are flexible.

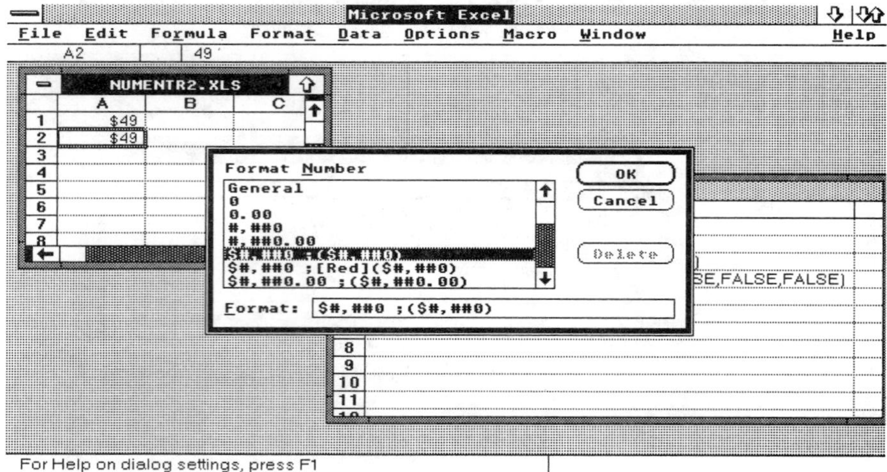

Fig. 11.4. The Format Number dialog box.

11.9 Tip: Use the Formula Paste Function command to enter macro functions quickly and correctly.

If you aren't familiar with a macro function and the order of its arguments, use the Formula Paste Function command. The macro using ? in the preceding tip is straight-forward, but not useful unless the only number you work with is 49. With a simple modification, you can make this or any macro request the user to type a number, date, text, or logical operator. To make a change, first select the item you want to modify. For instance, select 49 by double-clicking on it (see fig. 11.5).

Fig. 11.5. Selecting an argument.

Microsoft Excel
File Edit Formula Format Data Options Macro Window Help
A2 =FORMULA("49")
NUMENTR2.XLS
$49
$49
NUMENTR2.XLM
Num.Entry
=FORMULA("49")
=FORMAT.NUMBER?("$#,##0 ;($#,##0)")
=BORDER?(FALSE,FALSE,FALSE,FALSE,FALSE,FALSE)
=SELECT("R[1]C")
=RETURN()
Edit

To replace the selected 49 with an INPUT( ) function and text that prompts for the arguments, choose the Formula Paste Function command. Then select the macro function from the scrolling list box shown in figure 11.6, select the Paste Arguments option, and choose OK. The result is shown in figure 11.7. You can use the pasted prompts to enter the specific arguments for this function. (The next tip discusses entering these arguments.) Pasting functions can save you time because you do not have to look up syntax in a reference manual.

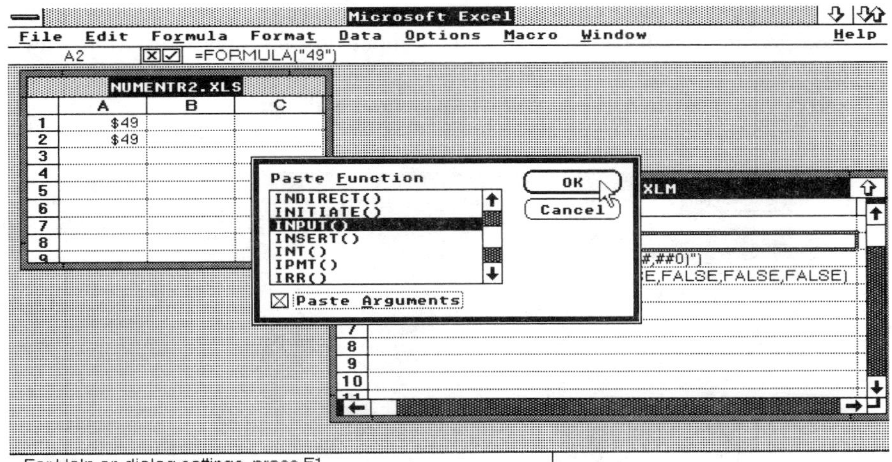

Fig. 11.6. The Paste Function dialog box.

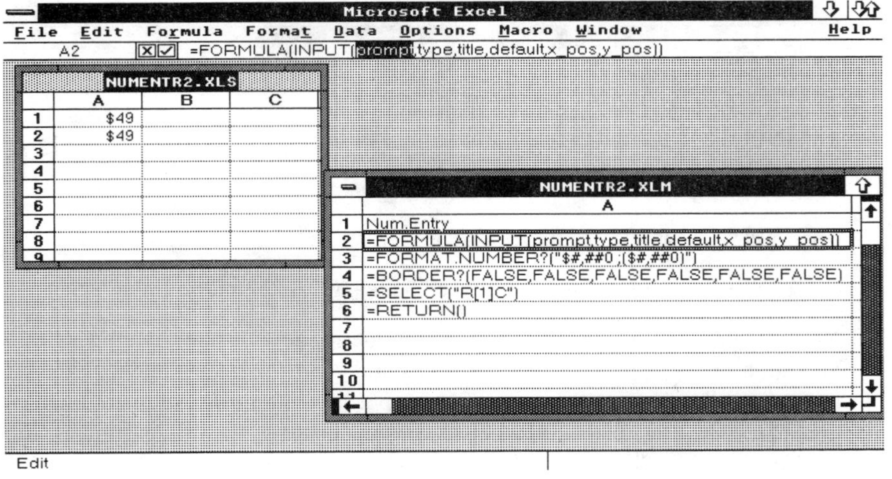

Fig. 11.7. Adding the INPUT( ) function to the macro.

11.10 Tip: **Replace FORMULA( ) with FORMULA(INPUT( )) to display an input box.**

When recording macros in which the user will be prompted for an entry, select the appropriate cell and enter a number, date, or text as the user would. Continue recording the entire data entry process. When you are finished, the recorded macro will contain FORMULA( ) functions for each manually entered data. These functions make excellent markers that indicate where input boxes should be added.

In figure 11.8, the FORMULA( ) command from figure 11.7 has been modified to contain an input box. This input box prompts the user to enter data, checks that the data is the correct type (such as numeric or text), and then enters that data where the FORMULA( ) command specifies.

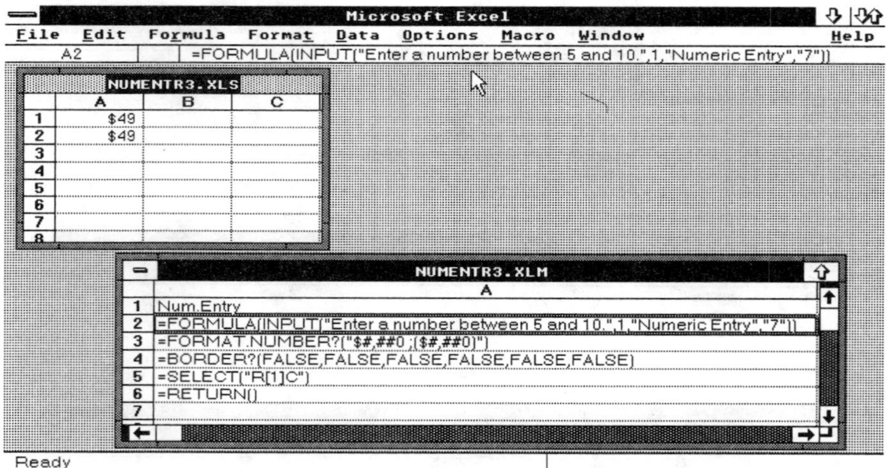

Fig. 11.8. Adding an input box.

The INPUT( ) function uses the following syntax:

=INPUT(*prompt*, *type*, *title*, *default*, *x_pos*, *y_pos*)

The INPUT( ) function in figure 11.8 is

=INPUT("Enter a number between 5 and 10.",1,"Numeric Entry","7")

Notice that text arguments and the numeric default are entered within quotation marks. You can omit the *x_pos* and *y_pos*; these arguments are used to position the upper left corner of the input box. The *title* argument enables you to add a title to the input box. If you do not enter this argument, the default, Title, is used. The *type* argument defines the type of input allowed. For example, a type-1 input box allows only numbers. If the input does not match the defined type, an error box appears.

The resulting input box is shown in figure 11.9. The default entry of 7 appears in the text box, and the prompt and title have been added to customize the box. Running the macro displays an input box that accepts only numbers and that enables you to format the number and border.

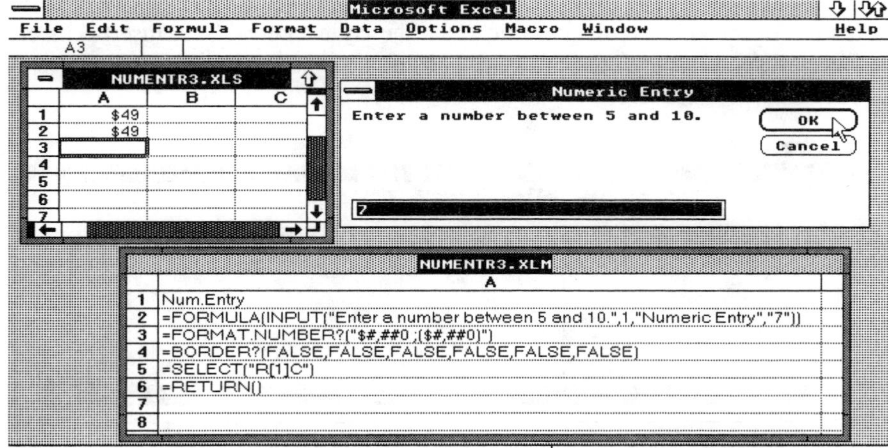

Fig. 11.9. *An input box.*

11.11 Tip: **Sum type numbers to allow the function to enter or accept multiple types of data.**

Many functions use an argument that specifies the type of number being accepted or returned. Often you can sum type numbers to enable the macro function to accept or return multiple types of data. The INPUT types include the following:

Type	*Data Type*
0	Formula
1	Number
2	Text
4	Logical
8	Reference
16	Error
64	Array

For example, you could enter **3** for the type argument if you want an input box to accept numbers (1) and text (2). If the user makes an entry that does not match the correct type, an alert box warns the user of the mistake.

Note that a formula can be entered only when the type is 0. When you sum types, this type (0) is not included.

11.12 Tip: Replace FORMULA( ) with IF( ), FORMULA( ), and INPUT( ) for data-checking macros.

You can further modify the macro in figure 11.8 so that the macro checks data entry. To do so, make the modifications shown in figure 11.10. Insert cells or cut and paste the macro to a lower position to make room for the inserted macro function.

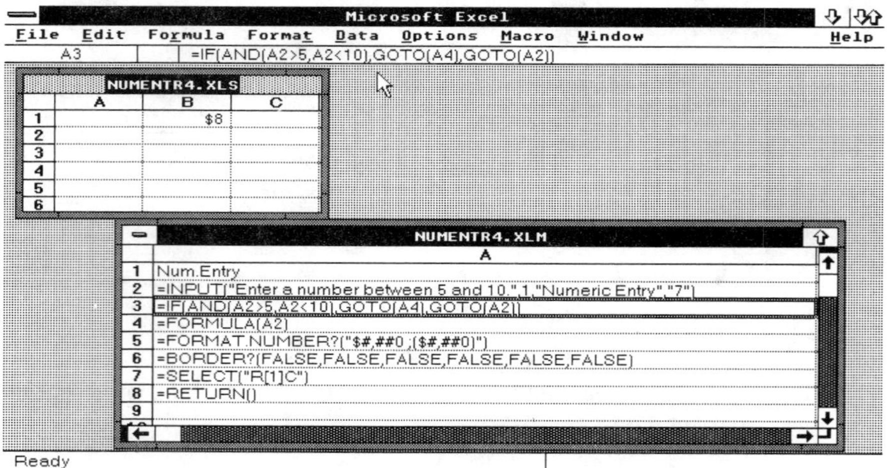

Fig. 11.10. A data-entry checking macro.

Cell A2 in the macro sheet presents an input box. The value typed by the user is stored in cell A2 when the user chooses OK or presses Enter. Cell A3 checks the value in A2 received by the input box. If the value is greater than 5 and less than 10, macro control goes to cell A4 where the FORMULA( ) function enters the value in the active worksheet cell. If cell A3 finds that the number is out of the set limits, macro control returns to the input box in A2 so that the user can enter an acceptable number.

11.13 Tip: **Use GOTO( ) to loop and repeat a macro.**

Use the GOTO( ) function to transfer macro control. For example, you can make the data-entry macro run in figure 11.10 continuously by putting a GOTO( ) function at the end of the macro; this function returns control to the top of the macro.

Figure 11.11 shows adding GOTO( ) to loop the data-entry macro. You can stop this macro by pressing Esc (PC) or Command+. (Macintosh).

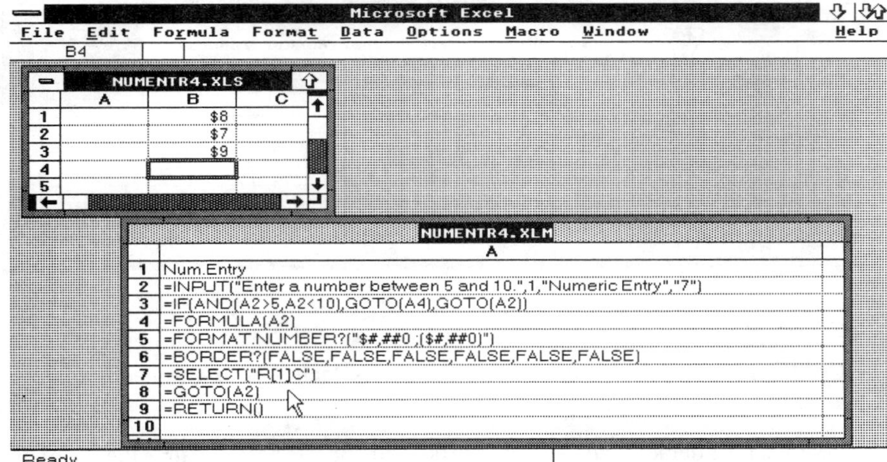

Fig. 11.11. Looping the macro by using GOTO.

11.14 Tip: **Use ALERT( ) type-1 dialog boxes to give users a choice.**

ALERT( ) functions display a dialog box containing text you specify and a button. The type-1 ALERT( ) function displays a box containing both an OK and a Cancel button, enabling you to prompt the user for a choice. The syntax for the ALERT( ) function is

=ALERT(*message_text*, *type_num*)

The *message_text* must be a reference to a cell or text within quotation marks. The *type_num* is the number 1, 2, or 3. Each number produces a different type of alert box. A type-1 box generates a caution message with two buttons: OK and Cancel. A type-2 box generates a note message with just the OK button. And a type-3 box produces a stop message with just the OK button.

You can modify the data-entry macro to include a box that asks whether additional entries are desired (see fig. 11.12). The next tip describes how to detect whether the user chooses OK or Cancel and shows how to change macro operation depending on that choice.

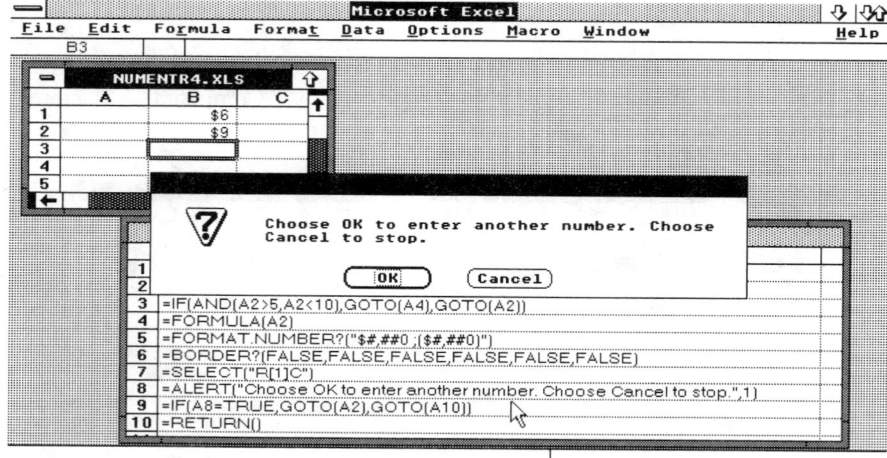
Microsoft Excel
File Edit Formula Format Data Options Macro Window Help
B3
NUMENTR4.XLS
A B C
1 $6
2 $9
3
4
5
Choose OK to enter another number. Choose Cancel to stop.
OK
Cancel
1
2
3 =IF(AND(A2>5,A2<10),GOTO(A4),GOTO(A2))
4 =FORMULA(A2)
5 =FORMAT.NUMBER?("$#,##0 ;($#,##0)")
6 =BORDER?(FALSE,FALSE,FALSE,FALSE,FALSE,FALSE)
7 =SELECT("R[1]C")
8 =ALERT("Choose OK to enter another number. Choose Cancel to stop.",1)
9 =IF(A8=TRUE,GOTO(A2),GOTO(A10))
10 =RETURN()

Fig. 11.12. An alert box with OK and Cancel buttons.

11.15 Tip: **Use IF( ) functions to test whether the user selects OK or Cancel in an alert box.**

Figure 11.12 demonstrates using an IF( ) function to test whether the user has selected OK or Cancel. When the user selects the Cancel button, the macro function returns FALSE. If the user selects OK, the ALERT( ) function returns TRUE. You can use the TRUE, FALSE, or value returned by a box to control macro operation.

In figure 11.13 the ALERT function( ) in cell A8 prompts the user to choose OK or Cancel from the alert box. If the user chooses OK, A8 contains the value TRUE, making the IF function( ) in A9 transfer macro operation back to the top, A2. If the user chooses Cancel, A8 contains FALSE, and control passes to cell A10, the end of the macro. Chapter 12 on advanced macros describes the returned values for one or more OK buttons in custom dialog boxes.

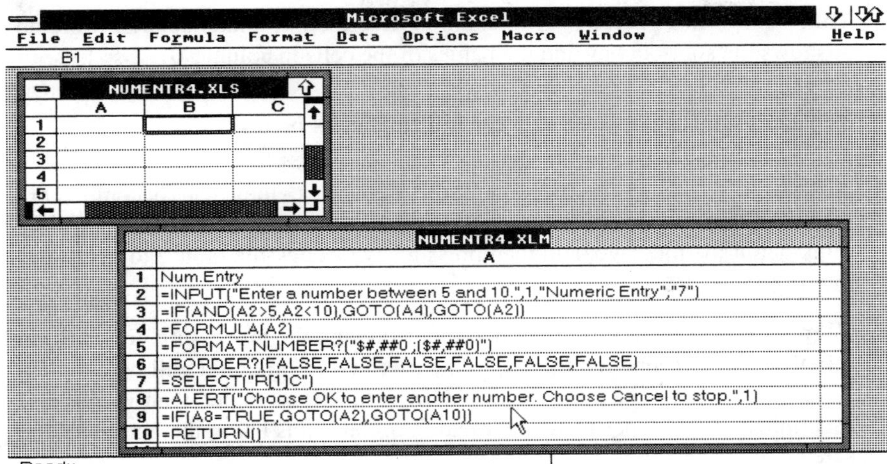

Fig. 11.13. Using an IF( ) function to check which button is selected.

11.16 Tip: Use modified alert boxes to inform the user about macro operation.

You can use values from other functions to create alert messages. For example, the ALERT( ) function in B5 in figure 11.14 uses the value from the INPUT( ) function in B2 to create a message. If the entry is within the set parameters, the macro bypasses the alert message in B5 with a GOTO command. Otherwise, the macro continues to run and generates the message. The &B2& in the alert formula calls for the value from B2.

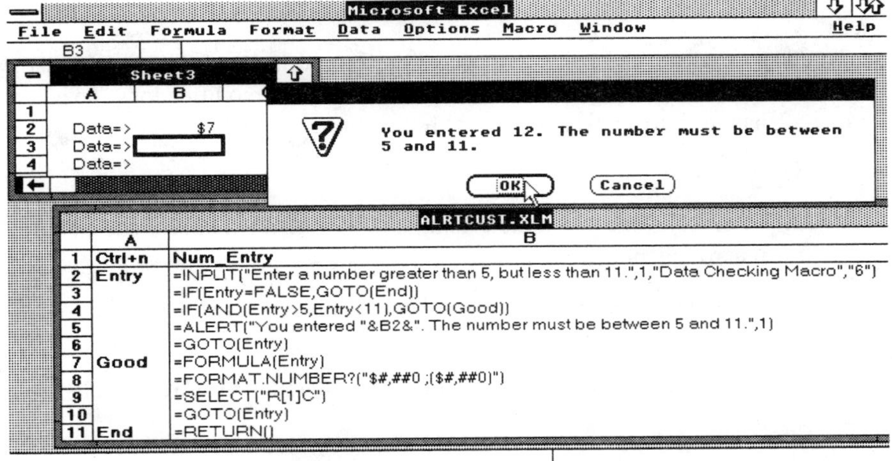

Fig. 11.14. Another alert box.

This macro shows partial documentation described in a later section. Column A shows the shortcut key and the names of the cells in column B.

11.17 Tip: **Substitute status bar messages for multiple alert boxes.**

As ALERT( ) functions become more numerous, they can become more annoying than helpful. Each alert box requires the user to look at the screen, think about the message, and then press a key or click the mouse to get things moving again.

To provide on-screen information without slowing the processing, try using an initial ALERT( ) function to remind the user that information will be provided in the status bar. Then use MESSAGE( ) functions rather than ALERT( ) functions to display pertinent information in the status bar at the bottom of the screen.

The MESSAGE( ) function syntax differs from that of the ALERT( ) function. The first argument in a MESSAGE( ) function must be either TRUE or FALSE. If the first argument is FALSE, the function clears the status bar. If the first argument is TRUE, the function takes a second argument—the message itself, enclosed in quotation marks. An example message is

=MESSAGE(TRUE,"Now updating the inventory records.")

A status bar message remains on-screen until it is either replaced by another message or eliminated with the =MESSAGE(FALSE) function. You should always clear the status bar before ending the macro.

11.18 Trick: **Use the macro recorder to modify existing macros.**

To add to existing macros, you don't need to type macro functions. Instead, you can use the macro recorder to record many of your modifications. To enter macro changes into an existing macro, follow these steps:

1. Activate the macro sheet.
2. Insert cells or rows in the existing macro to make room for additional macro functions.
3. Select the top cell in the inserted cells. This is where the new macro functions will appear.
4. Choose **M**acro Se**t** Recorder to specify where the macro should be placed.

5. Choose **M**acro **A**bsolute Record or Rel**a**tive Record.
6. Choose **M**acro **S**tart Recorder.
7. Choose commands, select cells, or type entries that you want to add to the macro.
8. Choose **M**acro Stop Re**c**order to stop recording.

If the recorder runs out of blank cells, the recording will stop, and a dialog box will warn you. In this case, follow this same procedure to insert additional functions.

11.19 Trick: **Use Print Preview to record print macros without waiting for a lengthy print job.**

Recording print macros can be time-consuming if you have to wait for each print job to complete. Get around this delay by recording the macro using the **F**ile **P**rint command with the **P**review option selected. When the preview appears, choose Cancel.

The print function uses the following syntax:

=PRINT(*range*, *from*, *to*, *copies*, *draft*, *preview*, *parts*)

Once you record the macro, you can leave it as is to give the user a chance to preview the command. Or you can change the preview argument from TRUE to FALSE, enabling the PRINT( ) function to print directly.

11.20 Trick: **Use named ranges to create macros that print multiple areas.**

To make easy-to-record print macros, follow these steps:

1. Name the ranges of the areas you want to print.
2. Set the recorder if necessary and start the macro.
3. Press the Goto key, F5 on the PC or Command+G on the Macintosh.
4. Select the name of the range you want to print and choose OK.
5. Choose the **O**ptions Print **A**rea command.
6. Choose the **F**ile Page Se**t**up command and select options.
7. Choose the **F**ile P**r**inter Setup command if you want to change orientation or font cartridges.

8. Choose the **F**ile **P**rint command.

9. Repeat the process from Step 4.

This process of selecting a named range, setting the print area, and then printing creates a macro that is easy to understand and modify.

Understanding References and Values Returned by Macros

Excel macro functions are the same as formulas in a worksheet. They return values according to the operations they perform. Understanding the values returned by macro functions is fundamental to building custom macros and to troubleshooting.

11.21 Tip: **To understand macro operation, understand the values that the macro returns.**

A macro sheet is almost the same as a worksheet. One of the differences is that a macro sheet normally displays the formulas in each cell. In a worksheet, the display normally shows the values in each cell.

Macro functions also return a value to their cell. The value depends on the action taken by the macro function, the value the macro function received when the action completed, or whether the macro function successfully completed. These values are important to understanding how macros operate, to being able to write macros without the recorder, and to being able to troubleshoot macros.

In figure 11.15, two windows have been opened in the data-entry macro sheet. To display the values in the macro sheet on the left, choose the **O**ptions **D**isplay command and unselect the Fo**r**mulas option. Notice that in cell A2 in the left window you can see the value 9; this value was typed by the user in the input box. The TRUE values indicate valid operation of that function. If a macro function fails to operate, it might return FALSE. If the macro receives incorrect data or is used incorrectly, it returns one of the #ERROR values. OK buttons return TRUE, and Cancel buttons return FALSE, like the result in A8 of the left window. You can use this procedure to diagnose macros that are not working correctly.

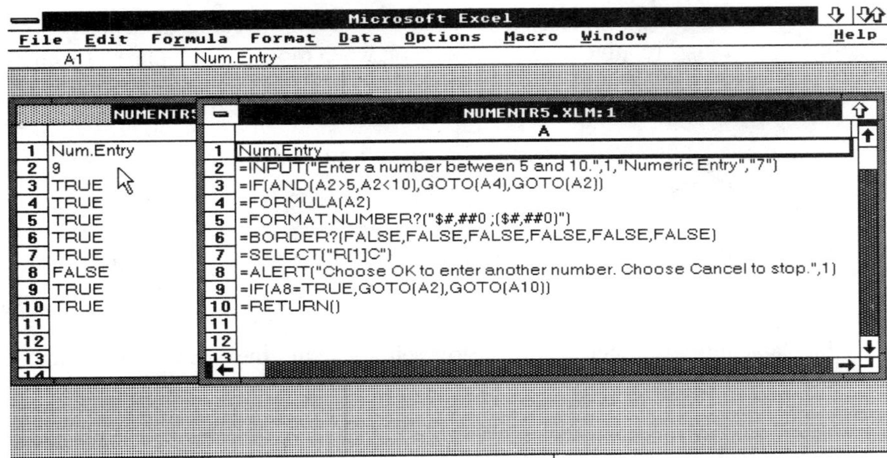

Fig. 11.15. Side-by-side macro windows showing return values.

11.22 Trick: Use a shortcut key to see macro values.

When you write or troubleshoot macros, it's important to see the values they return. Using the **O**ptions **D**isplay command to change the Formula option is cumbersome. Setting up two windows takes up too much room.

A much better alternative is to use the shortcut key that switches the display between formulas and values. On the PC, press Ctrl+‘ (the accent key, not the apostrophe). The accent key is located on the same key as the tilde (~). On the Macintosh, press Command+‘.

11.23 Tip: Understand macro cell references so you that you know the worksheet on which a macro is operating.

Excel macros can use either A1 type addressing or R1C1 addressing. A1 addressing uses columns lettered from A to IV and numbered rows. R1C1 addressing uses numbered rows, R, and columns, C. Both forms can use relative or absolute addressing.

Understanding the different reference types used within macros is important. Different types of references have different advantages and refer to different sheets. The following examples illustrate the different types of cell references:

The following absolute reference refers to cell A1 in the same worksheet. This reference does not change when moved to a new location in the macro sheet.

$A$1

The following relative reference refers to cell A1 in the same worksheet. This reference adjusts relative to its new location when moved in the macro sheet.

A1

The following absolute reference refers to cell A1 in the active worksheet:

!$A$1

The following relative reference refers to cell A1 in the active worksheet:

!A1

This absolute reference refers to cell A1 in the worksheet named FILENAME.XLS:

FILENAME.XLS!$A$1

This relative reference refers to cell A1 in the worksheet named FILENAME.XLS:

FILENAME.XLS!A1

The following absolute reference refers to cell R1C1 (A1) in the same worksheet as the macro:

R1C1

The following is a relative reference in the macro sheet to a cell relative to the cell containing this statement:

R[?]C[?]

The following is an absolute reference to a cell in the active worksheet:

!R1C1

The following relative reference refers to the active worksheet but its reference is relative to the location of the macro statement in the macro sheet. This reference can produce extremely confusing results.

!R[?]C[?]

This absolute reference refers to a cell in the active worksheet:

FILENAME.XLS!R1C1

The following is a relative reference to the cell in the macro sheet. The reference is not relative to the FILENAME.XLS worksheet.

FILENAME.XLS!R[?]C[?]

11.24 Tip: **Use the REFTEXT( ) or TEXTREF( ) functions to retrieve the value or the cell reference returned by a function.**

Functions such as ACTIVE.CELL( ) return a reference to a cell. When another macro function examines the cell containing ACTIVE.CELL( ), the function doesn't see the active cell's reference, but sees the value contained in the active cell. Before you can use the reference to the active cell, you must use a function such as the following:

```
=REFTEXT(ACTIVE.CELL( ))
```

This function converts the reference to the active cell's value into a text reference within quotation marks. The reference as text can then be manipulated or used by other macro functions that need a cell reference. The TEXTREF( ) function converts the text reference back into a normal cell reference. An example of the use of REFTEXT( ) and TEXTREF( ) is shown in Tip 11.28.

Selecting Cells and Ranges in a Macro

A basic concept in Windows applications such as Excel is to select items you want to change and then choose the command to make the change. If you are writing macros rather than recording them, you will need to know how to select ranges with a macro.

11.25 Tip: **Learn to use R1C1 references for better control.**

If you are an ex-Lotus 1-2-3 user, the R1C1 reference method may seem strange; however, this method makes complex programming in macros much easier to understand. In macros, relative references under the R1C1 reference system appear as R[?]C[?], where the question marks are the number of rows or columns different from the current selection. For example, R[2]C[-1] selects the cell 2 rows down and 1 column to the left. If there are no square brackets in a relative reference, the row or column is the same as the active cell. For example, RC[30] selects the cell in the same row as the active cell, but 30 columns to the right.

The tips in this section all use a similar case to demonstrate range selection. These tips show how to select a range, set the print area, and then print the range. The last three macro functions in each macro are the same; these include the print and end functions.

11.26 Tip: **Use range names in your macros.**

One of the easiest ways to select an area is to assign the range a name that the macro can reference. Before you create the macro, create a name for the cell or range you want to select. When you want to create the macro, use the Goto key, F5 (PC) or Command+G (Macintosh), to select the range name. Then choose the commands you want to affect the selected range. Range names are easy to use in macros. Also, range names will still refer to the correct area when you insert or delete cells through the middle of that range. Figure 11.16 shows a macro that selects and then prints the database range.

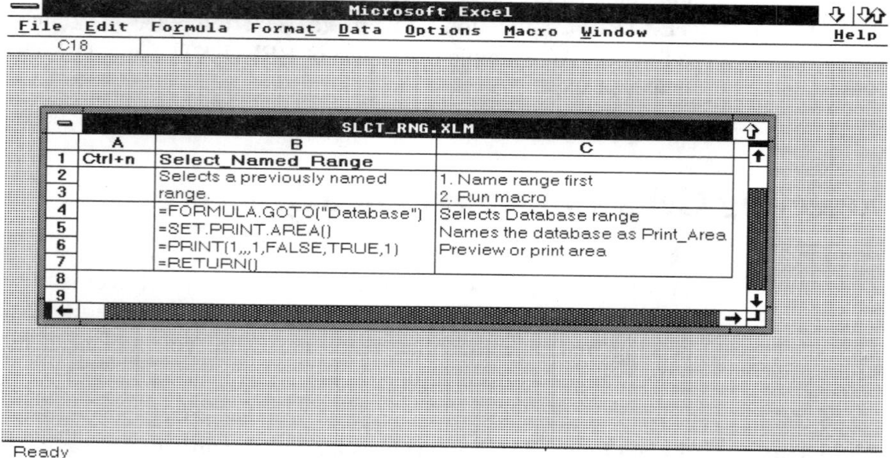

Fig. 11.16. A macro that selects and prints the database range.

11.27 Tip: **Select areas of adjoining cells with the Formula Select Special Current Region command.**

You can use another quick and convenient method of selecting areas. The Formula Select Special command with the Current Region option selects any group of filled cells that are surrounded by blank cells. In some cases, this command may select additional unwanted cells in your worksheet. If you design your worksheet ahead of time for this command, the command is easy to use.

The macro in figure 11.17 uses the SELECT.SPECIAL(5) command; this macro selects the region of filled cells that surrounds the current active cell. You must find a way to position the active cell within a region before running

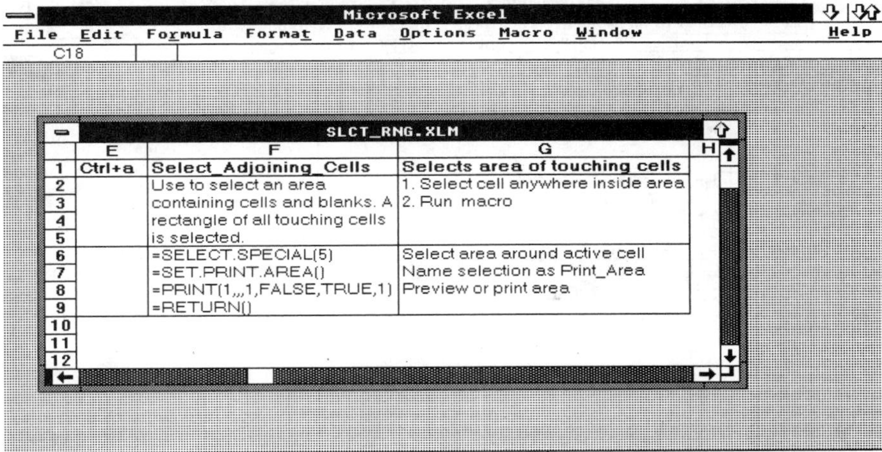

Fig. 11.17. *The SELECT. SPECIAL macro.*

this type of macro. You can record this macro by first selecting an active cell, turning on the macro recorder, and then selecting the Formula Select Special and **F**ile **P**rint commands.

11.28 Tip: **Select areas by their corner reference.**

You can select areas by finding the corner address of an area and then calculating the selection range from the corners. The macro in figure 11.18 works on ranges where the left column and bottom row are filled. A blank cell within the left column or bottom row prevents the macro from selecting the entire range.

Before running this macro, select the top left cell of the range. The names in column I are the range names of the cells to their right in column J. In figure 11.18 cell J7 finds the reference of the active cell and changes it to text. If the REFTEXT( ) function were not used, the value of the active cell would be returned. SELECT.END(4) moves the active cell down the column until a blank cell is reached. The REFTEXT(ACTIVE.CELL( )) again calculates the cell reference as text for this corner. SELECT.END(2) moves the active cell to the right until a blank cell is met; then the cell reference as text is calculated by another REFTEXT(ACTIVE.CELL( )).

The range is finally selected by the SELECT( ) function. The TEXTREF( ) functions change the text version of the cell references from text back into cell references that can be used by functions. For this macro to work, use the Formula Create Names command to name the cells in column J with the

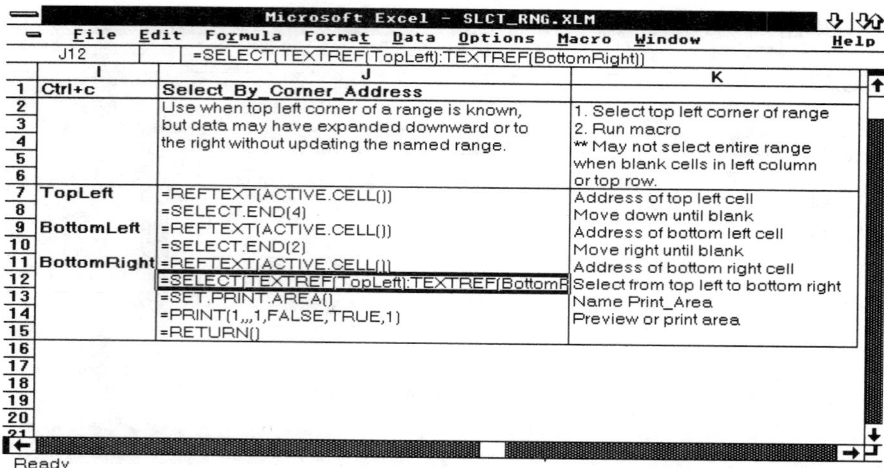

Fig. 11.18. Selecting a range by corner addresses.

names in column I. These names are then used in the formula in cell J12. You can see the full SELECT( ) function in the formula bar at the top of the window.

When using this macro, note that an entire range may not be selected if there is an unfilled cell in the left column or bottom row of the range. This macro works only if the range is at least two filled cells by two filled cells in size. The macro will not work on a single cell or a row or a column.

11.29 Trick: Select areas by macro duplication of keyboard shortcut keys.

This macro uses a trick to duplicate the PC Excel shortcut keys that move and select the active cell. The SEND.KEYS( ) function is used to record the same keystrokes that a user would press to select a range manually.

The macro in figure 11.19 duplicates the same Shift+Ctrl+arrow keys used to move across and select a row or column of filled cells. The macro also demonstrates how the ON.TIME( ) function is used to stop the macro, let the sent keystrokes work, and then restart the macro to finish the printing. As in the preceding macro, this macro may not select the entire range if the left column of data or the bottom row contains blanks.

In N6 and N7 the SEND.KEYS( ) function records the keystroke symbols for Shift+Ctrl+down arrow and Shift+Ctrl+right arrow. Notice that these keystroke symbols are enclosed in quotation marks. The appendix of the Microsoft Excel Functions and Macro reference manual contain a list of these keystroke symbols.

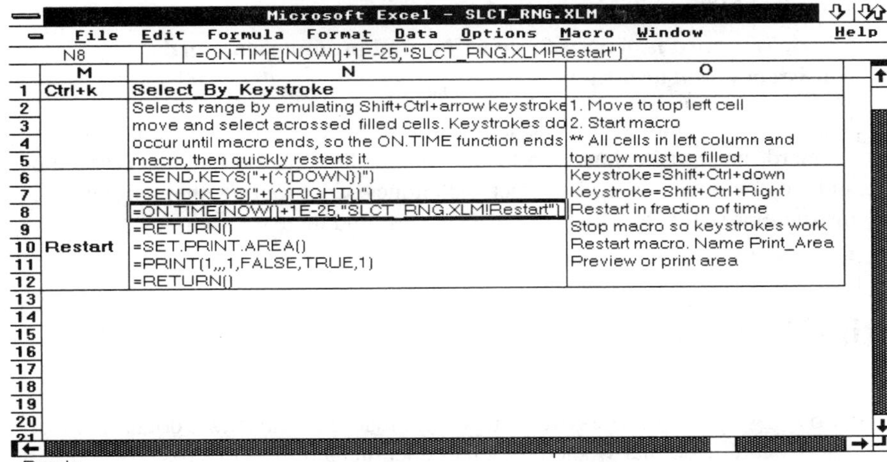

Microsoft Excel - SLCT_RNG.XLM
File Edit Formula Format Data Options Macro Window Help
N8 =ON.TIME(NOW()+1E-25,"SLCT_RNG.XLM!Restart")

	M	N	O
1	Ctrl+k	Select_By_Keystroke	
2		Selects range by emulating Shift+Ctrl+arrow keystroke	1. Move to top left cell
3		move and select acrossed filled cells. Keystrokes do	2. Start macro
4		occur until macro ends, so the ON.TIME function ends	** All cells in left column and
5		macro, then quickly restarts it.	top row must be filled.
6		=SEND.KEYS("+(^{DOWN})")	Keystroke=Shift+Ctrl+down
7		=SEND.KEYS("+(^{RIGHT})")	Keystroke=Shfit+Ctrl+Right
8		=ON.TIME(NOW()+1E-25,"SLCT_RNG.XLM!Restart")	Restart in fraction of time
9		=RETURN()	Stop macro so keystrokes work
10	Restart	=SET.PRINT.AREA()	Restart macro. Name Print_Area
11		=PRINT(1,,,1,FALSE,TRUE,1)	Preview or print area
12		=RETURN()	

Ready

Fig. 11.19. Selecting a range by keystroke.

The keystrokes sent by SEND.KEYS do not operate until a macro ends. Although this appears to present a problem, you can easily overcome the problem by using the ON.TIME( ) function to set a time to restart the second part of the macro. Following the ON.TIME( ) function, the RETURN( ) function stops the macro. In a small fraction of a second, the ON.TIME( ) function reaches its time limit and restarts the macro at Restart, cell N10. The second part of the macro prints the selection.

Working with Function Macros

Macro functions can save you considerable time and improve the accuracy of your work. These functions enable you to create worksheet or macro functions that aren't native to Excel. If you can't find a math, financial, text, or statistical function you need, you can create it with a function macro.

11.30 Trick: **Save typing time when duplicating ARGUMENT( ) functions.**

Use the Ctrl+" key combination to copy ARGUMENT( ) functions down from the preceding line in function macros. Once the ARGUMENT( ) function is in the formula bar, press F2 or click in the formula bar and change the arguments within the parentheses.

11.31 Tip: **Create standard functions to save time and promote standards, consistency, and accuracy.**

Your company can save time and increase accuracy by developing sets of standard functions that are in a locked macro sheet. These functions should be audited for accuracy and correct techniques. Distributing them freely with instructions will help reduce duplicate efforts and increase accuracy.

Documenting Macros

Two types of people work frequently with macros—those that document their macros and those that wished they had documented their macros. As you will see in the following examples, you can easily document macros. Documentation can save you and others a great deal of time if you ever need to make changes.

11.32 Tip: **Always name macros in the macro sheet.**

Always name macros. If you record a macro, enter a name when requested. If you write or add to a recorded macro, ensure that the name of the macro starts at the top of the macro code.

In the top row, to the left of the macro name, enter the shortcut key for the macro if one is used. This makes the associated shortcut key obvious.

11.33 Tip: **Use a three-column layout for command macro documentation.**

Figure 11.20 demonstrates one convenient way to document a macro within the macro sheet. The macro name is at the top of the column containing macro functions. The top row of the macro contains from left to right, the shortcut key, the macro name, and a description area. The top row is formatted as bold for easier reading.

The top areas above the macro describe how to operate the macro and what its limitations are. A description of what each macro function does is in the right column.

The left column is an important addition; this column contains the range names for the macro cells to the right. You can enter the names in column I

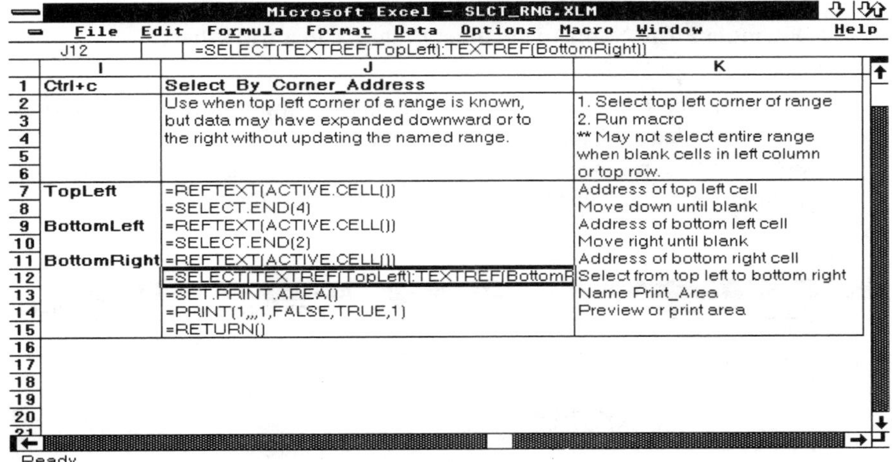

Fig. 11.20. A three-column macro layout.

and then use the Formula Create Names command to assign all the names at one time.

The outline around the macro is not entered until the macro is complete. The outline makes the macro easier to read.

11.34 Tip: Insert text subheadings and explanations in macros for clarification.

Excel macros attempt to process a cell's contents only if the cell starts with an equal sign (=). This means that you can enter text descriptions or add titles to macro subsections directly in the macro. As long as the cells don't contain an equal sign, they won't affect macro operation. Macros are a kind of programming language and should be documented as a program is documented.

11.35 Trick: To protect macros, hide them.

You can hide some or all the macro functions even if the macro window is open. This process enables you to hide proprietary information.

To hide macro functions in a macro sheet, select the cells containing the functions and then choose the Format Cell Protection command. Select the Locked and Hidden options and choose OK. Now choose the Options Protect Document command. Enter a password if desired and choose OK. The macro functions will no longer be visible even when the macro sheet is open.

11.36 Tip: **Use Formula Paste Name to document macros in a worksheet.**

To document the names and locations of macros, find a clear area in your macro sheet at least four columns wide and as many rows deep as there are names in the macro sheet. Select the top left cell of this area and choose Formula Paste Name. The result will appear similar to figure 11.21.

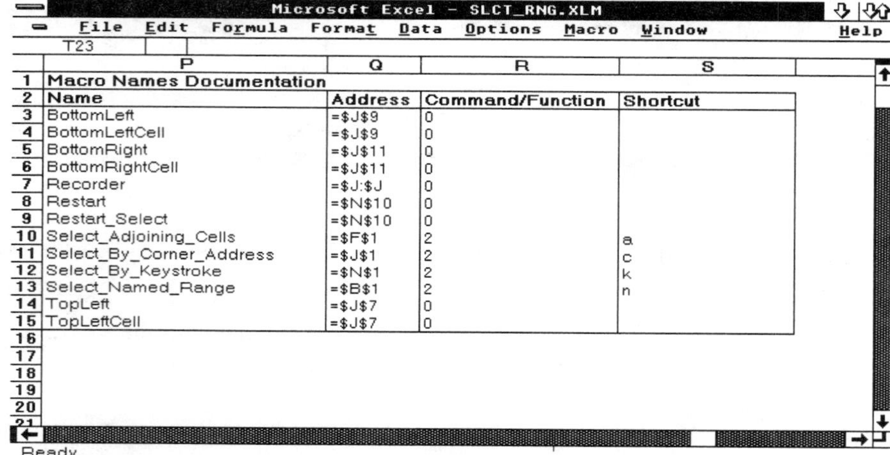

Microsoft Excel - SLCT_RNG.XLM

File Edit Formula Format Data Options Macro Window Help

T23

	P	Q	R	S
1	Macro Names Documentation			
2	Name	Address	Command/Function	Shortcut
3	BottomLeft	=$J$9	0	
4	BottomLeftCell	=$J$9	0	
5	BottomRight	=$J$11	0	
6	BottomRightCell	=$J$11	0	
7	Recorder	=$J:$J	0	
8	Restart	=$N$10	0	
9	Restart_Select	=$N$10	0	
10	Select_Adjoining_Cells	=$F$1	2	a
11	Select_By_Corner_Address	=$J$1	2	c
12	Select_By_Keystroke	=$N$1	2	k
13	Select_Named_Range	=$B$1	2	n
14	TopLeft	=$J$7	0	
15	TopLeftCell	=$J$7	0	
16				
17				
18				
19				
20				

Ready

Fig. 11.21. Macro names pasted in the worksheet.

In figure 11.21 the headings have been added for clarity. The first column in the pasted area contains the names. The second column contains the cell reference for that name. The third column contains a 0 for a cell reference name, a 1 for function macro names, and a 2 for command macro names. The fourth column displays the macro's shortcut key.

Troubleshooting Macros

Simple efficient macros add a great deal of productivity to the everyday work you do with Excel. But when you begin to create larger systems that are controlled by macros, you will run into macros that don't immediately run as you want. The tips in this section describe how to find and fix trouble spots in macros.

11.37 Trick: **Switch between formula and value display to see a macro function's result.**

Press the Ctrl+' (PC) or Command+' (Macintosh) key combination to switch the macro display between formula and value display. Check the results displayed for macro functions where a macro fails. Compare the value at the failure point to the values returned when the same macro function runs correctly.

11.38 Tip: **Check for undefined names or arguments when a #NAME error appears.**

If an undefined name or argument is used in a macro, the macro results in a #NAME error when used in the worksheet. To find these errors, use the Formula Find command. Type **#NAME?** in the Find **W**hat box, select the Values button, and then choose OK. You move to the first occurrence of #NAME. Using this process, you can find range names in the macro that have not been defined; then you can name the ranges using Fo**r**mula **D**efine Name.

11.39 Tip: **Insert a STEP( ) function to monitor macro functions.**

Insert a STEP( ) function a few cells before the location where you think a macro is operating incorrectly. When the macro reaches the STEP( ) function, the Single Step box is displayed (see fig. 11.22). This function enables you to single-step through the macro, seeing each macro function before it executes. If you want to continue with normal macro operation, choose the **C**ontinue

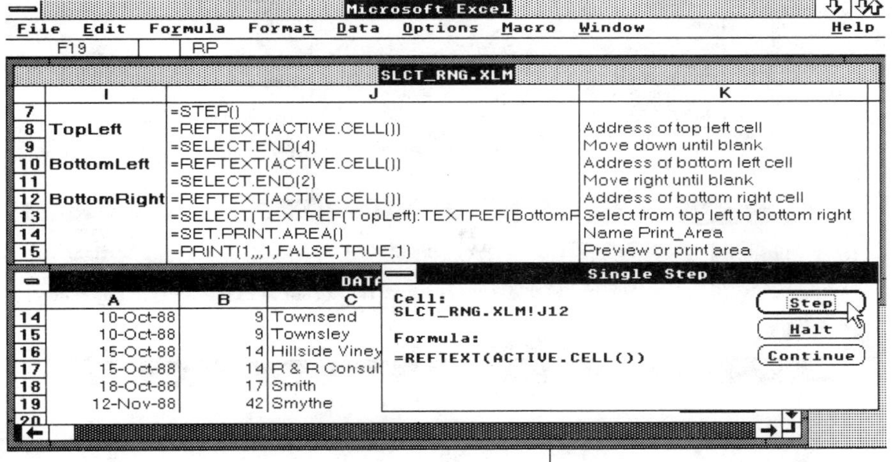

Fig. 11.22. The Single Step box.

button. If you want to stop the macro, choose **H**alt. To step forward to the next function select **S**tep.

Because the **C**ontinue button enables you to fast-forward through a macro, you can put numerous STEP( ) functions throughout a large macro. On reaching these points, choose the **C**ontinue button to go on.

Once your macros run correctly, you don't have to remove all of the STEP( ) functions. Use the Form**u**la R**e**place command to replace =STEP( ) with STEP( ) and change the function into text. At a later date, you can reinsert the equal sign if needed.

11.40 Trick: **See the macro function results in the Single Step box by holding down the Shift key.**

A valuable tip to all macro users is the Shift+Step combination. This key combination enables you to see the macro function before it executes, but it also enables you to see the result of each partial calculation with a complex macro function. For example, in figure 11.23 cell J13 contains a SELECT( ) function that has a calculated range. Figure 11.23 shows the SELECT( ) function when first reached in STEP mode. Figures 11.24, 11.25, and 11.26 show the progression of the calculation within SELECT( ) by holding down the Shift key as you select the **S**tep button. Each phase of the calculation is shown inside the Single Step box. The TRUE display in the Single Step box in figure 11.27 verifies the successful completion of the SELECT( ) function.

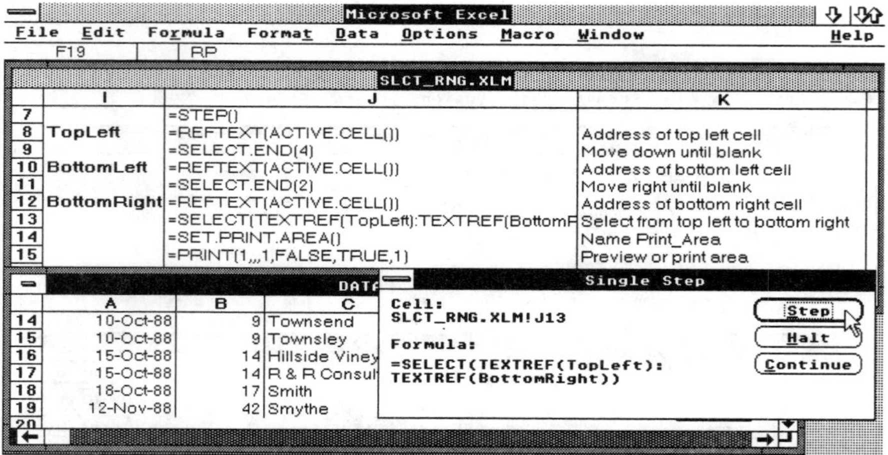

Fig. 11.23. Stepping through a macro.

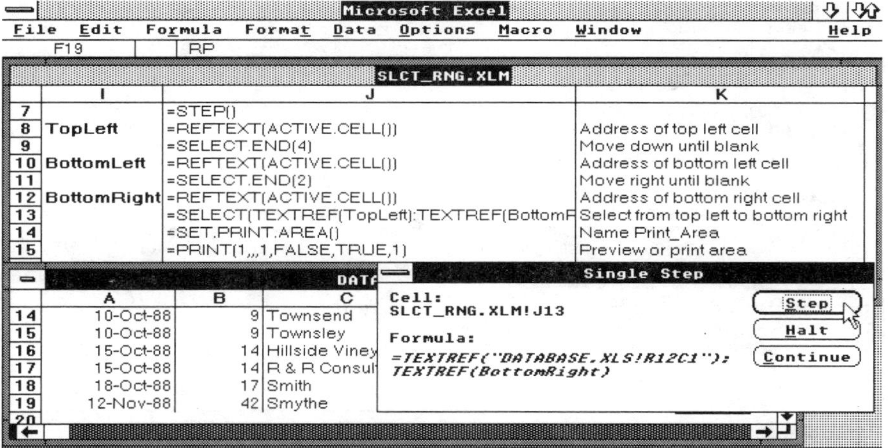

Fig. 11.24. Calculating the first part of the function.

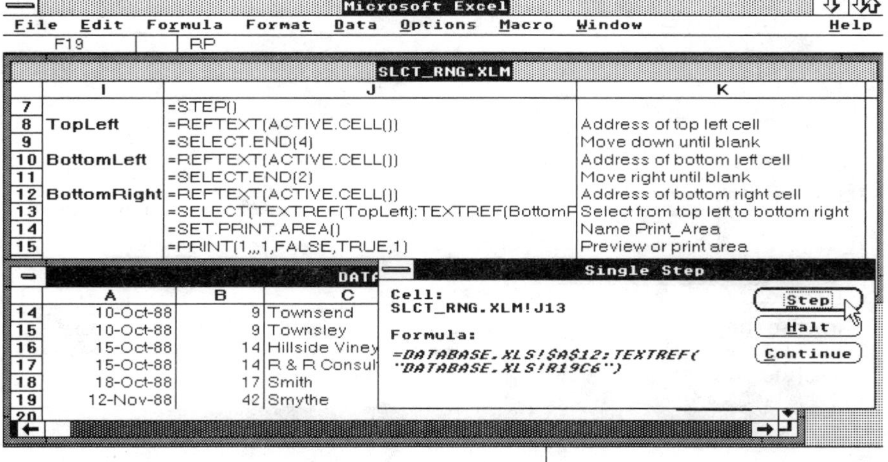

Fig. 11.25. Calculating the second part of the function.

To see the conversion of the names TopLeft and BottomRight into references and then the conversion into text references by the TEXTREF( ) functions, follow these steps:

1. Insert a STEP( ) function before the macro function you want to observe.

2. Run the macro.

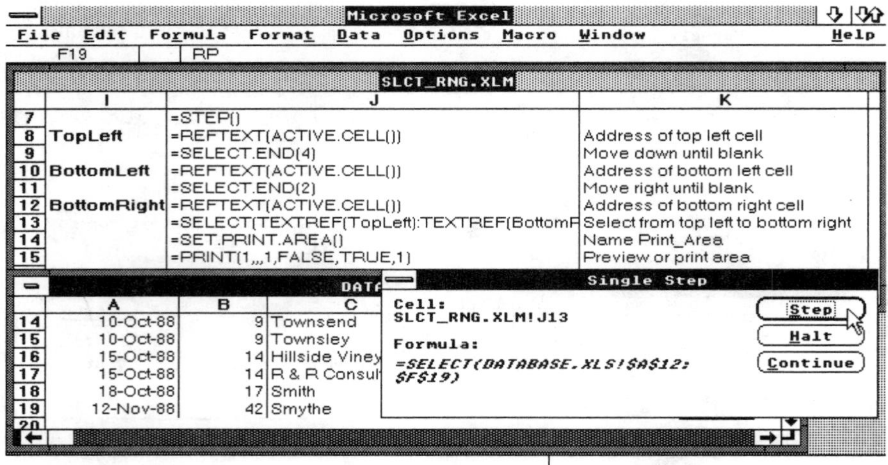

Fig. 11.26 Calculating the third part of the function.

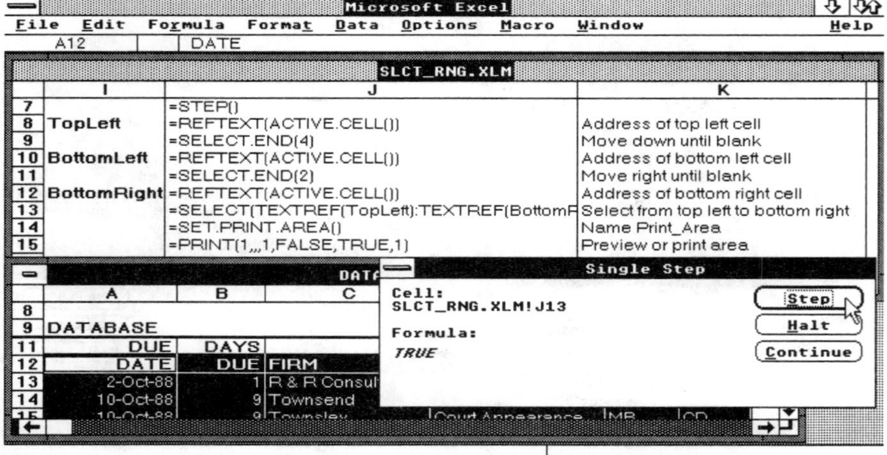

Fig. 11.27. The result of the function.

3. Hold down the Shift key as you press Enter or select the **St**ep button.

4. Observe the change to the function displayed within the Single Step box.

5. Repeat Steps 3 and 4.

Each press of Shift+Enter or Shift+Step completes a partial calculation of the macro function currently operating and displays the result of that partial calculation in the Single Step box.

11.41 Trick: **Use a simple macro to run STEP mode when you run any macro.**

When you test macros, it's convenient to start STEP mode without always having to insert a STEP( ) function at the beginning of a macro. You can do this with the following macro:

```
Run.Step
=STEP( )
=RUN?( )
=RETURN( )
```

Suppose that, for example, you are currently debugging a macro called Enter.Receipts and you want to run Enter.Receipts in STEP mode. When you run the Run.Step macro with a shortcut key, the macro starts STEP mode and then displays the Macro **R**un dialog box so that you can select a macro to run.

11.42 Tip: **Test fragments of a macro with another macro.**

The following short macro is great for testing fragments or sections of your macros before you assign names and shortcut keys. First, name and assign a shortcut key such as Ctrl+s to the Short.Test macro. Then select the cell where you want to start testing and press Ctrl+s to run that macro. Be sure that you have put a RETURN( ) or a HALT( ) function where you want the macro to end.

```
Short.Test
=RUN(ACTIVE.CELL( ))
=RETURN( )
```

12

Creating Advanced Macros

This chapter discusses tips, tricks, and traps you can use to create advanced macros. From this information, you learn how to use the dialog editor to create dialog boxes, how to increase macro performance, and how to implement other time-saving macro features. The first section includes tips to consider when designing macros.

12.1 Tip: **Create hidden macro sheets.**

Creating macro sheets and worksheets that are hidden when they open can help you produce polished applications. The Excel user never sees the macro or worksheet open and never sees the screen flicker; the user sees just the Excel screen or your custom menus.

One way to create a macro sheet that stays hidden when it opens is to make an entry or change to the macro sheet and then hide it using the **W**indow **H**ide command. With the macro sheet hidden, choose the **F**ile E**x**it command to close Excel. Because you did not save your change, you are prompted to save the macro sheet. Saving the macro sheet will save it as a hidden file. When reopened, the macro sheet will still be hidden.

The disadvantage to this solution is that you may want to continue working in Excel. Figure 12.1 shows a macro that keeps Excel open and saves the hidden worksheets. To operate this macro, make a small change in the macro sheet and then hide it with the **W**indow **H**ide command. Now press the shortcut key to run the macro. Excel closes all worksheets. If changes have been made but not saved, you are asked whether you want to save the changes. Respond yes, and the macro sheet is saved.

Fig. 12.1. A printout of a macro to hide worksheets.

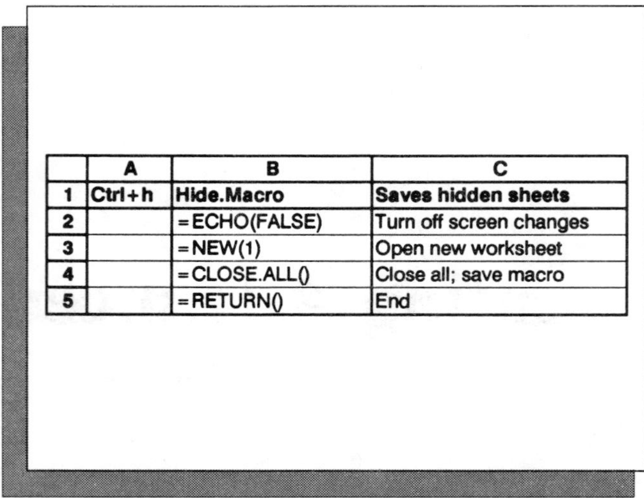

	A	B	C
1	Ctrl+h	Hide.Macro	Saves hidden sheets
2		=ECHO(FALSE)	Turn off screen changes
3		=NEW(1)	Open new worksheet
4		=CLOSE.ALL()	Close all; save macro
5		=RETURN()	End

12.2 Tip: **Create macros you can reuse.**

Whenever possible, break your macros into subroutines that can be reused. When correctly designed, an Excel macro can be called or run from another Excel macro. The macros do not have to be designated as subroutines.

If you design each macro so that it is generic, you can use the macro for different programs. For example, two macros that switch between landscape and portrait page orientation are provided later in this chapter. At the end of each macro, the current Print_Area is printed.

By removing the PRINT( ) function at the end of these macros, you can use them as page orientation subroutines by any other macro.

If you create generic subroutines, you can group and store them in libraries of macro sheets. For example, one macro sheet could contain print subroutines, another formatting subroutines, another menu subroutines, another dialog box templates, and so on.

Working with Macro Functions

Excel contains more macro functions than any other electronic worksheet. Excel has as many commands as most programmable databases. The number of functions may seem overwhelming; however, many functions duplicate commands you are familiar with from the menus.

12.3 Tip: **Note that some macro functions return their values in arrays.**

The DOCUMENTS( ) and WINDOWS( ) functions are similar in that they return information about open documents. Note some subtle differences between these functions. The DOCUMENTS( ) function returns the name of each worksheet once, even if you have four open windows of the same worksheet. Also, the worksheets are listed in alphabetical order. The DOCUMENTS( ) function stores the names in a horizontal array.

The WINDOWS( ) function also returns an array of names, but the active worksheet is listed first. Other worksheets are stored in a horizontal array in their order from top to bottom. Additionally, the WINDOWS( ) function returns a name for every open window you have. The next tip demonstrates how names are arranged in the array.

12.4 Tip: **Use the calculate shortcut key to cross-check the values returned by the DOCUMENTS( ) or WINDOWS( ) function to ensure that you have a complete list of all open worksheets and windows.**

To understand how DOCUMENTS( ) and WINDOWS( ) return names, enter and run the macro in figure 12.2. Enter DOCUMENTS( ) and WINDOWS( ) functions by either pressing Enter or by pressing Shift+Ctrl+Enter as you would to enter an array.

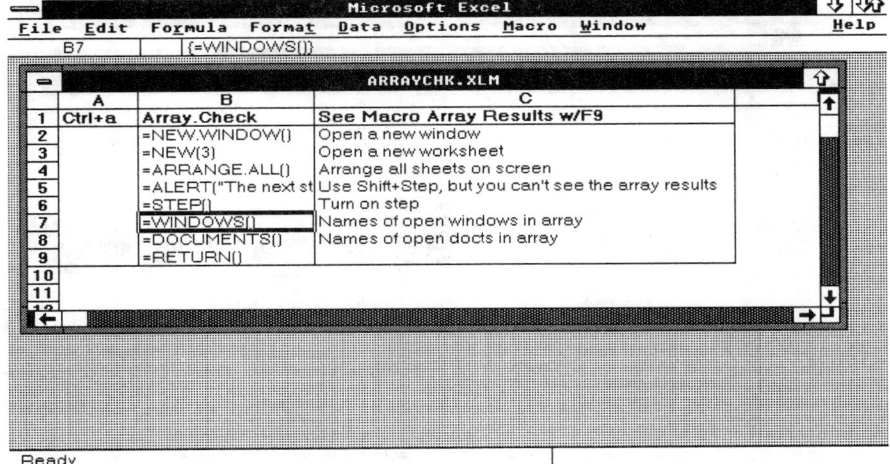

Fig. 12.2. A macro to check array results.

When you run this macro, two additional worksheets are opened and arranged. An alert box appears asking you to use Shift+Step to continue. Choose OK. When the next box appears, hold down the Shift key and choose OK.

In figure 12.3 notice that the WINDOWS( ) and DOCUMENTS( ) functions do not appear to return values as other functions do with Shift+Step. To find out what these functions do return, select cell B7, the cell that contains WINDOWS( ). Select the WINDOWS( ) formula in the formula bar and then press F9 or Command+= to calculate the formula. Figure 12.4 illustrates that the WINDOWS( ) function actually contains an array of names.

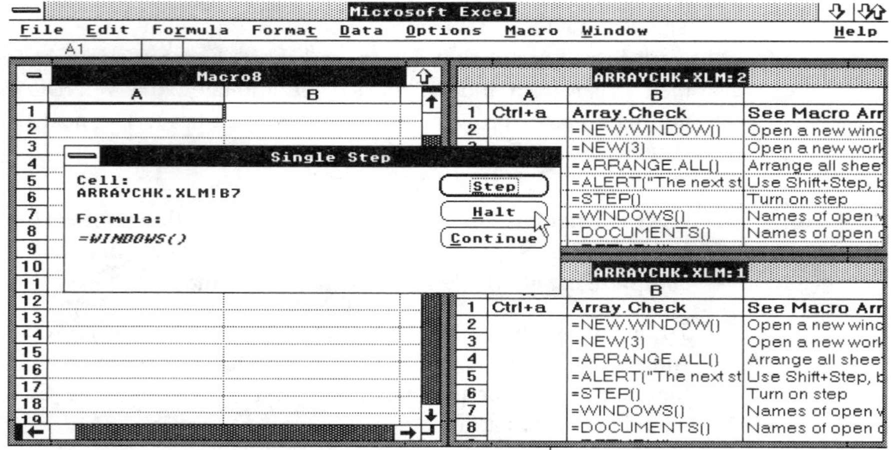

Fig. 12.3. The WINDOWS function in the Single Step box.

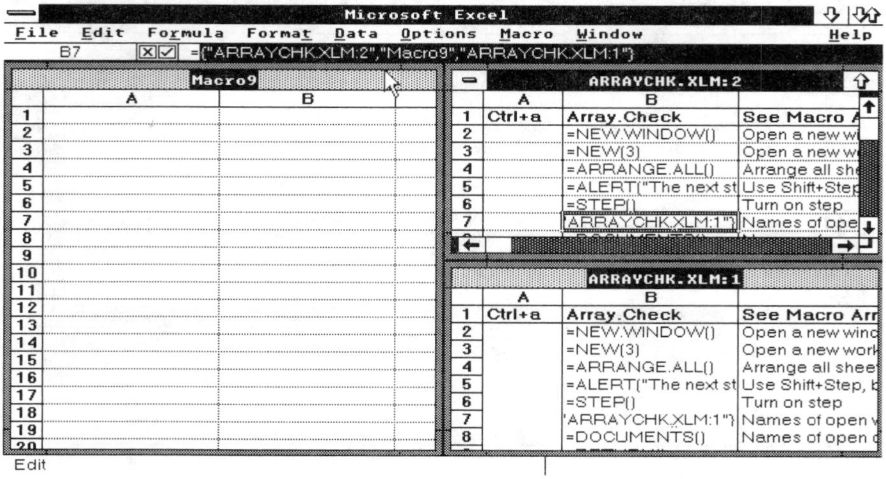

Fig. 12.4. The WINDOWS function evaluated as an array in the formula bar.

12.5 Tip: **Enter the WINDOWS( ) and DOCUMENTS( ) functions as arrays to separate the results into individual cells.**

To separate the names stored in the horizontal arrays of the WINDOWS( ) and DOCUMENTS( ) functions, enter the functions into the macro sheet as arrays. For example, to enter the DOCUMENTS( ) function, select the range B10:D10, type the function, and then press Shift+Ctrl+Enter. Then enter the WINDOWS( ) function in the same fashion (see fig. 12.5).

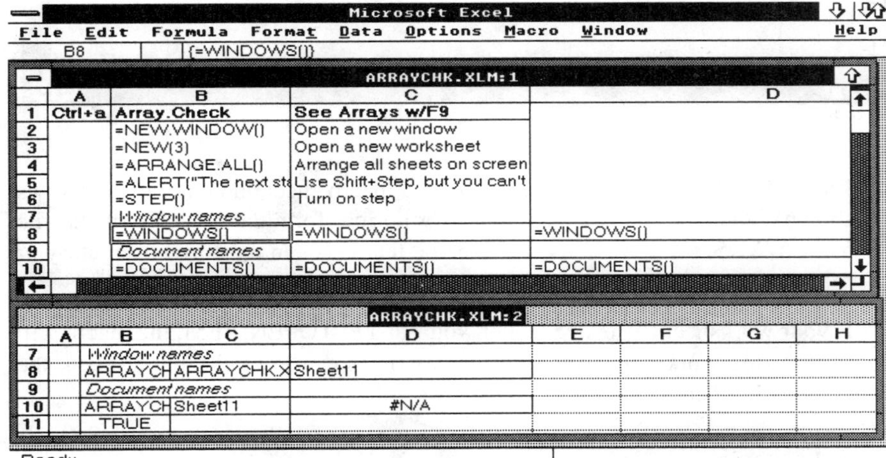

Fig. 12.5. Entering DOCUMENT and WINDOWS as arrays.

After running the macro, use Ctrl+' (accent) on the PC or Command+' (accent) on the Macintosh. Or choose **O**ptions **D**isplay and unselect Fo**r**mulas to display the values returned by the two arrays (see fig. 12.6). Notice that duplicate windows appear in the WINDOWS( ) array. The #NA error indicates that there were not enough array elements to fill the entire selection.

12.6 Trick: **Combine SUM( ), IF( ), and DOCUMENT( ) functions to test whether a worksheet is open; then activate or open the worksheet.**

A frequent need in macros is to test whether a worksheet is open. If the worksheet is already open, you may want to activate it so that it appears on top. Or if the worksheet is not open, you may want the macro to open it. This trick shows you how to check the contents of the DOCUMENTS( ) array to determine whether the worksheet you want is open.

Fig. 12.6. *Displaying the values returned by the two arrays.*

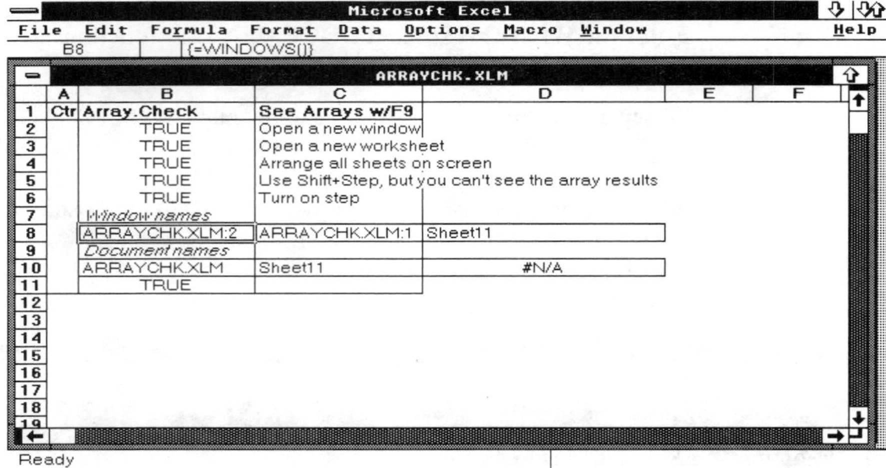

To create the macro in figure 12.7, open a macro sheet and enter the macro as shown. Enter the SUM( ) function as a normal formula. In place of the file name WRKSHEET.XLS, use a file name that exists in the current directory or folder on your disk.

If your worksheet file is open when you run TESTOPEN.XLM, the macro will activate the worksheet so that it appears on top. If your file is not open, the macro will open it.

Fig. 12.7. *A macro to test whether a worksheet is open.*

Microsoft Excel
File Edit Formula Format Data Options Macro Window Help
A1

TESTOPEN.XLM

	A	B	C
1	Ctrl+o	Test.Open	Test if sheet open
2		=SUM(IF(DOCUMENTS()="WRKSHEET.XLS",1,0))	
3		=IF(B2=1,ACTIVATE("WRKSHEET.XLS"),OPEN("WRKSHEET.XLS"))	
4		=RETURN()	
5			
6			

WRKSHEET.XLS

	A	B	C	D	E	F
1		Generic Quality Corporation				
2		Five Year Forecast				
3						
4		1988	1989	1990	1991	1992
5	Sales	$10,000	$11,000	$12,100	$13,310	$14,641
6						
7	Cost/Expenses					
8						
9	COG	3,000	3,300	3,630	3,993	4,392
10	G&A	2,000	2,200	2,420	2,662	2,928
11	Mktg	3,500	3,850	4,235	4,659	5,124

Ready

This macro works because the IF( ) function in B2 checks the value WRKSHEET.XLM against each element in the DOCUMENTS( ) array. The elements in that array contain the names of open files. If any one of those elements is WRKSHEET.XLM, IF( ) results in 1 (TRUE). If an element is not equal to the name, the function results in 0 (FALSE). Only one match is needed to produce a SUM( ) result of 1.

In cell B3, another IF( ) function checks to see whether the result is TRUE (the worksheet is already open) or FALSE (the worksheet is not open). If TRUE, the ACTIVATE( ) function brings the WRKSHEET.XLM file to the top. IF FALSE, the OPEN( ) function opens the WRKSHEET.XLM file.

You can use this same process to detect whether a file is still open. If the file is open, you can close it with a CLOSE( ) function.

12.7 Tip: **Use the + (plus) operator to place multiple operations in a single cell and therefore simplify writing macros.**

The concept of putting multiple operations in a single cell is exemplified by this simple macro:

```
Run.Step
=STEP( )+RUN(ACTIVE.CELL( ))
=RETURN( )
```

This macro uses the plus (+) operator to perform more than one function on a line. The plus operator can be helpful in IF( ) statements where you may want to produce multiple actions without having to run a subroutine. The plus operator works well when you want to execute two or more "action" commands. The Run.Step macro runs the macro that the active cell is on. As soon as the macro reaches the first function, STEP mode goes into effect.

Although this method is convenient for action commands, combining functions in this way may produce unusual returned values that are indecipherable to functions that try to read them.

Controlling Other Applications and Macros with SEND.KEYS

With SEND.KEYS( ) you can send keystrokes to Excel to produce an action for which there is no macro function. SEND.KEYS( ) will also send keystrokes to other Windows applications (or other applications open under

Macintosh Multifinder), enabling you to put Windows and other Macintosh applications under keyboard control during macro execution.

12.8 Trick: **Use ON.TIME( ) to send keystrokes and then immediately return to the macro.**

The keystrokes sent to the buffer by SEND.KEYS( ) don't take effect until the macro ends. If your macro must continue running, you encounter a problem. For instance, you may want a print macro to set the page orientation, print automatically, and then continue running.

You can take care of this problem by using the ON.TIME( ) function. Used with the NOW( ) function, ON.TIME( ) enables you to stop the macro so that keystrokes will be sent; the function then restarts another macro in a split second. The next tips describes using these functions in a printer setup macro.

12.9 Trick: **Use the SEND.KEYS( ) and ON.TIME( ) functions to control page orientation.**

Excel does not provide macros to change page orientation, select a different printer, or choose a different font cartridge. However, the SEND.KEYS( ) macro enables you to create your own printer setup macro.

Figure 12.8 shows two SEND.KEYS macros that change between landscape and portrait mode on HP LaserJet Series II printers. After changing orientation, these macros print the current Print_Area.

Fig. 12.8. Two print control macros.

Microsoft Excel - PRNTCTRL.XLM

File Edit Formula Format Data Options Macro Window Help

B2 =SEND.KEYS("%(s)%(n){Enter}{Enter}")

	A	B	C
1	Ctrl+l	Landscape	Print landscape
2		=SEND.KEYS("%(s)%(n){Enter}{Enter}")	Send keys: s n Enter Enter
3		=PRINTER.SETUP?()	Catches keys
4		=ON.TIME(NOW()+0.0000001,"PRNTCTRL.XLM!Print.Land")	Stop macro, then restart
5		=RETURN()	
6	Print.Land	=PRINT()	Restart here
7		=BEEP()	Beep
8		=RETURN()	
9			
10	Ctrl+p	Portrait	Print portrait
11		=SEND.KEYS("%(s)%(r){Enter}{Enter}")	Send keys: s r Enter Enter
12		=PRINTER.SETUP?()	Catches keys
13		=ON.TIME(NOW()+0.0000001,"PRNTCTRL.XLM!Print.Port")	Stop macro, then restart
14		=RETURN()	
15	Print.Port	=PRINT()	Restart here
16		=BEEP()	Beep
17		=RETURN()	
18			
19			
20			

Ready

Both of these macros work the same way. You can modify them for any printer that prints both portrait and landscape.

The first macro's SEND.KEYS( ) function contains these key codes:

"%(s)%(n){Enter}{Enter}"

These symbols translate to the following keys:

Symbol	*Key*
%	Alt
(s)	s
(n)	n
{Enter}	Enter
{Enter}	Enter

This function has the same effect as pressing Alt, s, n, Enter, Enter. The parentheses around the s and n indicate that the Alt key, %, should be held down. These are the keystrokes you would press from the Printer Setup dialog box to change an HP Series II printer to landscape: **S**etup, La**n**dscape, OK, OK.

The following sequence sends the keys to the buffer and restarts the macro:

```
SEND.KEYS( )
PRINTER.SETUP?( )
ON.TIME( )
RETURN( )
```

The SEND.KEYS( ) function sends these keystrokes to the keyboard buffer. But the buffer can't be read until the macro stops running. The keystrokes stay in the buffer until the macro pauses with the open command. Then the keystrokes flow from the buffer into regular memory. The next macro command will use these keystrokes as input. After SEND.KEYS sends keystrokes to the keystroke buffer, the Printer Setup dialog box is opened and held waiting with a ? mark.

Then the ON.TIME( ) function sets a time that is .0000001 of a 24-hour period from now. The RETURN( ) function ends the macro. After a brief pause, the macro resumes running at the location PRNTCTRL.XLM!Print.Land. During that interim pause, the keyboard buffer empties itself into the waiting Printer Setup dialog box and changes the page orientation.

When the time calculated by ON.TIME( ) is reached, macro control goes to the cell named Print.Land, B6. There the macro restarts beginning with the PRINT( ) function.

The portrait macro works in exactly the same fashion except that a different keystroke is used to select portrait. Be careful: the keystroke selections to change between orientation and landscape are different for different printers.

12.10 Trick: Use SEND.KEYS( ) to control Windows Write.

SEND.KEYS( ) enables you to control other Windows applications, even if those applications do not have DDE control. Using this function enables you to copy and paste data between Excel and other applications under macro control. You can even make the other applications print.

In figure 12.9, SEND.KEYS( ) is used to copy the active chart or selected cells from Excel and paste them into Windows Write. The Sheet.To.Write macro is used after worksheet cells are selected. The APP.ACTIVATE( ) function immediately activates Windows Write if it is already running and untitled. This application name, enclosed in quotation marks, must exactly match the application name in the application's title bar.

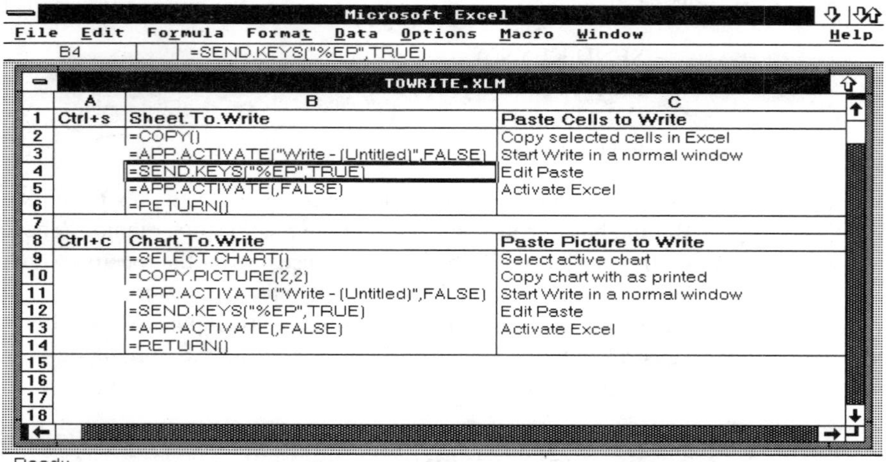

	A	B	C
1	Ctrl+s	Sheet.To.Write	Paste Cells to Write
2		=COPY()	Copy selected cells in Excel
3		=APP.ACTIVATE("Write - (Untitled)",FALSE)	Start Write in a normal window
4		=SEND.KEYS("%EP",TRUE)	Edit Paste
5		=APP.ACTIVATE(,FALSE)	Activate Excel
6		=RETURN()	
7			
8	Ctrl+c	Chart.To.Write	Paste Picture to Write
9		=SELECT.CHART()	Select active chart
10		=COPY.PICTURE(2,2)	Copy chart with as printed
11		=APP.ACTIVATE("Write - (Untitled)",FALSE)	Start Write in a normal window
12		=SEND.KEYS("%EP",TRUE)	Edit Paste
13		=APP.ACTIVATE(,FALSE)	Activate Excel
14		=RETURN()	
15			
16			
17			
18			

Fig. 12.9. *A macro to paste data to Windows Write.*

SEND.KEYS( ) then sends the keys Alt, E, P to Windows Write. These keystrokes choose the **E**dit **P**aste command and paste whatever is on the clipboard. The next APP.ACTIVATE( ) function reactivates the Excel application.

If you want to see the document in Write, press Alt+Tab to switch applications. If you paste tables of data into Write, you will probably have to format the document and set tabs. Pasting a chart into Write usually requires resizing the chart. You can perform all these tasks under SEND.KEYS( ) control.

The second macro in figure 12.9 (Chart.To.Write) allows you to copy a chart created in Excel into Windows Write.

Creating Dialog and Input Box Macros

Excel's dialog boxes are just one of the devices that set Excel apart. Intermediate and advanced macro programmers can create data-entry boxes that are attractive and easy to use. The following tips and tricks refer to the dialog box shown in figure 12.10. This dialog box enters student enrollment data into a database shown behind the dialog box.

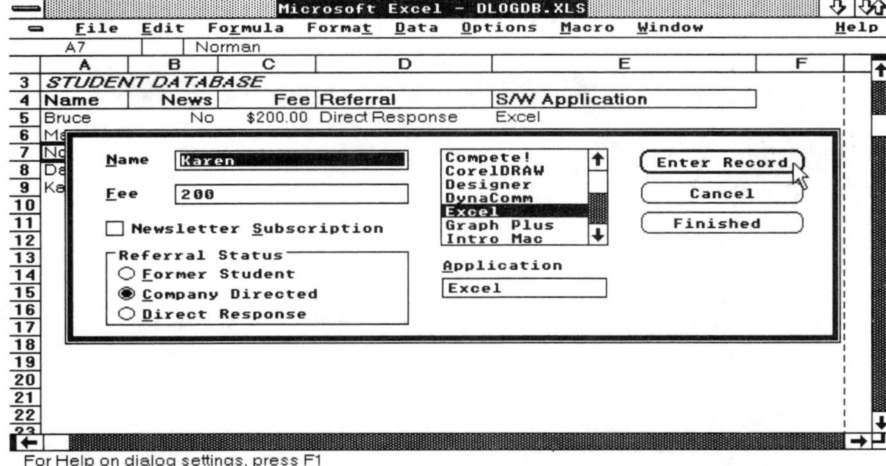

Fig. 12.10. A dialog box and database worksheet.

The macro that controls the dialog box and transfers data from the dialog box into the database is shown in figure 12.11. The dialog box range and its associated list for the scrolling list box are shown in figure 12.12.

Fig. 12.11. A printout of the data-entry macro.

	A	B
1	**Ctrl+e**	**Enter.Records**
2		ECHO(FALSE)
3		STEP()
4		*Set defaults, start dialog box*
5	**Restart**	=SET.VALUE($L$3:$L$18,{"";"Karen";"";"200";FALSE;"";"2";"";"";"";"";"Excel";"5";"";"";""})
6	**Dialog**	=DIALOG.BOX(F2:L18)
7		*Check command buttons*
8		=IF(Dialog=FALSE,GOTO(End))
9		*Data entry checks*
10		=Data.Check()
11		=IF(Chk.Fee=FALSE,GOTO(Restart))
12		*Insert Row in Database*
13		=FORMULA.GOTO("Database")
14		=SELECT("R[2]C")
15		=SELECT("R")
16		=INSERT(2)
17		*Insert Data in Row*
18		=FORMULA(Rslt.Name,OFFSET(ACTIVE.CELL(),0,0))
19		=FORMULA(IF(Rslt.News=TRUE,"Yes","No"),OFFSET(ACTIVE.CELL(),0,1))
20		=FORMULA(Rslt.Fee,OFFSET(ACTIVE.CELL(),0,2))
21		=FORMULA(CHOOSE(Rslt.Referral,"Former Student","Company Directed","Direct Respons
22		=FORMULA(Rslt.Appl,OFFSET(ACTIVE.CELL(),0,4))
23		=IF(Dialog=16,GOTO(End))
24		=GOTO(Restart)
25	End	=RETURN()
26		
27		
28	**Sbrtn**	**Data.Check**
29	**Chk.Fee**	=IF(AND(Rslt.Fee>=150,Rslt.Fee<=350),GOTO(Chk.Done))
30		=ALERT("Enter a number greater than $150, but less than $350.",2)
31	**Chk.Done**	=RETURN()

Fig. 12.12. A printout of the dialog box data.

	E	F	G	H	I	J	K	L	M	N	O
1	**Type**	**Item**	**X**	**Y**	**Width**	**Ht**	**Text**	**Int/Result**	**Result Names**		**List Box**
2	blank	12	0	0	552	177					Compete!
3	text	5	24	14	50	18	&Name				CorelDRAW
4	text edit	6	74	12	170	18		Karen	Rslt.Name		Designer
5	text	5	24	44	30	18	&Fee				DynaComm
6	number edit	8	74	42	170	18		200	Rslt.Fee		Excel
7	check box	13	24	72	220	18	Newsletter &Subscription	FALSE	Rslt.News		Graph Plus
8	group box	14	24	96	220	72	Referral Status				Intro Mac
9	radio group	11	24	114	180	45		2	Rslt.Referral		Intro PC
10	radio button	12	32	114	172	15	&Former Student				Lotus 1-2-3
11	radio button	12	32	132	164	15	&Company Directed				Mac Word
12	radio button	12	32	150	164	15	&Direct Response				PageMaker
13	text	5	268	108	88	12	&Application				Pres Mngr
14	text edit	6	268	126	120	18		Excel	Rslt.Appl		Q+E
15	linked list box	16	268	12	120	90	=REFTEXT(O2:O16)	5			Windows
16	default ok butto	1	412	12	120	21	Enter Record				WordPerfect
17	cancel button	2	412	39	120	21	Cancel				
18	ok button	3	412	66	120	21	Finished				

12.11 Tip: **Control dialog box default settings with the SET.VALUE( ) function.**

In the macro in figure 12.11, data entries into the dialog box are placed in the Int/Result column next to the appropriate item. For example, an entry for the Name field is placed in L4 in figure 12.12, the text edit box corresponding to &Name. The problem is that these entries write over any default settings you may have initially typed in those cells.

To reset default settings each time the dialog box appears, use the SET.VALUE( ) function shown in cell B5. SET.VALUE( ) is used in macros only to put a value into a cell. Rather than using multiple SET.VALUE( ) functions, one for each cell, B5 uses Excel's array capabilities to enter the array of values. The values are enclosed in brackets { } and entered into the range $L$3:$L$18. A set of quotation marks is used to mark cells that receive no default setting.

12.12 Tip: **Test a dialog box for check box selections.**

Check boxes, like the Newsletter Subscription check box in figure 12.10, return either TRUE if selected or FALSE if unselected. The value appears to the right of check box item. In figure 12.10, an unselected check box resulted in FALSE in cell L7 in figure 12.12. This is the same row as the check box definition.

12.13 Tip: **Test a dialog box for OK or Cancel.**

Many dialog boxes contain an OK and a Cancel button. OK buttons are a type-1 item if bold and selected or a type-3 if unselected. Cancel buttons are type-2 if unselected and type-4 if bold and selected. The selected button is the default when Enter is pressed.

Choosing the Cancel button produces a FALSE value behind the DIALOG.BOX( ) function in cell B6. Selecting any OK button produces an integer value in cell B6. The integer returned represents the position in the dialog box of that OK button.

In the Enter.Records macro, cell B8 checks for a Cancel selection by evaluating the name Dialog, which represents B6. If B6 is FALSE, the macro ends.

If the OK button defined as "Enter Record" in E16:L16 in figure 12.12 is selected, B6 will contain 14 in figure 12.11. This definition is the fourteenth item in the dialog box description. There is no test to see whether Dialog equals 14; therefore, the macro continues to run.

If the OK button defined as "Finished" in E18:L18 in figure 12.12 is selected, B6 will contain 16 in figure 12.11. This definition is the sixteenth item in the dialog box description. Cell B23 in the Enter.Records macro tests whether Dialog=16 and if so ends the macro.

Remember that you can have multiple command buttons each with a unique name. The result of their selection does not appear in the dialog box description, but in the cell with the DIALOG.BOX( ) function. The value returned for a selection is not related to the number of buttons, but rather is the button's position within the dialog box definition.

12.14 Tip: Test a dialog box for group results.

Grouping radio buttons together makes them act in concert. Only one button from the group can be chosen.

In figure 12.12, the range E9:L12 defines a group of radio buttons. Notice that the first item in the group has a type of 11 as shown in F9. The button chosen from the group appears in L9 on the same line as the radio group item. The number 2 in L9 indicates that the second radio button, Company Directed, was chosen. Cell M9 contains the name Rslt.Referral that names L9. The name Rslt.Referral makes it easier to refer to the button selection in formulas.

12.15 Trick: Transfer data out of a dialog box and into the worksheet using a macro.

Some users transfer data out of the dialog box and into the worksheet with the **E**dit **C**opy and **E**dit **P**aste commands. This method is painfully slow. A much faster method is shown in figure 12.11 in the cells B18:B22.

Before transferring data into the database, the macro functions from B12 to B16 move the active cell into the second row of the database and then insert a blank row. At that time, the active cell is the first cell in the blank row of the database. This active cell is used as a benchmark when data is entered into the blank row.

The FORMULA( ) functions in cells B18, B20, and B22 transfer the data from a named cell in column L into a blank row in the database in the active worksheet. The cell location in the blank row is defined as an offset from the active cell in the blank row. For example, in cell B18, the value in Rslt.Name is put in the cell defined as 0 rows down from the active cell and 0 rows to the right. All data are put in the same row as the active cell; therefore, the vertical offset from the active cell is 0.

To make it easier to write these FORMULA( ) functions, the cells in column L that contain entries returned by the dialog box are named with the names in column M in figure 12.12. These names are easy to create if you select both columns and then use the Formula Create Names command and specify the names in the right column.

A TRUE/FALSE response from the check box is handled in cell B19 with an IF( ) function. If the check box is selected, Rslt.News is TRUE, and the IF function( ) results in "Yes." If FALSE, the function results in "No."

Handling multiple-choice selections from the grouped buttons works differently. The formula bar in figure 12.13 shows a CHOOSE( ) function that selects a value from a list of text responses depending on the value of Rslt.Referral. Rslt.Referral can be 1, 2, or 3, each with different text results. In figure 12.13, CHOOSE( ) returns the value in the Rslt.Referral range name in L9. Therefore, CHOOSE( ) returns the value 2 or "Company Directed."

```
Microsoft Excel - DLOG08.XLM
File  Edit  Formula  Format  Data  Options  Macro  Window  Help
B21   =FORMULA(CHOOSE(Rslt.Referral,"Former Student","Company Directed","Direct
      Response"),OFFSET(ACTIVE.CELL(),0,3))
    A
4              Set defaults, start dialog box
5   Restart    =SET.VALUE($L$3:$L$18,{"";"Karen";"";"200";FALSE;"";"2";"";"";"";"";"Excel";"5";"";"";""})
6   Dialog     =DIALOG.BOX(F2:L18)
7              Check command buttons
8              =IF(Dialog=FALSE,GOTO(End))
9              Data entry checks
10             =Data.Check()
11             =IF(Chk.Fee=FALSE,GOTO(Restart))
12             Insert Row in Database
13             =FORMULA.GOTO("Database")
14             =SELECT("R[2]C")
15             =SELECT("R")
16             =INSERT(2)
17             Insert Data in Row
18             =FORMULA(Rslt.Name,OFFSET(ACTIVE.CELL(),0,0))
19             =FORMULA(IF(Rslt.News=TRUE,"Yes","No"),OFFSET(ACTIVE.CELL(),0,1))
20             =FORMULA(Rslt.Fee,OFFSET(ACTIVE.CELL(),0,2))
21             =FORMULA(CHOOSE(Rslt.Referral,"Former Student","Company Directed","Direct Resp
22             =FORMULA(Rslt.Appl,OFFSET(ACTIVE.CELL(),0,4))
23             =IF(Dialog=16,GOTO(End))
24             =GOTO(Restart)
Ready
```

Fig. 12.13. A formula to handle multiple-choice selections.

12.16 Trick: Use REFTEXT( ) to keep your scrolling list box accurate.

You can type the range for the scrolling list box in figure 12.10 as text in cell K15 in figure 12.12, but this method can cause trouble while you are developing the dialog box. If you change the size of the scrolling list range by adding or deleting items, the text range you've specified, O2:O16, does not adjust automatically.

Instead, enter the range of the list box using REFTEXT( ) as shown in K15 in figure 12.12. When you expand or contract the list by adding or deleting items, the range in K15 will adjust automatically.

Building Dialog Boxes with the Dialog Editor

The dialog editor does away with a great deal of the work involved in creating dialog boxes. With the editor, you select items for the box and then move them into place. When your dialog box is designed, you copy the dialog box and paste it onto the macro sheet. The pasted result is text and numbers that define the box. (The dialog editor was not available in the original release of Excel.)

12.17 Tip: **Use the dialog editor to save time creating dialog boxes.**

To create a new dialog box with the dialog editor, first activate the macro sheet that will contain the dialog box specifications. (This macro sheet can be blank.) Then choose the R**u**n command from the Application Control menu. Select the **D**ialog Editor option.

At this point, you can add whatever dialog box objects you want by choosing the **I**tem command and specifying the type of object you want. The mechanics of creating and editing dialog boxes are covered in the booklet, *Microsoft Excel Dialog Editor*, included with the Excel version 2.1 documentation.

When you are done editing your dialog box, do the following:

1. Choose the **F**ile E**x**it command. The dialog editor then asks whether you want to save the dialog box specifications to the clipboard.
2. Select **Y**es.
3. Select the cell in your macro sheet that will be the upper left cell of the dialog box description area.
4. Choose the **E**dit **P**aste command.

The information in the clipboard translates into dialog box specifications which are pasted into the macro sheet. You usually need to fine-tune the box to align text and entry boxes accurately.

12.18 Trap: **Select items in the dialog editor in an orderly manner.**

You must place certain types of dialog box items in adjacent rows in the dialog box description area in the macro sheet. For instance, a linked list box (object type 16) must be preceded by a text box (type 6), and groups of option buttons (type 12) must be in adjacent rows and preceded by an option button group (type 11). However, the dialog editor does not always arrange the specifications in the required sequence. (The location depends on the chronological sequence in which the objects were created in the dialog editor.)

You should, therefore, familiarize yourself with the sequencing rules that apply to the particular dialog box you are designing, and look over the dialog box description area after adding new objects in the dialog editor. Doing so can save you time by preventing macro errors when the DIALOG.BOX( ) function is calculated.

12.19 Trap: **Adding items in the dialog editor creates new rows that may destroy existing dialog data.**

To avoid losing data, always leave extra rows at the bottom of your dialog box description area. Do not specify these rows in the DIALOG.BOX( ) function. These rows will prevent the dialog editor from pasting additional items over areas of your worksheet should you later add more dialog items.

12.20 Tip: **Add additional items of the same type by pressing Enter.**

When you start with an empty dialog box in the dialog editor, the only way to add an object, an **E**dit Box for example, is to choose the **E**dit Box command from the **I**tem menu. Once you have created that first text box, though, you need only select that box and press Enter to add another one just like it. The next one will align directly below the first. This procedure works for most dialog box objects.

Note some exceptions, however. Pressing Enter while an OK or Cancel button is selected creates alternating OK and Cancel buttons rather than several of either kind. Selecting a group box and pressing Enter creates option buttons within the group box. (Incidentally, creating option buttons in this way ensures that the option buttons will be positioned perfectly within the group box.)

12.21 Trick: **Use a group box as a measuring device.**

If you want to line up the edges of dialog boxes to the exact pixel, you can use the **E**dit **I**nfo command. This command allows you to enter precise position and dimension information. As a faster method, you can create a group box and use its horizontal and vertical edges as rulers. To line up items vertically, just move and resize the group box so that the right edge of the group box is positioned where you want the right edges of all your objects. When you finish, delete the group box.

Group boxes also can come in handy as spacing devices. To provide the same amount of white space between the edges of the dialog box and the objects within it, just measure the space at one end with a group box and then move the group box to the opposite edge and line up the objects accordingly.

12.22 Tip: **Align items to present an attractive dialog box.**

Align items in dialog box editor by doing the following:

- Press Enter to duplicate items and align them directly below.
- Hold down Shift and drag the mouse to move multiple items and keep them aligned.
- Edit the positioning numbers in the dialog box definition range. For example, if multiple related items have X values of 57, 57, 56, 58, change them all to 57.

Increasing Macro Performance

Recorded macros are easy to create, but they may not run with optimum performance. By changing recorded functions such as CUT( ) and PASTE( ) to functions such as FORMULA( ), you can significantly increase speed. You also can use techniques that make macros seem faster, when in reality they are not.

12.23 Tip: **Make macros seem faster even though they operate at the same speed.**

You can get apparent performance improvements during macro operation by doing the following:

- Divide macro operations into segments that operate at dead times in the program. For example, while someone is reading directions, turn off the screen and format other parts of the worksheets or load hidden files.
- Load multiple files at one time. Unneeded files should be loaded as hidden files. When worksheets or charts are needed by the user, the file can be unhidden for quick display rather than waiting to load from disk.
- Consolidate long calculations and present the user with a box showing how long the calculations will take. The user can then work on something else.

12.24 Tip: Use FORMULA( ) and SET.VALUE( ) to transfer data.

Rather than using the COPY( ) and PASTE( ) functions in a macro, use FORMULA( ) to transfer any cell contents to another cell in any type of worksheet. To change cell contents in a macro sheet, you also can use SET.VALUE( ).

12.25 Tip: Use the FORMULA( ) function to copy cells more quickly.

Excel's macro recorder is easy to use, and because the recorder duplicates commands chosen from the menu, the recorder produces macro functions that are relatively easy to understand. But often a recorded macro is not the fastest way to do something.

One way of significantly speeding up your recorded macros is to replace COPY( ) and PASTE( ) commands with a FORMULA( ) function to transfer data. For example, figure 12.14 shows a recorded macro that transfers data between worksheets.

Even without the window activation functions, the macro in figure 12.15 is faster because it doesn't have to copy data into the clipboard before transferring the data to the cell being pasted. Figure 12.15 shows the significantly faster macro that uses the FORMULA( ) function.

The seven code lines of the first macro are replaced by the single line in the fast macro. Another advantage to the FORMULA( ) function is that the worksheets being transferred among do not have to be active, although they must be in memory.

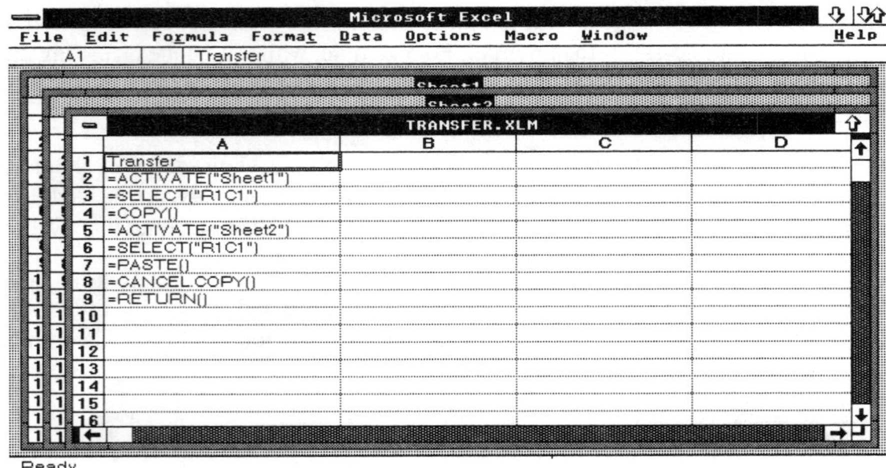

Fig. 12.14. *A macro that transfers data.*

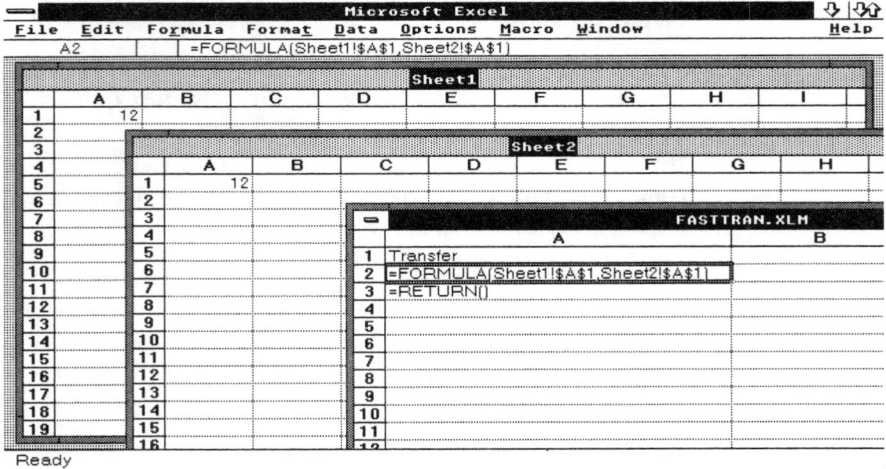

Fig. 12.15. *A faster data-transfer macro.*

12.26 Tip: Replace some PASTE.SPECIAL( ) functions with faster FORMULA( ) functions.

You can replace functions such as PASTE.SPECIAL( ) by the faster FORMULA( ) functions. Figure 12.16 shows a macro that combines cell A1 from SHEET1.XLS into cell A1 of SHEET2.XLS. The two cells are added together. A faster FORMULA( ) version of the same macro appears in figure 12.17.

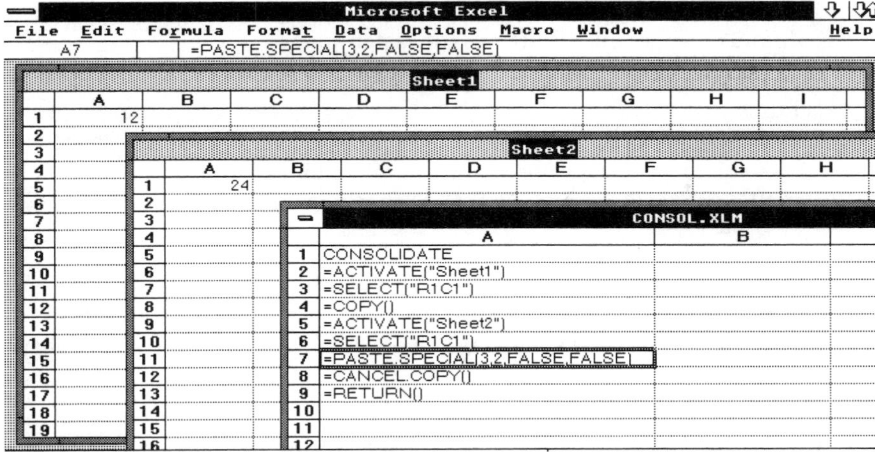

Fig. 12.16. *A macro that consolidates data.*

Microsoft Excel
File Edit Formula Format Data Options Macro Window Help
A2 =FORMULA(Sheet1!$A$1+Sheet2!$A$1,Sheet2!$A$1)
Sheet1: 12
Sheet2: 24
FASTCONS.XLM

```
Fast.Cons
=FORMULA(Sheet1!$A$1+Sheet2!$A$1,Sheet2!$A$1)
=RETURN()
```

Ready

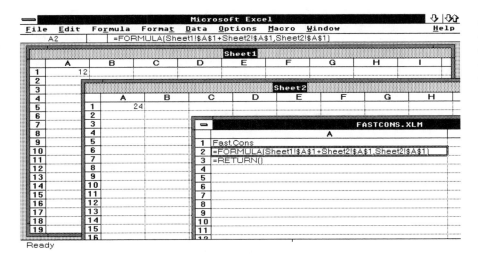

Fig. 12.17. *A faster data-consolidation macro*

The syntax for the FORMULA( ) function is

=FORMULA(*Formula_Text,ref*)

In figure 12.17, *Formula_Text* is the actual formula you want to result in the target cell using external references to the cells involved in the equation. *ref* is the cell location where the equation will be placed. By changing *ref* to a third worksheet or a different cell reference, you can place the formula in another location.

12.27 Tip: **Create your own looping functions for faster macros.**

Excel uses FOR/NEXT( ) and WHILE/NEXT( ) functions to create loops in macros. Although these functions are easy to learn, set up, and use, they are not as fast as loops that you program yourself. Building your own loops with IF( ), SET.VALUE( ), and GOTO( ) functions can significantly speed performance.

Figure 12.18 shows two loops that each repeat the loop 100 times and then beep when finished. The first macro, Slow.Loop, uses the FOR( ) and NEXT( ) functions. While easier to understand, this macro is significantly slower than the second macro.

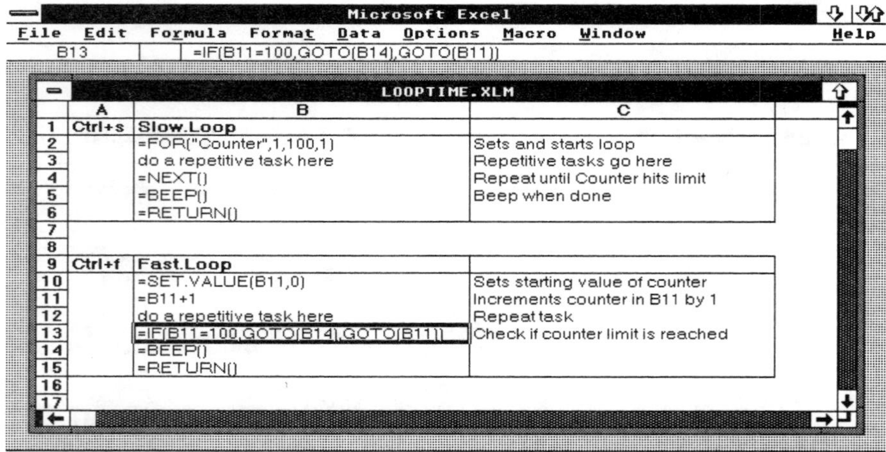

Fig. 12.18. Two looping macros.

The second macro, Fast.Loop, builds a counter and loop using the SET.VALUE( ), IF( ), and GOTO( ) functions. In B10 the SET.VALUE( ) function sets the value of cell B11 to 0. The formula in B11 then increments the value in B11 by 1 each time the macro operates. Cell B12 is where you enter repetitive macro functions, formulas, or subroutines. The macro repeats itself under the direction of the IF( ) function in cell B13. The IF( ) function in B13 checks whether B11 has reached 100. If it has, the GOTO( ) function sends the macro to B14, which contains the BELL( ) function. If B11 has not reached 100, the second GOTO( ) function sends control back to cell B11, and the process repeats again.

12.28 Tip: **Use SET.VALUE( ) rather than SET.NAME( ) for faster performance.**

Although the SET.NAME( ) function is a good way to assign values to names and to keep your macros readable, this function slows macro operation. As a faster alternative, use the SET.VALUE( ) function to set the value in a cell reference. Then use that cell reference in formulas.

13

Improving Performance

Humans are adaptable and demanding creatures. The event that initially impresses you is soon normal, then boring, then ignored. The nervous system evolved to ignore the predictable so that it could focus intently on new, stimulating, and possibly dangerous events.

The advantage in the capacity for the new is curiosity and the need for mental stimulation. When it comes to computer systems, such as Excel, the disadvantage is that no matter how good a system is, you eventually want the system to be better and faster. In this chapter, you learn to conserve memory in Windows and Excel so that you can build more powerful systems, and you learn to make Excel run faster.

Conserving Memory

Memory is money. You can buy all the memory you need to handle multiple applications and worksheets, but in many situations, planning and design considerations will conserve memory (and therefore money).

13.1 Trick: Select the Minimize MS-DOS option in the Windows MS-DOS Executive to reduce overhead memory.

Regain the use of approximately 15K of memory when you use Windows and Excel by modifying the MS-DOS Executive so that this program takes less memory while other applications run. To do so, activate the MS-DOS

Executive. Choose the File Run command, select the **M**inimize MS-DOS Executive option, and then choose OK.

13.2 Tip: **Remove terminate-and-stay-resident programs before starting Excel or Windows.**

Terminate-and-stay-resident (TSR) applications, such as SideKick, take memory away from Windows and Excel. These programs are not designed to work in the Windows environment and may cause Windows to freeze. If Windows or Excel freezes due to a TSR application, you will lose all work since the last save.

To avoid this problem, remove TSRs before you start Excel or Windows. Do not attempt to remove a TSR while Windows is running. Instead, exit Windows, quit the TSR program using the commands for that program, and then restart Windows.

Some TSR applications can be configured to run as standard DOS applications. If your TSR will run as a stand-alone DOS application, you may be able to write a PIF file for Windows that will enable your TSR to run in its own window.

TSR programs are a temporary and inelegant solution to the problems they attempt to solve. As you use more applications within the Windows or Presentation Manager environments, you will find less need for TSR programs.

13.3 Tip: **Regain memory in PC Excel by removing unneeded device drivers.**

Check your CONFIG.SYS file for device drivers you may no longer need. If you use the mouse only in Windows, for example, you can remove the MOUSE.SYS driver. Windows includes its own mouse driver.

13.4 Tip: **Close unneeded applications in Windows Presentation Manager or Multifinder (Macintosh) and close worksheets in Excel to regain memory.**

Every open application and every open worksheet in Excel uses memory. If you need to conserve memory, close unneeded applications and worksheets.

13.5 Tip: **Enter formulas or constants as arrays to conserve memory.**

You can enter formulas that are copies of one another or a constant number or text that fills adjacent cells as a single array. Arrays use significantly less memory than individual formulas or constants. Instead of a formula or constant being entered in every cell in a range, an array is stored only once, but used by all cells in the array. Chapter 4, on functions, describes how to enter functions and formulas as arrays.

13.6 Tip: **Keep worksheet and macro sheet data and formulas arranged in a rectangular fashion.**

When creating a worksheet to conserve memory, you face a trade off between having a well designed and arranged worksheet and one that conserves the most memory.

Rows that are blank take no memory; however, rows that are partially filled use almost as much memory as full rows of the same width. With this in mind, you can conserve memory by building worksheets and macro sheets that keep data and formulas in rectangular blocks of nearly full cells. A trade off in using this layout is that rectangular blocks of densely packed data and formulas make the worksheet or macro sheet more difficult to edit and rearrange.

13.7 Tip: **Use small linked worksheets rather than large worksheets to build large systems.**

You will find many advantages to using small linked worksheets over building large inflexible worksheets. One major advantage is that small linked worksheets use less memory. Linked worksheets are discussed in Chapter 5.

13.8 Trick: **Use a consistent set of worksheet fonts to save memory.**

Excel requires memory for each different font or font size used in open worksheets. By consistently using the same fonts across multiple worksheets or by opening only a few worksheets with different fonts, you conserve memory.

13.9 Trick: **Format entire rows and columns to preserve memory.**

Save memory by formatting entire rows and columns with the most frequently used format in that row or column. This formatting method stores a 6-byte format code once for each row or column. If you format each cell individually, each cell contains a 6-byte format code.

To format the entire row or column, click on the row or column header to select the row or column. From the keyboard, press Shift+space bar to select the row that contains the active cell. Press Ctrl+space bar (PC) or

Command+space bar (Macintosh) to select the column that contains the active cell. Then format individual cells in the row or column that differ.

13.10 Tip: **Don't format blank cells.**

Formatting takes memory. If you are concerned about saving memory, don't format blank cells unless they will later contain data.

13.11 Trick: **Save memory by writing formulas that reference entire rows or columns.**

Just as formatting an entire row or column saves memory, formulas that reference an entire row or column also save memory. A common use for this trick is summing a column of numbers. For example, if column C contains only the numbers you want summed and no other data, you can use a formula like the following:

=SUM(C:C)

Do not enter the SUM( ) formula in column C, or you will create a circular reference. Formulas that reference an entire row or column should not be entered in the row or column they reference.

To sum a row of numbers, use a formula like the following:

=SUM(5:5)

When entering this type of formula, clicking on the row or column heading after typing the first parenthesis enters the row or column reference. Type the second parenthesis and then press Enter.

13.12 Tip: **Change formulas to values to conserve memory.**

If some formulas in your worksheet are not going to change, you can save memory by copying the formulas with **E**dit **C**opy. Then paste the selection back on top of the original with **E**dit Paste **S**pecial with the **V**alues and **N**one options selected.

To prevent later confusion and possible mistakes, use the Fo**r**mula **N**ote command to mark formulas that were changed to values. Save the worksheet under a new name.

13.13 Trick: **Delete range names when opening Lotus 1-2-3 worksheets to conserve memory.**

Excel reads and translates Lotus 1-2-3 worksheets when you open them. As Excel translates the 1-2-3 worksheet, it builds a dependency list that tracks relationships in the worksheet. Excel reserves memory for *each time* a range name is used in the 1-2-3 worksheet, not just the first time. This reservation method wastes memory. For example, if you open a 1-2-3 worksheet that uses only a few names, but that uses the names frequently in many formulas, Excel reserves memory for each use of the names.

To preserve memory in Excel, delete range names from the 1-2-3 worksheet before you open it in Excel. Once you open the worksheet, you can add the names back to the Excel worksheet with the Formula Create Name and Formula Define Name commands.

13.14 Trick: **To regain inefficiently used memory, save, close, and reopen the worksheet.**

For Excel to regain memory after you have followed some of the techniques described in this section, you should save, close, and reopen the worksheet. This procedure makes Excel reallocate memory to the worksheet. Use the following process to help you regain wasted memory.

1. Use Edit Clear or a shortcut key to clear the formatting from blank cells.
2. Remove blank columns that separate columns containing data. Although you may want to retain some blank columns for appearance, remove those you can to conserve memory.

   Check whether a column is blank by selecting the column and then choosing Formula Select Special. Select the Constants option and choose OK. If that displays a dialog box showing nothing found, repeat the process with the Formulas option selected.
3. Apply other tips and tricks described in this chapter.
4. Reallocate memory by saving, closing, and reopening the worksheet.

13.15 Tip: **Make a change to WIN.INI to store wide worksheets more efficiently.**

If your worksheet is composed primarily of wide rectangles of data that exceed column FD, the 160th column, you may be able to improve memory efficiency. Use a word processor to edit the WIN.INI file to include the following statement under the Excel section:

BLOCK=2

This statement enables Excel to handle wide worksheets more efficiently.

If your worksheets are tall, the BLOCK=2 statement may cause Excel to run out of conventional memory before running out of expanded or extended memory. If this occurs or if you use worksheets with a vertical orientation, remove the BLOCK statement from WIN.INI.

When you save the WIN.INI file from a word processor, save it as an ASCII or DOS text file. You must restart Windows to make the changes to WIN.INI take effect.

Improving Speed

Excel is more powerful than its predecessors, yet the program is easier to use and learn. And its capabilities require faster computer processors, more memory, and a hard disk. Even if you already have a fast, powerful system, you can use several ways to increase Excel's performance.

Check Chapter 12 on advanced macros for techniques that improve macro performance.

13.16 Tip: **Continue working and let Excel calculate in the background.**

When the hourglass (PC) or watch (Macintosh) appears on-screen telling you to pause while Excel works, you don't always have to heed its command. If the hourglass or watch appears because Excel is recalculating formulas, you can continue to work by selecting a cell, choosing a command, or scrolling the worksheet. As soon as you continue working, the hourglass or watch disappears. If you pause briefly, Excel again displays the hourglass or watch and returns to calculating. Excel catches up with any calculations affected by your recent entries and then continues with its total recalculation.

You cannot interrupt a data table from recalculating nor can you interrupt the automatic calculation that occurs before saving an uncalculated worksheet. (You can interrupt a worksheet save by pressing Esc, but this action erases any existing file on disk with the same name.)

13.17 Tip: **Control calculation with the Options Calculation command.**

You can turn off automatic calculation. Normally, when you enter data on which a formula depends, Excel recalculates all cells and tables that depend on the changed data. This recalculation can slow data entry. Even if you take advantage of Excel's background calculation by continuing to type, there will be a slight pause before you can work again. However, you can turn off calculations.

To stop calculations, choose the **O**ptions **C**alculation command. Select the **M**anual or Automatic except **T**ables options. The **M**anual option stops all calculations. The Automatic except **T**ables option recalculates formulas but does not recalculate data tables.

When you want to recalculate, choose **O**ptions Calculate **N**ow or press F9 to calculate all worksheets in memory. To calculate only the active worksheet, press Shift+F9. In Macintosh Excel, you also can press Command+= to calculate the worksheet.

13.18 Tip: **Calculate only the active worksheet.**

In most cases, you will want to recalculate only the active worksheet. Instead of pressing F9, which calculates all worksheets in memory, press Shift+F9. Pressing this key combination calculates only the active worksheet which may take considerably less time.

13.19 Trick: **Calculate single cells while automatic calculation is off.**

Recalculate single cells while automatic calculation is off by selecting the cell you want to recalculate. Then press the F2 key or click in the formula bar so that you can edit the formula. Delete and then retype something in the formula. For example, delete and then retype the equal sign. Then press Enter. The formula recalculates. Other formulas in the worksheet will not recalculate because automatic recalculation is turned off.

13.20 Trick: **Calculate a range of cells while automatic calculation is off by using Formula Replace to replace all equal signs.**

You can recalculate all cells within a range even when automatic calculation is off. Select the range of cells you want to recalculate. Choose the Formula Replace command and enter an = (equal sign) in both the Replace and **W**ith text boxes. Choose **F**ind Next and **R**eplace to recalculate individual formulas or choose Replace **A**ll to recalculate all selected formulas at once. Because the formulas contain equal signs, they are all changed, causing the formulas to recalculate. Cells outside the range will not recalculate.

13.21 Trick: **Use simple external references to retrieve data from slow-to-calculate tables.**

If you are creating a system involving worksheets that depend on complex tables and the tables are independent of calculations you are doing, you may want to put the tables and calculations in separate worksheets. This placement enables you to calculate the tables once and then save them to disk. Once on disk, the calculation worksheet can refer to the tables with links. Because the tables are not in memory, they will not slow down recalculation time if you calculate all worksheets in memory.

To create a simple external link between an entire table and the calculating worksheet, open both the table worksheet and the calculating worksheet. Activate the table worksheet and select the table; then choose **E**dit **C**opy. Activate the calculating worksheet, move to where you want the copy of the table, and choose **E**dit Paste **L**ink. Close the table worksheet.

The calculating worksheet now contains an image of the table that you can reference and use in calculations. The table's image is linked to the real table on disk so that it remains up-to-date, but will not recalculate if you recalculate worksheets in memory. With complex data tables that analyze large mainframe downloads, this method can reduce calculation times from an hour to a second.

13.22 Tip: **Suspend unused applications in Windows/386 to regain CPU performance.**

Windows/386 can multitask. This capability splits your computer's processing power between applications in memory. If you have three applications running, each gets one-third of your computer's processing power.

Splitting the processing power drags down the performance of your computer so that calculations and macros run more slowly. If this happens, you need to give more of the processor's power to Excel. You can use one of several ways to do this.

You can close applications you are not using. This method removes the applications from memory so that the computer does not have to share processing power with them.

Or you can suspend needed applications that do not need to calculate when they are inactive. For example, applications such as word processors usually need processing power only while you are typing in the program. To suspend applications so that they will not continue to process in the background, follow these steps:

1. Switch to the application you want to suspend by pressing Alt+Tab or Alt+Esc.
2. Activate the Control menu by pressing Alt+space bar and choosing the Settings menu.
3. Select the **S**uspend option.
4. Choose OK.

Return a suspended application to normal processing by following the same process but selecting the **R**esume option in Step 3.

As another method, you can designate that Excel receives all the power of the processor and that other applications receive none. To do this, you must tell Windows/386 you want a program to run exclusively so that it receives all the processing power:

1. Switch to the application you want to have all the power by pressing Alt+Tab or Alt+Esc.
2. Activate the Control menu by pressing Alt+space bar and choosing the Settings menu.
3. Select the E**x**clusive option.
4. Choose OK.

13.23 Tip: **Improve PC Excel and Windows performance by improving your disk performance.**

PC Excel and other Windows programs are too large to fit completely in 640K of memory. As a consequence, parts of program code are stored on disk until needed. When needed, selected parts load into memory and "overlay" unused portions of code already in memory. The time it takes to retrieve an overlay portion of code from disk can make Excel seem slow. (Hard disks are mechanical; therefore, they access data thousands of times slower than electronic memory.)

Improving the performance of your hard disk improves the speed of overlays. You may not have to buy a faster hard disk. Try using a program that rearranges data on your hard disk to make it operate more efficiently. These programs, called defragmenters or "defraggers," align similar data on disk in contiguous blocks, making data easier and quicker to read. Always make a copy of important information on your hard disk before using a defragmenter.

13.24 Tip: **Use HIMEM.SYS to give Excel in Windows 2.1 more conventional memory and to improve speed.**

You can give 45K of conventional memory to Excel under Windows 2.1 to increase the speed of operation. To do so, you use HIMEM.SYS. HIMEM.SYS uses 64K of extended memory to store 45K of Excel's application code that would normally be stored in conventional memory. This action increases performance because overlayed program code will not have to be brought in from disk as frequently. The remaining 19 to 20K of extended memory is used to increase the speed of pull-down menus.

If you have an 80286 computer with at least 64K of extended memory, you can use HIMEM.SYS. If you have an 80286 computer that does not have extended memory, you may be able to reconfigure your memory board to convert expanded memory into extended memory. Some memory boards can have both expanded and extended memory with extended memory configured in blocks of 128 or 512K.

If you have extended memory, Windows asks you during the installation process whether you want to take advantage of extended memory. Answer yes, and the installation program copies HIMEM.SYS onto your hard disk and changes the CONFIG.SYS file for you.

If you have Excel without the full version of Windows, you can reinstall the run-time version of Windows by changing to the EXCEL directory and typing **WINSU**. When asked whether you want to take advantage of extended memory, answer yes.

If you want to install HIMEM.SYS manually and you have extended memory, copy the HIMEM.SYS file to the root of your hard disk. HIMEM.SYS is on one of the Utilities disks that came with Excel. Edit the CONFIG.SYS file to include the following line:

```
DEVICE=HIMEM.SYS
```

This line should be the first entry in the CONFIG.SYS file. Restart your computer to take advantage of HIMEM.SYS.

If you have an 80386 computer, you do not have to use HIMEM.SYS.

13.25 Tip: **Use MEMSET.EXE and the READMEEM.TXT files to add performance to Windows 2.1.**

Multiple versions of Windows are available, and each computer has different configurations and memory capabilities; therefore, every version and configuration cannot all be discussed here. To get the optimum performance from Excel and Windows, read the separate manual that comes with Excel or Windows. This manual lists recommended configurations for specific hardware.

If you have extended or expanded memory, the installation program asks whether you want to take advantage of that memory. Answering yes runs the program MEMSET.EXE, which installs programs that increase the performance and memory capability of Excel and Windows. To run MEMSET.EXE, you should know the manufacturer and brand name of the expanded or extended memory board in your computer.

You can run MEMSET.EXE after installing Windows or Excel by changing to the WINDOWS or EXCEL directory where MEMSET.EXE is located. From DOS, type **MEMSET** and press Enter. Answer the on-screen questions.

MEMSET helps you install HIMEM.SYS and SMARTDrive, a disk-cache program that increases the performance of your hard disk. You should not run another disk-cache program if you use SMARTDrive; SMARTDrive takes the place of all other disk-cache programs. MEMSET also helps you install RAMDrive. RAMDrive acts as an electronic hard disk, taking the place of any other RAM disk in your computer. You must restart your computer after installing these programs for them to take effect.

In addition to MEMSET, read the READMEEM.TXT file that comes on the installation disks. You can use a normal word processor to load this ASCII file and read or print it. The READMEEM.TXT file describes how to customize your computer for different extended and expanded memory configurations.

Index

B

C

D

E

F

G

H

I

K

L

M

N

O

P

Q–R

S

X–Z

More Computer Knowledge from Que

Lotus Software Titles

Title	Price
1-2-3 Database Techniques	24.95
1-2-3 Release 2.2 Business Applications	39.95
1-2-3 Release 2.2 Quick Reference	7.95
1-2-3 Release 2.2 QuickStart	19.95
1-2-3 Release 2.2 Workbook and Disk	29.95
1-2-3 Release 3 Business Applications	39.95
1-2-3 Release 3 Quick Reference	7.95
1-2-3 Release 3 QuickStart	19.95
1-2-3 Release 3 Workbook and Disk	29.95
1-2-3 Tips, Tricks, and Traps, 3rd Edition	22.95
Upgrading to 1-2-3 Release 3	14.95
Using 1-2-3, Special Edition	24.95
Using 1-2-3 Release 2.2, Special Edition	24.95
Using 1-2-3 Release 3	24.95
Using Lotus Magellan	21.95
Using Symphony, 2nd Edition	26.95

Database Titles

Title	Price
dBASE III Plus Applications Library	24.95
dBASE III Plus Handbook, 2nd Edition	24.95
dBASE III Plus Tips, Tricks, and Traps	21.95
dBASE III Plus Workbook and Disk	29.95
dBASE IV Applications Library, 2nd Edition	39.95
dBASE IV Handbook, 3rd Edition	23.95
dBASE IV Programming Techniques	24.95
dBASE IV QueCards	21.95
dBASE IV Quick Reference	7.95
dBASE IV QuickStart	19.95
dBASE IV Tips, Tricks, and Traps, 2nd Edition	21.95
dBASE IV Workbook and Disk	29.95
dBXL and Quicksilver Programming: Beyond dBASE	24.95
R:BASE User's Guide, 3rd Edition	22.95
Using Clipper	24.95
Using DataEase	22.95
Using Reflex	19.95
Using Paradox 3	24.95

Applications Software Titles

Title	Price
AutoCAD Advanced Techniques	34.95
AutoCAD Quick Reference	7.95
AutoCAD Sourcebook	24.95
Excel Business Applications: IBM Version	39.95
Introduction to Business Software	14.95
PC Tools Quick Reference	7.95
Smart Tips, Tricks, and Traps	24.95
Using AutoCAD, 2nd Edition	29.95
Using Computers in Business	24.95
Using DacEasy	21.95
Using Dollars and Sense: IBM Version, 2nd Edition	19.95
Using Enable/OA	23.95
Using Excel: IBM Version	24.95
Using Generic CADD	24.95
Using Harvard Project Manager	24.95
Using Managing Your Money, 2nd Edition	19.95
Using Microsoft Works: IBM Version	21.95
Using PROCOMM PLUS	19.95
Using Q&A, 2nd Edition	21.95
Using Quattro	21.95
Using Quicken	19.95
Using Smart	22.95
Using SmartWare II	24.95
Using SuperCalc5, 2nd Edition	22.95

Word Processing and Desktop Publishing Titles

Title	Price
DisplayWrite QuickStart	19.95
Harvard Graphics Quick Reference	7.95
Microsoft Word 5 Quick Reference	7.95
Microsoft Word 5 Tips, Tricks, and Traps: IBM Version	19.95
Using DisplayWrite 4, 2nd Edition	19.95
Using Freelance Plus	24.95
Using Harvard Graphics	24.95
Using Microsoft Word 5: IBM Version	21.95
Using MultiMate Advantage, 2nd Edition	19.95
Using PageMaker: IBM Version, 2nd Edition	24.95
Using PFS: First Choice	22.95
Using PFS: First Publisher	22.95
Using Professional Write	19.95
Using Sprint	21.95
Using Ventura Publisher, 2nd Edition	24.95
Using WordPerfect, 3rd Edition	21.95
Using WordPerfect 5	24.95
Using WordStar, 2nd Edition	21.95
Ventura Publisher Techniques and Applications	22.95
Ventura Publisher Tips, Tricks, and Traps	24.95
WordPerfect Macro Library	21.95
WordPerfect Power Techniques	21.95
WordPerfect QueCards	21.95
WordPerfect Quick Reference	7.95
WordPerfect QuickStart	21.95
WordPerfect Tips, Tricks, and Traps, 2nd Edition	21.95
WordPerfect 5 Workbook and Disk	29.95

Macintosh/Apple II Titles

Title	Price
The Big Mac Book	27.95
Excel QuickStart	19.95
Excel Tips, Tricks, and Traps	22.95
Using AppleWorks, 3rd Edition	21.95
Using AppleWorks GS	21.95
Using dBASE Mac	19.95
Using Dollars and Sense: Macintosh Version	19.95
Using Excel: Macintosh Verson	22.95
Using FullWrite Professional	21.95
Using HyperCard:	24.95
Using Microsoft Word 4: Macintosh Version	21.95
Using Microsoft Works: Macintosh Version, 2nd Edition	21.95
Using PageMaker: Macintosh Version	24.95
Using WordPerfect: Macintosh Version	19.95

Hardware and Systems Titles

Title	Price
DOS Tips, Tricks, and Traps	22.95
DOS Workbook and Disk	29.95
Hard Disk Quick Reference	7.95
IBM PS/2 Handbook	21.95
Managing Your Hard Disk, 2nd Edition	22.95
MS-DOS Quick Reference	7.95
MS-DOS QuickStart	21.95
MS-DOS User's Guide, Special Edition	29.95
Networking Personal Computers, 3rd Edition	22.95
Norton Utilities Quick Reference	7.95
The Printer Bible	24.95
Understanding UNIX: A Conceptual Guide, 2nd Edition	21.95
Upgrading and Repairing PCs	27.95
Using DOS	22.95
Using Microsoft Windows	19.95
Using Novell NetWare	24.95
Using OS/2	23.95
Using PC DOS, 3rd Edition	22.95

Programming and Technical Titles

Title	Price
Assembly Language Quick Reference	7.95
C Programmer's Toolkit	39.95
C Programming Guide, 3rd Edition	24.95
C Quick Reference	7.95
DOS and BIOS Functions Quick Reference	7.95
DOS Programmer's Reference, 2nd Edition	27.95
Power Graphics Programming	24.95
QuickBASIC Advanced Techniques	21.95
QuickBASIC Programmer's Toolkit	39.95
QuickBASIC Quick Reference	7.95
SQL Programmer's Guide	29.95
Turbo C Programming	22.95
Turbo Pascal Advanced Techniques	22.95
Turbo Pascal Programmer's Toolkit	39.95
Turbo Pascal Quick Reference	7.95
Using Assembly Language	24.95
Using QuickBASIC 4	19.95
Using Turbo Pascal	21.95

For more information, call

1-800-428-5331

All prices subject to change without notice. Prices and charges are for domestic orders only. Non-U.S. prices might be higher.

Using Excel: Macintosh Version

by John Annaloro

Complete with an introduction to Excel worksheets and macros, this combination of tutorial and reference shows readers how to create spreadsheets, databases, and graphics with this powerful Macintosh spreadsheet program. Covers the latest version of Excel!

Order #1031
$22.95 USA
0-88022-494-0, 650 pp.

Using Excel: IBM Version

by Ron Person and Mary Campbell

Que's *Using Excel: IBM Version* helps users master Excel. Includes **Quick Start** tutorials plus tips and tricks to help improve efficiency and troubleshoot problems. Also includes a special section for 1-2-3 users making the switch to Excel.

Order #87
$24.95 USA
0-88022-284-0, 804 pp.

Excel QuickStart

Developed by Que Corporation

Excel QuickStart takes readers step-by-step through basic Excel operations—including spreadsheets, databases, and graphs—with more than 100 two-page illustrations. Covers both IBM and Macintosh.

Order #957
$19.95 USA
0-88022-423-1, 400 pp.

Using PageMaker: Macintosh Version

by C.J. Weigand

Covering both program fundamentals and basic design principles, this informative text helps users produce professional-quality documents. Includes numerous applications and examples.

Order #949
$24.95 USA
0-88022-411-8, 600 pp.